tango

An Argentine Love Story

CAMILLE CUSUMANO

SEAL PRESS

Tango
An Argentine Love Story

Copyright © 2008 Camille Cusumano

Published by Seal Press
A Member of Perseus Books Group
1700 Fourth Street
Berkeley, CA 94710

Library of Congress Cataloging-in-Publication Data
Cusumano, Camille.
  Tango: an Argentine love story / by Camille Cusumano.
    p. cm.
  ISBN-13: 978-1-58005-250-4
  ISBN-10: 1-58005-250-9
  1. Tango (Dance)—Argentina. 2. Women—Psychology. I. Title.
  GV1796.T3C87 2008
  793.3'3—dc22
                                    2008018647

Cover design by Susan Koski Zucker
Interior design by Tabitha Lahr
Printed in the United States of America
Distributed by Publishers Group West

To Argentina's creole stew of gauchos, African slaves, Cuban mariners, Andalusian *zapateados* (heel stompers), and Italian immigrants, who simmered to perfection, yielding a contemplative's consummate nourishment called tango.

Contents

Chapter 1

Goddess of the
Tango Galaxy

*Strictly speaking, there are no enlightened people, there is
only enlightened activity.*

—*Shunryu Suzuki*

*He has no name. He is the first of a thousand strangers.
We stand a few inches apart facing each other. I press my
chest that contains my broken heart gently, slowly into
his. We form an embrace with our arms, much in the way
lovers do, even as his raised left palm meets my right one.
The first thing I'm aware of is the heat of his body. His
level of warmth is an indication that it hasn't been long
since he left his last partner. He sweats, and I will carry his*

moisture away in my hair and on my bodice when I leave him. I smell him—his cologne, worn by most Argentine men, and the scent of his clothes and skin. I can tell by subtle wafts of ammonia that he's a big meat eater. I will absorb his smells, too, like a blotter. He stands still for a few seconds, then, almost imperceptibly, rocks to locate me and my weight. I await his salida, *the entrance step to tango.* Salida, *which means "exit" in Spanish, is precisely the right word to describe this step. It's the moment we exit real time. There is no past or future, only a numinous present, while dancing tango. Who, what, when, where—all the measurable aspects of my life—are still present when I dance tango but only in some distant, unified way, as if I were on the moon, or a cloud, or atop a lofty mountain looking down and marveling at how I fit so perfectly with the world.*

I flow with him like quicksilver on an incline. I am the passive element, shifting with his center until we share one sweet spot, wordlessly agreed upon. The energy that sets us in motion transforms us from two particles into one wave. At first I am just a nanosecond behind where he wants me to be, and then, seamlessly, with no apparent force, his will is gone and we are one stroke of autonomous motion. We are each other's whole world, front to back, for three minutes.

He is faceless, like the unknown soldier, someone in whom I have blind faith and gratitude. He is one of the thousands of men I will dance with over a year's time. He is my dark shadow Self, unwittingly helping me navigate

*my difficult inner journey with the clarity and vision I lack
when I'm not on the dance floor.*

I am living in Buenos Aires, Argentina, dancing tango both day and night. Self-imposed exile, I'd half-jokingly told my friends at my bon voyage party in August before I left San Francisco, California. I had braved it all with a big smile, but underneath I was drowning in a pit of despair and self-doubt.

"You're going to have the time of your life," they had said. "We're so envious." I'd just nodded. You bet—the time of my life.

My original plan had been in place since May, during a more peaceful time in my life. I would travel to Argentina to improve my tango skills, write about the dance, and do other travel research, a vital component of my freelance job since leaving my full-time magazine-editor post in late 2005. I had allotted myself two and a half months for this pleasurable business. But it took only a few days before I decided that I could not leave this country that once harbored Nazis, waged a Dirty War (1976–1983) against its own citizens, and wasted their money—and which gave us *dulce de leche*, empanadas, yerba maté, and tango—until I was cured of my horrible, energy-stealing, soul-murdering emotions.

I've chosen to come to a country also in crisis. The 2001 *crisis financiera* was still on the lips of Argentines when I arrived. Runaway inflation, imbalance of trade, and pegging the peso to the dollar on a one-to-one basis derailed the entire country. Argentina had suddenly faced a $142 billion foreign debt it couldn't pay. Global trade, which makes the rich richer and the poor poorer, as opposed to fair trade, which benefits everyone, was bad for the country's economic health. It came at a time when Argentina was still in the early stages of rebuilding its democracy after its brutal military regime had fallen. As always, economic violence hit the poor and lower middle classes the worst. Thousands slipped below the poverty line and became homeless and hungry overnight. The "Talibans of orthodox finance" was what *Le Novel Observateur* called those who invested their money abroad with the complicity of corrupt politicians. The nation is still recovering. Like me, its citizens have known sudden ruin. And in their admirable resilience and gentle introspection, they are a good people to be among.

I arrived in Buenos Aires in late August, the tail end of Argentina's winter. Despite—or maybe because of—my constant companion, anxiety, I take comfort in the big-city buzz. Buenos Aires has New York City's energy with San Francisco–like neighborhoods and a touch of Paris in its architecture. I'm in awe of the beautiful French and Italian Renaissance–style buildings with their balconies, grillwork, friezes, caryatids, columns, and capitals, often punctuated by homely construction from the 1960s. Trees are bare, skies are gray, the ground in parks near my rented apartment is still hard and cold. I have no friends or family here. I do not know a soul. I have traveled often over the course of my fifty-five years. I've loved popping up in new places that await my discovery, but never in my life have I felt this alone or desolate.

This is not my first time in Buenos Aires. I was here for three weeks in the spring of 2005, traveling in a group with my San Francisco–based tango teacher, Christy Cote, and her other students.

I took many classes—with well-known teachers, such as Fabian Salas and Carolina del Rivero, Chiche and Marta, Osvaldo and Coca. I walked the streets of Buenos Aires's best-loved barrios—San Telmo, where tango was born on those bumpy cobbled streets that train your feet to dance better; Palermo, with its sycamore-lined avenues; Recoleta, with its chic boutiques; and La Boca, one of the barrios where tango was danced among the lowest classes—immigrants.

In La Boca, I met an artist named Guillermo Alio, who had combined his love of tango and art to create fantastic tableaux with his feet. I watched him and his partner dip the soles of their shoes in paint and dance tango upon a blank canvas. I wondered if their whimsical artistry was a way to capture the elusive pleasure of tango— the equivalent of making a body print of lovemaking, or an X-ray of enlightenment, or a mimeograph of joy. As I recall that experience my thoughts shift back to Dan, the person I most want to avoid thinking about, the person to whom my thoughts always return.

During that first trip, Dan, my partner for nearly fifteen years, had been waiting for me at home in San Francisco, sending emails and supporting my adventure and crazy "thing" I had for tango. It wasn't even a year after that first trip that I had a brief affair with a tango partner I'd known for barely three months. It occurred during a period when Dan and I were having a serious lull in our intimacy. Dan had suggested we have a breather, and during our time apart I gave in to the ever-present temptation to practice more than tango with a dance partner. As if to compensate for his distance from me at that time, Dan wanted to marry me right away. But even as I watched his body armor of defenses erode, I said, "I'm not ready." We weren't ready. An affair shouldn't be a catalyst to marriage, I told him. I needed time to get over the affair.

He waited three months before beginning a relationship with Evelyn, a woman who'd been a mutual friend. He'd told me right away. "It looks like Evelyn and I are going to have a relationship," he said. This pronouncement was surreal. Loyalty was never an issue in our many years—prior to tango.

Then it was my turn to vaporize. At times in the weeks after his revelation, I followed at his heels like a duckling clinging to its mother, chanting, "I'll give up tango, please don't go with her, I'll give it all up, forever, promise." He had smiled and hugged me, knowing this untruth was simply a measure of my desperation.

Until my tango-induced dalliance, Dan and I had had a pretty good relationship. We shared a love of nature and the outdoors. He's a feminist, supportive of women's and other civil rights. Unlike me, a product of nuclear patriarchy, he comes from a matriarchal family. He even irons his own clothes. His mom, the breadwinner, held advanced degrees in math and chemistry and was a schoolteacher. We were both the fifth child in big families that we liked spending time with. I took Dan, who's half Irish, to Sicily to meet the relatives. They fed him every part of the lamb they had just slaughtered, including the genitals, along with pizza, pasta, wild fennel, and fire-roasted artichokes. It was an initiation greater than any marriage certificate. It made him *mia familia*. We lived together for eight years until I moved to a quiet one-bedroom so I could write. We talked about getting married, but it never seemed necessary. We had no clocks ticking. We had always nurtured each other's dreams.

Before leaving for Buenos Aires, I had cried out to my friend Alan, "Tango wrecked my life!" He firmly replied, "Tango will save your life." Somehow, I think we both were right. Only in dancing tango do I find that meditative space of solace, where time stops, where I stop measuring and weighing my self-worth against the *other woman* or anyone, because in tango there is no Self—there is just that boundless oneness, a unity so divine, so beautiful, it's impossible for me to hate or feel any of the tumult I now feel off the dance floor.

I have rented a lovely furnished loft apartment from tango friends Adrian and Andrea, who live in San Francisco. It is in the Palermo barrio, which takes its name from the Italians, the dominant group of European immigrants who settled in Buenos Aires during the late nineteenth and early twentieth centuries. When my trip turned into a need to get away from the mess I had made of my love life, Dan had suggested I go to Sicily—"Where they love you," he'd said—instead of Argentina, where I know not a soul. But I'm discovering that Sicily is here. Most of the original tango lyricists, composers, and dancers were Italian. I find half a dozen people in the Buenos Aires phonebook with my last name (I'm the only listing in San Francisco) and wonder if I am genetically predisposed to do tango. My ankles, calves, and thighs were tempered strong as steel long before I was born. My grandparents walked their formative years on steep cobbled hills in villages just south of Sicily's capital city, Palermo. Thinking about my heritage immediately conjures up the image of Evelyn, the woman who suggested that I might actually have put a contract out on her. It wasn't the first time my being Sicilian has sparked an allusion to the Mafia and their penchant for rubbing out enemies—but heretofore it had always been made in jest.

I hear a man's voice singing "Cafetín de Buenos Aires," one of tango's most popular anthems, and it feels like my own voice singing about my own past. The song's lyrics, written by Italian immigrant son Enrique Santos Discépolo, are charged with melancholy, loss, and a sense of failure. It is I, not the crooning singer, who have lived in this place long ago and who have his memories of falling in and out of love in this old café, *shooting dice amid wise and suicidal fools, learning about cruel poetry and how to no longer think about myself.* This sudden sense of déjà vu doesn't seem so odd when I think that my grandparents could just as easily have sailed south to this New World.

It's as if I can recall growing up in Buenos Aires, saturated with the music described as *"dos por cuatro,"* or "two by four," for its early influence from the habanera beat that arrived around 1870 with Cuban seamen. My grandfathers could have been among those resourceful immigrants in La Boca who took the shipyard's castaway red, blue, green, yellow, and orange paint and poured it over the drab buildings whose primary colors today draw camera-snapping tourists. My grandparents would have lived in a *conventillo,* one of the tenements where it is said some of the first tangos were improvised among immigrants on the common patio. My parents, excellent beat dancers, would have naturally taken to tango.

Even before I know them, I decide I will love the people of Argentina, heart and soul. I decide to embrace this culture and these people with a whole heart, in part, I think, to atone for my sins. At the end of life, they say, we fall back on religion. What is a spiritual crisis but the death of some part of us? I am falling forward. On boundless love for whatever is in my path. Whether that be the next thousand dancers I encounter. Whether that be a whole nation.

My loft is Juncal Street, across from one of the city's many red-lighted *otelos*, love hotels, where you can rent by the hour. In the wee hours, when I return home after long nights of dancing, I pass the ladies of the night (many of them transvestites), standing in spike heels, thongs, plunge bras, and little else.

The loft has a beautiful wooden floor, upon which I will practice tango and do urgent sessions of yoga and meditation. A black wrought-iron staircase leads to the loft level with a king-size bed.

Sliding glass doors open to a small back terrace. I have limited views, but the white noise of my neighbors in surrounding high-rise buildings drifts in—a flute player, a tenor sax player, a woman running her vocal cords through scales, and a bird that sings even in the dead of night. I position my laptop so that I'm facing outside as I write. I have always cherished a clean well-lighted place of solitude, the fertile ground from which my creations spring. But now my writing is the source of discomfort. I confront only the memories of my love life, fifteen years with Dan, crashing in.

To stave off my blues, I prepare for my debut *milonga,* the venue where tango is danced, and treat myself to a manicure and pedicure. Not since I attended Barbizon modeling school at age nineteen have I invested so much time in personal glamour. Now my five-inch suede-sole dance shoes are dwarfing my hiking boots. In the salon, I read a women's magazine with a short piece on Paris Hilton. The story translates into Spanish what is written on the front of Hilton's blue T-shirt: Soy la diosa de esta jodida galaxia. (I am the goddess of this fucking galaxy.) I write it down on a notebook and memorize it. It is my first full sentence in Spanish.

Buenos Aires has more than a hundred *milongas,* old and new, big and small, *nuevo* and traditional, many listed in guides, others known only by word of mouth. The free Tango Map guide, tacked to a bulletin board in my loft, helpfully plots them all. I stick pushpins in the ones I want to attend—until I run out of pins. Tango is everywhere in Buenos Aires: on the streets where young couples dance spectacular stage-style tango to crying violins and weeping *bandoneónes,* the concertina or squeezebox instrument that is the sine qua non of tango music. It emanates from the iconic white smile under the pulled-down fedora of tango's patron saint, singer Carlos Gardel, who died in his midforties in a plane crash in 1935. It's on the airwaves on Todo Tango radio and on the TV in the subway. Many taxi drivers love and play the music in their cabs and chuckle when I sing a few bars of a classic, "Malena," a song about an archetypal broken woman who drinks too much but sings like a lark.

For my debut, I choose an afternoon *milonga* called El Arranque, a spot whose name comes from the verb *arrancar*—to uproot. I slip into a black dress with some sparkles on it and pace the floor of my heart and loft. Finally, I call Nicholas, a man whose card was given me by Christy Cote before I left. He is what is called a taxi dancer, one of those *tangueros* who charge to be your escort (not in the sexual sense) and dance with you for several hours at the *milonga*. He's expensive by Argentine standards, about $50 for three hours, but my tango dancing needs a "jump start," another meaning to the verb *arrancar*.

I notice a lot of white and gray hair at El Arranque—much more so than in San Francisco *milongas,* where tango has only begun to take hold in the past dozen years or so. It is said that in Argentina you'll find the very old dancers and the very young; fewer baby boomers dance because the military dictatorship banned group meetings during their coming-of-age years. Nicholas tells me that some smug dancers call El Arranque the *camposanto*—the "graveyard." As a group, however, the older *tangueros* far outshine the younger set, who don't have the long-term body memory the dance requires.

I enjoy this *milonga,* but Nicholas likes to sit, eat, and talk during some *tandas*—a series of three or four like-themed songs that can be pure tango, tango-*vals* (waltz), or tango-*milonga*—and it is the custom that you dance the entire *tanda* with the same partner. I like getting to know a local, but I'm eager to keep dancing. I have a quantum need to fill when it comes to tango. Once I'm up and moving, I don't rest. Luckily for Nicholas, another dancer, who introduces himself as Agosto, invites me to dance.

He's quite good. He knows how to show off my follower's technique. Agosto executes a move called *sacada*, and I respond with the slackness of a Hacky Sack, which lets my legs fly in a pretty arc. Then I reclaim my muscle tone to keep my balance. It's a follower's challenge, this switching on and off of your muscles, perhaps in a thousand cycles a minute in response to the leader, who must also switch on and off, allowing you space to receive his energy. This multitasking occurs so seamlessly and automatically if you bring to the tango partnership complete presence minus willfulness—the exact sort of detachment I want so badly in the rest of my life.

I will see Agosto many more times at El Arranque and other *milongas*. He reeks of tobacco—a major drawback—but I will dance with him often. In the beginning, I tell myself, it's important to always *accept what is offered*. This is one of the guiding precepts distilled from my Zen practice into my tango dancing. I am here to take what comes my way. I am here to give myself over. And already in my very first *milonga* I come to an important realization: I don't need Nicholas at all. I am tango-centric enough to go out on my own.

When I am not lost in my tango trance, I watch other couples lost in theirs. I catch the pain and vexation as well as the melancholy and euphoria on their faces and feel a kinship with all shades of emotion. I enjoy being a voyeur, watching secrets exchanged in plain sight. No other dance has tango's *charla*, or chat, a period of a minute or less between songs. It's like "speed relating." A room that was just silent but for music and the sweep of shoes across the floor erupts into a loud fest of chattering couples engaged in *chamuyo* (exaggerated smooth talking), *piropos* (flirtatious remarks), and other small talk. The original purpose of *charla* was to give the leader a few seconds to assess the next song and to decide how he might execute his *salida*.

I never tire of studying the women's feet, envying the delicate-boned ones, in so many variations of gorgeous shoes: suede, leather, a rich palette of color, some with silver, gold, or rhinestone accents.

I make a mental list of the styles my collection needs—a nine-centimeter heel with crisscross straps around the ankle; a sparkling red pair; and the latest rage—the sandal-foot, very open. Mine (when I can afford them) will be in metallic aquamarine and royal blue.

I watch both the men's and women's feet do *adornos,* or adornments, the decorative punctuation in a tango sentence. I watch and learn, taking notes on ones I like enough to incorporate as my own. The best male dancers can trace *lápices* (literally "pencils"), or circles, with the balls of their feet as they turn the follower, all in fluid, seamless motion. I take ceaseless pleasure in watching the men of this so-called "macho" culture show their feminine side in the way they move their bodies. The women do quick *amagues* (nervous clicks), amazing deft footwork in those spike heels, and high and low *voleos* that show off their legs and sometimes their thighs.

There is incredible competition in tango, but I am never jealous of other dancers. Never threatened. This is my other deep dark secret—my good secret—that I have never shared with anyone. I am nameless and faceless, but nobody can touch me in tango. When I step onto the floor, I go from broken to whole, from a flimsy self-confidence to a self-assurance of steel. Off the floor I am an average-pretty woman, in good shape. On the floor, I am a goddess. *Soy la diosa de esta jodida galaxia.*

Back at the loft, I sit for forty minutes of meditation before trying to sleep. I have been plagued by bad dreams. In one, a few months ago,

I was sentenced to death, forced to swallow berry-flavored poison. When I awoke, I knew the elixir was the berry-scented perfume Poison that I had sprayed all over Evelyn's locker at the Dolphin Club where she, Dan, and I were members.

Rational or not, Evelyn became the object of the purest hatred I have ever tasted. This betrayal, by a woman I considered a friend, drew the overarching focus of my ire. One day, about two weeks before I arrived in Buenos Aires, I called Blanche Hartman, a former abbess at San Francisco Zen Center, to ask for a *dokusan,* a formal discussion of one's Zen practice. Blanche was my kind of guru. She grew up in Berkeley; she sat *zazen,* the Japanese name for Zen meditation, like a mountain, but she had a regular life with kids and grandkids outside the *zendo,* the inner sanctum of the temple where *zazen* is sat.

I met Blanche at the Zen center and we bowed deeply to each other. We turned and bowed to the small altar where a cone of sandalwood incense burned before a little Buddha. We sat facing each other in lotus on *zafu* cushions and tatami mats. I waited with my hands in the prescribed mudra—left resting in right palm, thumbs forming a bridge—as Blanche tucked her flowing black Zen priest robes under her legs.

"My hatred is so overpowering," I told Blanche. "I'm sleeping with a would-be murderess!" I didn't have to explain to her that I meant my own shadow Self. Nothing I could have said would have shocked Blanche who, at eighty years old, had seen much. She closed her eyes calmly, her shaved head nodding knowingly. She began to tell me about some of her challenges, which indeed rivaled my own. Blanche told me about how she worked through her confusion and accepted the things about her life that she wished were not so. And then she recited:

"This is what should be done
By one who is skilled in goodness,
And who knows the path of peace."

"The *Metta Sutta?*" I said. She nodded. These are the first lines in the Buddhist's Sutra of Loving Kindness. She recommended I memorize and chant it.

I was no stranger to it or to many of the sutras that I had chanted over the past eighteen years at the Zen center. Chanting in Japanese or English with a roomful of people had the same effect on me as my tango dancing—both always made me feel high and cleansed. Both produced some sort of endorphins. I knew the power of chanting as well as I knew the power of tango.

I went home and memorized the *Metta Sutta*. A fundamental teaching of Zen is "detachment," not to be confused with disassociation, an unhealthy cutting off of part of yourself. Detachment was a state I wanted more than anything right then and there, the state of being present for all that was happening, all that I could not change or control, feeling my pain, and *not* acting on it. Just being with it. But my poisonous feelings, as much as I wanted them gone, did not abate.

In Aquatic Park, at San Francisco's Fisherman's Wharf, I ran into Evelyn again a week before I was to leave for Buenos Aires. She did not appreciate my lack of warmth toward her. "You have to accept that Dan is with me now," she told me.

The comment, while true, cut me deeply. It reminded me of the serious consequences of having neglected my relationship with Dan. I recalled how I had told her, "Dan is my rock. I hate to lose him," and she'd launched into a long diatribe on how her sister, who was going through a divorce, didn't like losing either. "But, you know, things change."

So despite my years of a practice based on cultivating compassion, I found myself to be no poster girl for detachment or the serenity that Zen could bring. My response to her comment was lightning quick and spring-loaded. I grabbed a fistful of her long hair and pulled—really hard. She withered dramatically to the ground like the wicked witch in *The Wizard of Oz* and I let go. In the many times I've relived that moment since then, I hear the witch's lament as my own: "Oh, what a world, what a world."

Strangely, while I was still shaking with anger and fear over what I'd done, two young men and one young woman passing by stopped to shake my hand, as if I'd won a duel.

But nothing inside of me admired or rewarded my action. I should not have pulled her hair. She was not a bad person. I kept wishing for her to have someone like Olympia Dukakis's straight-talking Sicilian mother in *Moonstruck* to tell her, "You don't shit where you eat." Had I been calm or coherent, I might have tried explaining that as a person I'd called my friend, she'd transgressed my only Golden Rule. She wanted to go to the police and file a restraining order. "For all I know you have a contract out on me," she said. Dan, suddenly the unlikely middle guy, talked her out of it.

On my third night sleeping in the loft, I draw a tarot card before turning in. The Hanged Man. It reads: "He is in suspension, tortured by anxiety and the fear that his sacrifice might in the end come to nothing." Perfect. Drawing the card means "an acceptance of waiting in darkness." It augurs the need for giving up something. Such as "unforgiving hatred," says the card.

I fall into a fitful sleep. My dream is in a dark desert place of nothing but mounds and mounds of stones. There is to be an execution of some man and me, for capital crimes. I keep marching to my execution. Just like Evita, perpetually condemned to march up Avenida de Mayo to a dirge of tango, as I saw in scratchy film footage at the Evita Museo. I awake in the black still of the night and hear a few curling notes from the unseen bird. Having to negotiate this dark labyrinth between grief and rage makes me want to delay dreamtime. I can do that with a simple folk dance called tango. I get up and put on another tango-black dress, no sparkles this time. It's midnight. The *milonga* is calling.

Chapter 2

Tango Bleeds the Bad Blood

Toda mi vida es el ayer
Que me detiene en el pasado.

All my life is the yesterday
that keeps me in the past.

—*Naranjo en Flor (1944)*

I am sitting on the plaza at Mercado de Frutos in El Tigre, a town on the delta of the Río Paraná, an hour's drive north of Buenos Aires. Despite its name, the market does not sell fruit. It sells local artisanry and touristy souvenirs, lots of them, and you can spend hours going from booth to booth, collecting, gathering, or just admiring wicker, cane, pottery, leather, Indian wear, weavings, batik, jewelry, and so much more. I have come here for the day with my friend Lina, who is visiting from California for two weeks of tango.

We've hired Dante, a *tanguero* we met at Porteño y Bailarin *milonga,* to drive us. Peruvian by birth, he speaks fluent English with an American accent in fast, clipped sound bites like Al Pacino or Robert De Niro in one of their hood movies.

I met Lina and her tango partner, James, in San Francisco after admiring their dancing for months from afar. Together they embodied the lyricism of tango, the flesh and blood incarnation of the music that grabs you profoundly, the high art of it. They were refined. They were awesome. They were so smooth you could put a glass of milk on James's head and it wouldn't even splash—that was the magnificence of their mutual smoothness. James and Lina's eyes were never on the ground but always down at a forty-five-degree angle, softly inward, as in Zen meditation. Lina had the lighter presence—always with an angelic smile on her face. James was more serious in his rimless specs, with the demeanor of a tweedy professor.

I finally got up the nerve to say hello to this high priest and priestess of tango for the first time at an afternoon *milonga* at the Chinese Pagoda in Golden Gate Park. It was a most auspicious day. Normally cold and foggy, this July day was warm, sunny, and welcoming, just like Lina. To my surprise, she had an accent. "French?" I'd asked. Her ensemble was always flawless as a Parisian's. "No, but it's a good guess," she replied. "I like France, but I'm from Syria."

I leaned against the railing, feeling like a wallflower as I watched my two new friends and others dancing round and round the small circle of the pagoda. Not seeing any leaders I knew, I had made up my mind to leave at the very moment I noticed a handsome stranger with black hair and black eyes coming across the pagoda toward me. He was a good dancer: the perfect height for me, with the full, slightly barrel chest I love to push against to find my lead. He seemed a little nervous. Or maybe it was me. Maybe it was something else. He told me his name was Dave and that he was from the Napa Valley, that maybe he'd see me at Verdi Club some Thursday. When it was time for me to go I had a distinct feeling I'd never see Dave again, and I couldn't help but wonder what that feeling was about. It was the feeling of a destined meeting—something I've since learned not to take too lightly.

Lina is off looking for the perfect yerba maté *calabaza* (gourd) and companion *bombilla* (sipping straw) amid the daily market's dozens of booths. She is a much more thorough and patient shopper than I, and before she leaves she will have the best the city has to offer in maté, leather, shoes, and clothes.

I think of the street artist's work I bought on my carefree first trip to Argentina: a couple in a passionate tango embrace painted in oils over faded sheet music. Their dipping *corte* covers all but one word on the music score: *duele*. How many times did I let that pretty word swivel off my tongue as if it had nothing to do with my life? Now I know too well that *duelle* means "it hurts"—as in pain, the most liberal spice of tango lyrics.

As I sit and wait for Lina on a bench in the plaza, a couple of older women come and sit down next to me, so close I have to sidle over a bit. I find this bewildering—that they have chosen to sit so close to me when there are about four other empty benches nearby. My North American sense of entitlement to personal space has already been challenged on the subway and in the streets of Buenos Aires. These women are fleshy, voluptuous, like many of my Italian relatives, so I make a point of receiving their body warmth with an openness I don't have toward strangers back in San Francisco.

As they chatter, heedless of me, I open my little black journal, but I have no desire to write. Instead, I let my black felt-tip pen sketch what my hand "sees," a little exercise my art therapist has encouraged me to practice. When it's done, I have a pen-ink drawing of the plaza's three-tiered fountain with three *palomas,* mourning doves, hovering over the pools of water. Water cascades from their beaks in tear-shaped drops. I have drawn some drops upside down, as if they are floating up into the beak of one bird.

"Give it a name," I hear my art therapist, Gail, saying to me. I had seen her periodically over the past four years to flush my muse and keep my creative juice flowing. I started going to her at a time when it felt as if I had nothing but frazzled energy and not an iota of inspiration left over for "real" writing after giving my all to my work as an editor day after day.

In her bright office, I learned to use various media—pastels, ink, charcoal, tempera or watercolor paints, and crayons—on big empty sheets of white paper. I've always deplored my visual art skills, but with Gail's guidance, I've learned to appreciate how one can use free-association images to get beneath the same old words. She's helped me channel feelings, vivid dreams (often nightmares in my case), or past history (god, how many times did my father come up?) into artwork that we'd then deconstruct. She was skilled in finding the corner of a drawing that had a gap or black spot that pointed to my split selves. It annoyed me, but egged me on deeper to introspection—in both my meditation and my life. In this way, Gail was like a midwife who helped me birth new parts of my Self.

During our final session several weeks before my trip I sank into her comfy beige leather couch. I was blaming Evelyn for everything wrong in my life. I did not want to indulge or even divulge the level of my venom, but I couldn't contain it. I railed against the so-called friend who'd betrayed me, though I blamed myself for Dan's devastation over my affair with Dave. He blamed himself, took refuge in the easiest piece of ass in sight—oh how I railed and railed. As soon as I said these things, though, I felt more disgusted with myself than with her.

Gail just took it all in. She did not encourage me to draw during that last session. Instead, she brought out the big guns. She suggested we try EMDR (eye movement desensitization and reprocessing), a therapeutic modality that we did, not infrequently, especially when my too-skillful verbal expression was masking the underlying problem.

"Okay," I said, "crucify me. Let it bleed." This was an inside joke of ours because the practice involves two small plastic devices that rest in each hand and vibrate, sending signals to stimulate the brain. The process is supposed to "bleed" you of trauma by facilitating an interaction between both hemispheres of the brain as you relive a stressful situation. I was fond of referring to the little orbs as stigmata, which always made Gail laugh. If only she could have known how very serious I was when I said it that day.

At Gail's prompting, and with the orbs still vibrating alternately in my closed palms, I closed my eyes and relived Dan's telling me about Evelyn. Blow by blow. When the process was over I did not feel desensitized or reprocessed. I had a deep desire to have my split selves rejoined. I wished to be bled dry of hate. The "stigmata" had never felt like more than magical thinking to me. I left Gail's office, calmly, for the final time, telling her I was fine. But I was anything but fine. It was just one week later when I yanked Evelyn's hair.

If only we could have figured out how to make my tango bliss bleed me dry. I have no idea what part of the brain tango stimulates for me, but it feels like sped-up meditation. Each dance is a chance to let go completely. Each dance is a rebirth. You receive and let go a thousand times a minute—that's the only way this dance of dances works. If EMDR was my stigmata, tango is my resurrection.

"Fountain of Renewal," I label the sketch in a fit of wishful thinking. I see myself as that lone dove with the drops floating back up into my beak. The only way I can survive is by retaining the belief that there must be some long-distant nourishment in this struggle.

Lina comes back with her goods. Dante comes back from his stroll.

We board a boat that takes us deep into the delta, through El Tigre's calm oasis. We glide past rushes and moist, green banks with darling little cottages. I am suddenly overwhelmed with how heavy I feel inside—like lead—and don't want to chitchat as I slip into a memory of the Alaska ferry cruise Dan and I took together a few years back. We'd leaned against the railing together for hours watching for whales, bears, eagles, and other wildlife.

Sometimes my memory takes me back to one solitary week in October 2005, when I had never felt more content, more present, or more whole in my life. It was a place or time within myself that I experienced briefly, and which I believe is still there, but it's as if I've lost the combination.

Oddly enough, it was a week during which Dan and I had had a little falling-out and he had asked for a "breather." This was nothing new. It was a pattern in our relationship, but the intervals between tiffs seemed longer and longer as time went on and our relationship got stronger. So when he suggested the weeklong hiatus, I remember thinking, *Here we go again,* only this time it was followed by some of the saddest and loneliest feelings I'd ever felt in my life.

Then—maybe it was my tango dancing—but the circle of understanding got just a little bigger and I realized that after fifteen years I loved Dan exactly for *this,* for *who he was,* not for who he *should or would be.* It was as if a slightly blurry lens came into clear focus, or as if my lungs had suddenly cleared of chronic congestion. I breathed deeply, cleanly. I came into the present moment and stopped living in conditional tenses. It was the exhilaration my Zen teachers had told me about, of accepting things the way they are.

With this newfound insight, I decided that this time away from Dan had its upside—I would simply dance every evening. And that was what I did—and I did it with a light heart. If I could have anticipated what was about to unfold and how it would change our lives, I would have talked with Dan about how my circle of understanding of us had just gotten bigger. I would have taken him into it and shared with him the now-lost combination.

I attended an early evening *milonga* at the San Francisco Ferry Building on the Friday of our week apart. It was a convivial *milonga.* Shoppers pursuing the world's finest foodstuffs—from sustainably harvested California caviar to scrumptious artisan cheeses—stopped and watched the dancers in the open corridor. Across the hall, I recognized the guy from the pagoda. Dave. He bounded across the room and found me. We danced. He said he was staying in the city a few nights—could we practice? I gave him my email address without hesitation. I got a message from him the very next morning. Though Dave gave me no reason to believe he wanted anything more than dance practice from me, I stared at his email for thirty minutes, trembling, wishing it would go away, wishing I could ignore it. But I couldn't. And so I hit REPLY, setting up a time and place to meet.

Two weeks later, by mid-November, I was seeing Dave regularly. We'd practiced and danced several days a week. We would share some morning coffee and scones on my porch in the Presidio. I'd convinced myself that the chemistry I felt with Dave was all about our dancing, until I got an email from him in which he confessed the way he felt about me.

My eyes ran over the words: *The truth . . . the truth is I am dying to slide my lips slowly down your back . . . covering your skin with full kisses . . . and, reaching the lowest point of your back, your hips and legs in my hands, turn you over, and continue . . . Yes, basically you're driving me nuts.*

We had flirted, but this brash directness took me by surprise. I can't say I was put off by it, though. I was lured in. He had told me he was separated from his wife for the third time in their twenty-nine-year relationship and was moving into the city for a while to find himself anew. I told him about Dan, and some of our troubles, but added that our relationship was too important and that I had no intention of leaving him. I'd be lying if I said I didn't enjoy Dave's attention and overtures, especially at a time when Dan was physically and emotionally distant. I had the strong conviction that Dave and I should not make love . . . and I held my ground, for a while. I held my ground, held my ground, I swear I held my ground (but Heaven rest us, I'm not asbestos).

I finally gave in less than six weeks after that first email confessing how he felt about me, but I swear it felt like a lifetime. I felt like a piece of chocolate dying to melt in his mouth but that's kept chilled way beyond its shelf life.

On December 9, the morning after, I wrote in my journal: . . . *it was wonderful . . . such stamina. To relegate it to words is to defile it.*

That last sentence is from a Zen sutra, used in reference to the dharma or enlightenment, phenomena so rarefied and evanescent they cannot be held in words. But what's clear now is that so much of the sacredness that I experienced making love to Dave was about tango rather than sex. We had that ineffable chemistry, or as it's called in dance, "connection." People who watched us dance together saw it instantly. His torso felt like a cloud—that indescribably delicious male impetus. We could dance forever without arms, just sharing the give and take of energy. To have a fit that good ranks right up there with finding your soul mate. I have had lots of good connections with dancers, but none rival the "undefiled" one I had with Dave.

We practiced hard. I had access to big wood floors throughout the Presidio and at the Dolphin Club. Dave always brought an extra T-shirt because of how much he would sweat. We worked on various *colgadas* and *volcadas,* two advanced steps that involve an intrinsic understanding of how to share an axis, a center of gravity that is greater than your two. It requires trust and surrender. Because leaders (usually men) initiate the moves, it's been my experience more often than not that they want to tell me what I'm doing wrong when the step goes awry. But Dave and I never had words of recrimination. We understood instinctively there was always a third higher presence, the Dave-Camille partnership. In tango, we had the kind of rapport I'd always longed for in my relationships.

We laughed as much as we danced. I fantasized about joining the Palm Springs Follies, a group that only accepts performers over age fifty. (I still dream of joining the Follies "when I grow up"— they've had performers in their nineties!)

Dave followed me to Paris during part of my stay there in January 2006. I had planned a solo trip strictly to dance tango. (Dan took the opportunity to go to Guatemala to study Spanish.) Ah, Paris. I've loved it since my maiden voyage in 1971 (only two short weeks after I could officially no longer be called a "maiden"). It never lets me down. Dave and I enjoyed Saint-Germain-des-Prés, where I'd rented a friend's cute little walk-up (six flights, no elevator). We visited the Latin Quarter, cafés, restaurants, parks, streets I love, and a writing friend, Melinda, and her husband in their luxurious sixteenth arrondissement apartment. We took a private tango lesson with well-known teacher Jean-Sebastien Rampazzi at Casa de Tango but didn't dance nearly enough. Dave was getting sick, probably from stress over his marriage. We did not make love very much, but that was not important to me. I grasped at that elusive connection. It was a deluded thing to do; tango and Zen both show how "grasping" is the quickest way to fall off your axis (be it physical or spiritual).

By the time we got back to the States we downgraded to friends. I felt withdrawal symptoms, but I honored the one lucid thought I had expressed from the start: to protect the dance. I both regret and cherish the brief interlude. Dave was a good man and friend, if a bit confused. No, wait. We were both confused. Intoxicated. This was a symptom we both shared, he and I, as offspring of alcoholic parents. His mom, my dad. In our figurative drunkenness we bonded over all the stuff our mates were not giving us, getting loaded on how we would give it all to each other. There was a sweetness. We felt an effortless familiarity with each other.

What a tangoed web we wove.

By the time Dan returned from Guatamala, he knew something was off. When I confirmed his suspicions, he fell apart. I wanted us to go on, I told him, but I needed time. He blamed himself because we were having a breather. I never anticipated the strength of his reaction. Even as I realized how much he loved me, I felt frozen, lockjawed, and straitjacketed, the polar opposite of that magnificent week in late October. I wish I could reach back in time and have said something more than "I need time."

Dante, Lina, and I disembark on an island and take a path through the deciduous forest to the outdoor patio of a café for lunch. I force myself back to the present moment and take pleasure in listening to Dante speak. God, I love his name, how it resonates with circles of Hell and Heaven and maybe, ultimately, redemption. He is telling Lina how the Argentine *milongueros* do not like when foreign women flaunt custom and ask them to dance, but they tolerate it.

I make a mental note not to flout that custom. I want this whole country to love me back.

Lina's presence and her eagerness to see Buenos Aires get me out of my funk. The following day, the two of us ride the #150 bus to the Feria de Mataderos in a working-class barrio. We push through the crowds past the Mercado Nacional de Hacienda, where livestock is corralled for auction. We separate to walk the packed streets and sidewalks and plan to meet up for dinner. I see a lot of gaucho paraphernalia, including star-studded spurs and the ornate silver belts they love to wear. There are lovely earrings, rings, and other jewelry. Nothing tempts me but the food.

I make one purchase—a bottle of homemade *chimichurri*, made with variations of parsley, oregano, garlic, salt, hot pepper, olive oil, and vinegar. I'll add some spice to life. I love Argentine food already: the *parrilla* (or grilled meats of every muscle and organ); the Italian pastas and pizzas; the Spanish fish stews; the empanadas stuffed with savory fillings; the *dulce de leche;* the hearts of palm, fresh beets, and carrots added liberally to salads. My one complaint is the lack of the assertive spice and seasoning that you would expect in a predominantly Italo-Hispanic culture. I have yet to hear a reasonable explanation for the lack of piquancy (they don't even put black pepper on the table in restaurants, only salt).

Later on, my Spanish teacher would attempt to explain this by saying that the people were too poor. "The food is simple," she says, a simplistic response. "But it was precisely because of poor immigrants in the U.S. that our cuisine was so enriched," I tell her. My poor Sicilian grandparents grew hot peppers, fennel, mint, chard, basil, and more in their small garden in New Jersey long before these became widespread supermarket items. I attribute the mildness to something a Porteño man once told me—that as a nation they feel perpetually like the little brother to Europe and the United States. It's time they start thinking about biting back—starting with the food.

Lina and I meet up again amid the hushed excitement along the gaucho course of the Mataderos's main drag, Lisandro de la Torre. The horsemen quietly prepare for the competition. They are grooming horses, petting them, whispering to the beasts and to each other in an idiom that eludes us. My sense is of baseball players who have their set of superstitious hand-body movements. Lina wants to know why some horses have their manes and tails cut. I formulate the question in Spanish to one of the gauchos, who tells us, "For decoration." We gesture to him that we don't like it; it's unnatural. But he shrugs and ignores us. Later I learn what the gaucho may have wanted to tell us but didn't think we gringas would understand—that this custom of cutting sawlike designs in the criollo-breed horse's mane came with some of his country's forebears, the Moors.

We position ourselves alongside many other spectators on the sidewalks, on curbs, near the frame that holds the *sortija,* a half-dollar-size metal ring that dangles from a ribbon tied to the top of the frame. The cowboys must gallop their horses like the devil from about two blocks back as they carry a stick in hand. They must place the spike at the end of the stick through the ring—it's on a level just above their heads—as they pass beside the ring at speeds as high as sixty miles per hour. We watch and cheer excitedly for the two dozen gauchos, one after the other, as they kick up the street dust with their horses and make their charge toward the hanging ring. Four of them, including a little boy of about ten, get the spike in the little ring to thundering applause. It's quite amazing, no less a feat of coordination than the smoothness of Lina and James's tango moves.

As Lina and I walk to find the perfect *parrilla*, we are swept into the conviviality of music and dance in the streets, including tango and the folk dance *chacarera*. I am learning how the gaucho culture has seasoned tango. Gauchos of the pampas, the treeless plains, played polka-like *chamame* music on a button accordion in the early nineteenth century that prepared the way for the seventy-one-button *bandoneón*. Some of the heel-stomping *taconeos* you will see tango leaders do today come from gauchos. The stomping hitchhiked to South America with flamenco-dancing immigrants from Andalusia, Spain. Like many tourists, I'm a pushover for the almost-cliché art you can find nearly everywhere that portrays tango-dancing couples of old in Andalusian-influenced garb. Men appear in wide-lapelled suits, homburgs, and *lengues,* or white scarves, around their necks. The women, in flower-topped hats, wear fitted long bouffant dresses with crinolines showing as they arc their lower legs in *voleos.*

Over the next week, Lina dances deeper into the wee hours than I do. By day we meet up and enjoy great meals. We get a private tour of the glorious Dandi Royal mansion in San Telmo. We know its owner, *tanguero* Hector Villar, from his regular visits to San Francisco *milongas*. His tango-themed hotel is belle époque-style, with broad curving staircases of dark wood, Renaissance bronzes, frescoed walls, tiled skylights, three-tiered chandeliers, a pool on the roof, and one of the most elegant dance salons in town.

We ride the city's old wooden A train, South America's first subway car, to the Almagro, another working-class barrio. We consider eating at a famed hole in the wall where, for a few pesos, you can ravenously down hunks of grilled Argentine beef. But despite the tantalizing aroma of charcoal-roasted meat, the joint looks too *crudo,* or raw, for our taste, especially as full as it is of brawny men. We head to Las Violetas, a historic café, like Tortoni but brighter with French windowpanes and stained glass scenes that recall France's nineteenth-century school of pastoral painters. Its sophistication and intelligence better reflects the sensibility of my friend.

I will miss Lina when she leaves. I've enjoyed watching the way the men are drawn to the magnet that is her natural beauty. Her singular devotion to tango parallels my own. It's something you do regularly, like going to church, or praying silently. You go to *milongas,* you work the room with your smile, your eyes, silently. We are not the type of friends who banter and dissect our night out, the men, the other women. I know that under her hush, Lina is like me, like Paris Hilton, *la diosa de esta jodida galaxia,* when she dances. I know she feels the same way I do. I imagine her out there on the floor, enraptured, and thinking to herself, *Nobody dances tango the way I do.*

Chapter 3

Accidental Tanguera

Stay close and do nothing or you might miss it.

—Tenshin Reb Anderson, Zen monk, speaking on enlightenment

"Very few people do tango casually," my San Francisco tango teacher, Christy Cote, once told an audience during a lecture on tango and Zen. "People sabotage their own careers so they won't go anywhere, so they can dance tango."

I came to tango reluctantly, though curious about why people put their hands over their hearts and got this silly beatific look on their faces when they mentioned Argentine tango. I told a friend that beginner tango classes look like scenes from *Night of the Living Dead* because of the zombielike concentration and anxiety-ridden faces of "novitiates." They move with heads bowed to watch their feet, as if that were where the dance came from.

Before I got swept up by tango, I'd danced ballroom, swing, and Latin dances. I performed twice at the Metronome's annual showcase at Cowell Theater. At my last performance, Dan's family and mine filled two entire front rows. My teacher, Eldon Bryce, and I did a duo—a mix of foxtrot, quick step, and West Coast swing—to Van Morrison's "Moondance." We threw in some yoga leg extensions because, as Eldon told the show's surprised art director, "She can do them." My personal audience went nuts, my mother among them.

"I wish your father could be here," she told me afterward. My father had died two months earlier, so she was visiting my brothers and me out West.

"He is," I said, pulling his photo out of my shoe. "I put him there for good luck." I smiled.

⚜

Dan had never been a dancer, and we had already been together eleven years when I took up ballroom and swing. I was fond of coming home from dancing and announcing, "I had multiple partners again tonight." He would just laugh. He knew he had nothing to worry about. So did I, until Dave came along. But without tango, there wouldn't have been a Dave. Tango's spell for me was gradual, not sudden, but when it hit home, it moved into my life like a long-lost relative. No other dance takes you over so completely. More than a dance, it becomes a way of life.

When I started taking tango classes, I was surprised and delighted to find one of my longtime Zen teachers, Reb Anderson, and his wife, Rusa, in my first class. Reb told me that he'd been teaching Zen Buddhism for so long (more than thirty years) that he was ready to experience his "beginner's mind" again.

If dharma talks were tango compositions, Reb's would be those of Rodolfo Biagi or of Juan D'Arienzo, the King of Rhythm. Reb has the kind of voice that makes your pulse rise. He has a way of always touching on exactly what I need to hear at the moment. In the first dharma talk I heard him give, nearly twenty years ago, he recited from memory the sonnet by Renaissance poet George Herbert, "Love bade me welcome (but my soul drew back guilty of dust and sin . . .)." It's a poem about self-love. I have since memorized it and brought it out lately to guide my silent meditations.

Tango added a new dimension to my relationship with Reb. Instead of facing his raised podium from my place on a black *zafu*, I danced beside him. We were two sentient beings in equal darkness learning to dance tango. We only practiced open embrace in that beginner class series, which spared us the awkwardness many beginner tango students feel the first time they tell you to hug and hold a stranger to your bosom. I loved practicing with Reb, regardless. Having long followed the eightfold path, he had right concentration down.

Christy Cote was our teacher. She'd been an account executive for the Hertz Corporation, negotiating rental car contracts for a portfolio of Fortune 500 companies before giving up the high-paying job and the company car for her love of tango. She had been teaching ballroom dance when she took an interest in Argentine tango after seeing the Broadway smash hit that sparked tango's comeback some fifteen years ago, *Forever Tango*. She started taking classes with one of the stars from that show, the late Carlos Gavito, who mentored her and encouraged her to teach. But it wasn't until a breast cancer diagnosis two years later that she took the leap to become a full-time tango dancer, teacher, and performer.

It was an impulsive move, but it paid off. A brilliant, gentle, and soft-spoken cancer survivor, she is one of the few people in the San Francisco Bay Area who make a living at tango.

⚜

After a few months of tango lessons, Reb, like me, couldn't help but make the undeniably strong connection between Zen and tango. So he invited Christy and her two assistants to the Green Gulch Zen center in Marin, north of San Francisco. He gave a lecture titled "Exploring the Dance of Buddha."

One of the first things that Reb noted in his lecture was how the lotus flower appears suddenly out of muddy water and is the symbol of enlightenment arising from a confused mind. This was reminiscent of how tango arose from a "muddy" source, the brothels and slums of Argentina.

Reb proceeded to talk about why he joined his wife in dance lessons. He said, "Growth and wisdom require that we enter areas of unskillfulness. . . . We must enter realms of darkness and anxiety in order to grow." Reb is a giant of a teacher in my eyes, so I admired his humbleness.

My own attraction to these two seemingly unrelated practices seemed to unfold before me over the course of the lecture. Reb continued, "We need to train in movement and stillness to enter realization," which affirmed my gravitating more and more to tango. "When you sit in meditation," he pointed out, "you learn to do so with no expectation. To sit still with no anticipation, with no plan. This is exactly what seems to be the case in tango." My mind clicked with how Zen, which drew from my masculine energy—the discipline, stoicism, and restraint that both my parents gave me—was already merging in a happy marriage with my tango, the feminine energy awarded me by those same parents who knew there was a time to drop work and indulge their bacchanalian love of dancing.

Other comparisons did not escape, like how in tango, as in Zen, we traditionally wear dark clothes so as to blend in and not detract attention from the dance. We lower our eyes in concentration in both practices as well. In both tango and Zen, you must transcend the dualistic idea of a separate Self. Or, as Reb said, "When you get over the idea of leader and follower, there is tango." But it's not easy to let go of this duality. It wasn't until much later that I'd recognize how deeply my connection to Dave hinged on the simple fact that we were able to do this so seamlessly.

In Zen, we say, "There is nothing to get—you already know all you need to know." Similarly, tango is nothing but a series of improvised patterns. It can be broken down to a vocabulary of a mere six basic steps, each like a separate phrase:

1) *el básico*—the basic eight-step box step—is often called *dos por cuatro,* or two by four; 2) *caminando*—walking; 3) forward *ochos,* or figure eights; 4) backward *ochos;* 5) *voleo*—or a fan "throw" of the lower leg; 6) *molinetes*—windmills, or grapevines (also called

giros, or turns). And that's all there is. Every fancy step—*volcadas, colgadas, sacadas, media lunas*—is a compound sentence or dangling modifier that originates from one of these six "words." Adornments are pretty but unnecessary extras.

The interpretation we each bring to the dance is what makes no two dances the same, each as unique as fingerprints or snowflakes. In a 1998 essay entitled "The Tango and Trapeze Acts," famed Argentine *tanguero* Cacho Dante writes of the *milongueros* of Buenos Aires, "When they didn't really know how to dance, they did 20 steps; when they knew a bit more, they did 10; and when they really knew what they were doing, they danced five, but with real quality."

I was destined to love a dance whose pinnacle of achievement paralleled my midlife philosophy: The less clutter, the richer the experience.

I took six months of group classes with Christy before I started venturing out to dance socially at Bay Area *milongas.* There was one for every night of the week, many of them in San Francisco's South of Market, or SoMa, area, which I've since renamed Tango Gulch.

I was still dancing Lindy and ballroom, dances whose lead and follow rely not on the heart chakra (or energy hotspot, Sanskrit for "wheel") as in tango, but on compression conveyed down the arms, through the hands, and mediated by a dynamic tension in the elbows.

It didn't take too long before everything but tango fell off my schedule. I cannot locate the exact moment when this happened. The same passion that led me to these ramshackle dance halls in Buenos Aires also took me to Paris, Prague, and New York, and to neighborhoods in Baltimore and Philadelphia I would have never sought out if it hadn't been for the dance.

Looking back to my early classes, I can see how Christy's assistant, Pier, helped me find the key to my own inner tango in what I learned to recognize as my "hover" zone. Time after time, just when I felt, often too smugly, that I had a pattern down, Pier would deflate me: "Slow down! Wait, hold back, milk that step!"

"The man *invites* his partner to take an *ocho* or to do a *molinete*," Pier would gently explain. It was my prerogative to dilly-dally a bit, make him wait. I both loved and feared this, that I could forge such an attitude. I had never been good at feminine wiles, making men wait or guess. I was always prompt or early, forthcoming with feelings. My primal love was a man who didn't invite me, who ordered me to do things, to make me jump when he spoke. This dance, considered so "macho" by many, was turning out to be my *great robe of liberation,* a phrase in a sutra that we lay-ordained Zen practitioners chant each morning over our mini Buddha robes.

It took me a while to trust that it was okay to make the man wait, as Pier urged. But by and by I did, and I discovered my hover zone—a place where my weight feels suspended, as in my dreams, where I fly at will and wake up believing my body has truly defied gravity. My hover zone is a flashing-strobe place between steps where I hang out, totally present, ready to go in any of a thousand plausible directions for my leader.

It is the space between breaths, between beats of the heart, between pulses of energy. It is the Tao-like place of particles ruled by quantum physics' uncertainty principle. I have never heard any teacher talk of the "hover," but I know I go there, and I'm sure all good dancers know it by other names. One of my biggest pet peeves occurs in a class when a teacher stops me in the hover zone, when my weight is suspended in animation, to make a verbal correction. The hover is as far from verbal cues as you can get; it is the place of trance, of alpha brain waves, of surrender to the present. As tango's parallels to Zen became increasingly more apparent—an ever-shifting center of trueness, anticipation killing the moment, ego leading to grasping and suffering—I began to sit *zazen* less and to pursue tango more. I didn't even realize it at the time. But that silly beatific look was soon to be mine.

In the States, tango attracts mainly highly paid professionals who have the disposable income to splurge for expensive private lessons. For reasons that escape me, many techies are drawn to tango. I often marveled at the way they'd analyze it and deconstruct it, oftentimes lamenting how difficult and technical a dance tango is. Being left-handed, or right-brain dominant, I didn't see its difficulty as technical at all. I saw it as child's play, a returning to an innocence we all have. You subtract your adult, or conditioned, Self and there you have it. Tango is ever-present. From the start, I felt it as a place of numinous presence more so than with any other dance. *To relegate it to words is to defile it.*

Daniel, Christy's other assistant, is still one of my favorite teachers. He's an artist who teaches more through his body than his mouth. I love how he'd always say to the leaders, "The center of the universe is the follower. You forget about yourself." He often wordlessly led me in complex patterns my body had never experienced. But there was nothing to do but follow, free of thought, expertise, and anticipation. Beginner's mind, as Reb might have called it, is often lost and refound as we learn.

At Reb's lecture, Daniel had proclaimed himself "not the least bit spiritual." He said tango was a pursuit of art and beauty for him. But he sounded as spiritual as Reb to me when he confided that he thought men were needy. "We can't do this by ourselves," he said. "I've had my heart broken. I keep running into getting my feelings hurt. If you don't find a place where nobody hurts you, you won't grow." Rare is the leader who recognizes this.

Here in Buenos Aires, outside the so-called "tango for export" scene, I meet hundreds of dancers who just lay their heads and brains to rest, next to mine, and dance from the neck down. These are the descendants of tango's originators, who were mostly uneducated nineteenth-century immigrants. They packed together, one family to a room, into cheap tight quarters in tenements called *conventillos* (mentioned often in tango lyrics). Bathrooms and kitchens were communal, as was the patio, where neighbors were forced to be in touch with each other. There, some of tango's first steps were born of primal necessity, a language of bodies longing to convey love and feeling through music with *bandoneónes,* crude instruments; or perhaps it was the language of Rainer Maria Rilke's two "solitudes" longing to "protect, touch, and greet one another."

Tango's genealogy is much debated, but most agree that tango traces its roots to a melting pot of nationalities. Africans brought as slaves were dancing the *candombe,* a very get-down, rhythmic beat marked by strong percussion. The slaves faced each other, but did not embrace. Throughout the 1800s, various other influences appeared. The gauchos who sang *payadas,* or ballads, added some moves, particularly with their loose-jointed feet, that show up as adornments. Cuban mariners introduced the habanera, a slow dance in 2/4 time, and there was the Andalusian tango, a variation on the habanera. Finally, the Italian immigrants who loved to sing and play instruments added their heart and soul, and the dance solidified. It is said that tango was also done in the brothels and saloons where men, called *compadritos* (old-fashioned ruffians), imitated the contortions of *candombe* and vied with each other for prostitutes.

It's interesting to note that early tango music was more spirited than sad. "Mi Noche Triste," written by Uruguayan Pascual Contursi in 1915, marks a major turning point in tango lyrics. It's the first tango song to have sad lyrics and a storyline—it tells of a pimp dropped by his *percanta* (shady lady). The drama of unrequited love had universal appeal. Around the 1920s, Italian musicians and composers injected their nostalgia and melancholy.

There are numerous styles of tango, although they fall broadly into the three most popular: *milonguero* (very close embrace with tight, small moves); *salón* (close embrace, but with occasional opening, longer strides); and *nuevo* (mostly open embrace, with lots of fancy moves). A fourth category might be added—*fantasía,* or show tango—but as a choreographed dance, it's in another league. Within each category there are so many variations and personal styles, it's as my old friend Annie Hoffman used to say (quoting Heraclitus): "You can never step into the same stream twice."

During my first trip, I was like a kid in a candy shop. Tango was everywhere, and I was just at the start of my fixation. I scarfed up shoes (five of the pairs I still dance in, including my candy-apple blue metallic ones, worn to the lining), artwork, clothing (a slinky red dress and feline leopard one), and jewelry—a silver tango shoe charm I wear around my neck.

Now, that little doll-size shoe is a touchstone for me, a conversation piece when my dance partners compliment its artistry between dances. I'll flirtatiously suggest that they might be my Prince Charming by saying, in my best Mae West voice, "I'm looking for the other one . . . "

One elderly man shocked me by saying, "I have it." Marcelo pulled out his card to show me he was a jeweler and the maker of the tiny shoe around my neck. His shop was on Libertad, a few blocks from the *milonga* where we were dancing.

During that 2005 stay, I took three to four master classes a day. I went to the famous Teatro Astral and other theaters on Corrientes ("the street that never sleeps") and watched famous dancers, many of whom I'd been taking classes with, give dazzling performances. I threw good dollars after bad at tango for twenty days running. It was such a different time in my life. I was working full-time at *VIA* magazine as a travel editor, a job coveted by many. I had Dan waiting for me at home. I look back at that as my acquisitive phase.

Now I am divesting. In the pursuit of happiness, I am stripping my life of possessions, stripping my tango practice down to its purest elements. It's a deeply personal process, and one that seems limitless in its depth. It's spiritual hedonism. I limit my purchases of new clothing and shoes, of lessons. They are distractions from my path.

My path indeed seems so much less cluttered than it did even a few short months ago. I like the simplicity of my life here on Juncal Street. I am suddenly liberated from daily piles of junk mail. I am no longer plagued by telemarketing calls. In fact, I receive almost no phone calls. I've paid off my credit cards and live on cash. When I realized that $193, my Blue Cross monthly premium, could be my food bill for two months here in Buenos Aires, I dropped health insurance. I got rid of my cell phone.

My spare closet and drawers are no indication that I am going to spend a year on this continent. My tango apparel is from Goodwill, vintage and thrift shops, or bargain chains. It is Cinderella clothing. In daylight you don't have to look closely at the synthetic fabrics, black or garishly dyed, to see the pulls and pilling from friction against so many male chests. My beaded tops cling to men's shirts and ties, pulling at their fine fabrics. I am not dissatisfied with my glad rags, with the motion of my body they transform magically into stunning garments. Tango alchemy.

In a drawer with my showy tops, I keep the one precious garment—my *rakusu*, the layperson's version of a Buddha robe, which I sewed in part myself. It's a twelve-by-eight-inch navy blue cotton rectangle composed of several small rectangles (representing rice paddies of Asia). Hundreds of knobby stitches in special powder blue thread hold the geometric patterns together with a white silk panel lining the backside. Each of these stitches was made to the chant of *namu kihei butsu,* which is an aspiration of reverence for my own awakening to what is.

Dan was with me in June of 1996 at the Jukai ceremony (lay ordination), where I and five other lay ordainees were presented with our matching silk-lined blue cotton robes. We vowed to keep the ten precepts: 1) not killing; 2) not stealing; 3) not misusing sex; 4) not lying; 5) not giving or taking drugs; 6) not discussing others' faults; 7) realizing Self and Other as one; 8) giving generously, not withholding; 9) not indulging in anger; and 10) not defaming the Three Treasures (Buddha, Dharma, and Sangha, or Self, Truth, and Others).

In the ten years since, I have sat *zazen* many mornings at the Zen Center and chanted, "Great robe of liberation, field far beyond form and emptiness, wearing the Tatagatha's teaching, saving all beings," while hanging my *rakusu* around my neck. I could have never imagined then that I would commit such major transgressions against the seventh and ninth precepts, and feel so close to transgressing the first.

I've woken up nearly every morning I've been here feeling wrung dry by tears of hurt and anger. This morning, though, still just a couple weeks into my stay, I stare through salt-burned eyes at the *rakusu*'s backside, on which my teachers, Paul Haller and Blanche Hartman, had written my new Buddhist name in black calligraphy.

In Japanese, DAI KO AN SHIN, in English, INNER FLAME, PEACEFUL
HEART. A haiku of sorts reads:

PURE GOLD

IN THE FIRE

BECOMES EVER

BRIGHTER

Zen alchemy. Suffering can end, the Buddha said. It can
transform into pure happiness. All you have to do is stop clinging
and grasping, surrender to the moment, give up your ego. As I
contemplate the Japanese character for *an* (peaceful), I see that it is
unmistakably the image of two tango dancers in motion. One head,
two bodies, kinetically swirling, the female yin and male yang. Shiva
and Shakti spinning in an indistinguishable embrace.

My tango precepts are:
1. Just show up.
2. Accept what's offered.
3. Remain present.
4. Be kind and compassionate to Self and Other.

If Blanche and Paul could see me now. The rigors of the many
sesshins (seven days of sitting *zazen* morning through night) that
they led me through over the years are nothing compared to how
tango is working my body over. Keeping it in a state of low-grade
fatigue has a valium effect, dulling the edge of anxiety.

My feet are being reconfigured with thicknesses in new places
that make the floor feel bumpy when I walk barefoot. I have a pair of

black flats, between-*milonga* street shoes, that were once loose and are now tight. Each morning I soak my burning feet in a bucket of ice water followed by a bucket of warm water with seaweed salts. I have concocted new yoga poses for my toes and metatarsals to counter the effects of overuse. I speak to my feet like pets—my "dogs"—and ask them to bear with me. But after countless nights of dancing, they wake me in the middle of the night, like purring and keening pets, throbbing, pinging, nerves tingling, muscles twitching, stinging. *Go to sleep*, I speak soothingly and rub them. This will pass. All suffering does. I promise. A year at most. I promise.

And then we can all go home.

Chapter 4

El Príncipe Azul

Primero hay que saber sufrir,
Después amar, después partir,
Y al fin andar sin pensamiento.

First you have to know how to suffer
then love, then leave,
and finally wander without thought.

—*"Naranjo en Flor" (1944)*

Just as time's dimensions change when I enter into the dance with a partner, something magical happens for me when I cross the transoms of Argentina's most famous tango venues. I step into Club

Gricel and it's like entering a Candyland. Its sunshine-yellow walls and pink neon sign over the bar make me feel as if I've stepped into a time and place so far away from my real life that it's easy for me to get wholly and completely lost. I have a power spot in Gricel, near the second column on the right. It's a table that seats six women, all of whom usually arrive solo to sit and wait for invitations from the men's section. Nine-centimeter-high stilettos, sometimes my own, write *ocho, ocho* on the slightly uneven floorboards. Occasionally my heel catches. I improvise a false step—to my partner's relief. (Another maxim in tango: If a step goes wrong, it's always the leader's fault—talk about macho.)

In a club called Porteño y Bailarin, I find myself inside a brightly painted "tank." I'm a fish in an aquarium, weightlessly skimming the floor past a table that holds a cackling clutch of old *milongueros*. There's a lot of friction in tango—trunks rubbing trunks, feet heating the floor, couples brushing each other on the tightly packed floors—and the air crackles with electricity.

Another night, across the street at the magnificent El Beso, the air is crackling with the intensity of men and women holding each other's gazes across the small and intimate room. Because of the closeness, a unique civility reigns at El Beso—as if we're all proper guests at a private country club. Sitting near the edge of the dance floor, you can hear people breathe *"¡Que lindo!"* at the end of a dance.

A few blocks away is the Confitería Ideal, with its ancient marble staircase, the hum of violins, and the moan of *bandoneón* already raising my gooseflesh. This is the venue where Madonna was filmed dancing for *Evita,* and soon I'm gliding carefree amid this old salon's dark wood, beveled mirrors, and lavish chandeliers. With each step I'm sashaying back through tango history.

In Palermo's Salon Canning, I'm in some kind of heaven, moving under lasers of light thrown from a glitter ball. One partner, Jorge, says brusquely, *"¡Juega!"* ("Play!") and I give his pant leg a slow *lustrada* (shine) with my foot.

Club Fulgor stands solitary and nearly hermetic in nearby Villa Crespo barrio. When I enter I feel as if I've stepped onto a *Twilight Zone* set. It's a *milonga* where the same sort of people have been dancing since the 1940s. I imagine that they've not aged or changed with the times, that this is a *milonga* whose doors have created an impervious seal to the outside world. Club Fulgor is the type of place that makes you feel as if you've discovered a time capsule, and it's the *milonga* that's inspired me to assign it a theme song: *"Así se baile tango"* (This is how you dance tango).

Thursday nights, Niño Bien is the *milonga* with the highest concentration of *superoperados*, women and men who have had so much plastic surgery they look like dolls or mannequins who can't stop smiling. I go there early and satisfy my need for three perfect *tandas*, then leave with my euphoria—and unimproved smile— intact before the floor gets too crowded.

There are many others—La Nacional, Villa Malcolm, La Viruta, and more—and each one comes alive with its own distinct persona. I sit at linen-covered tables around the "altar" of the dance floor and watch legs fly in *voleos* or hook each other in *enganches*. I get close-up views of the body mechanics of tango's advanced steps as two bodies with four legs sway and dip as one.

Another person might take valium or antidepressants, but my relief comes from the *milongas*—the best tranquilizers not on the market. I automatically forget my suffering as soon as I step through the door into a salon. It's been just several weeks and I've already steeped my burning soles and ailing soul in many of them.

Though my nights are full of energy and life, my days require that I find other distractions. One of my commitments is to Joel Fox, an inmate at Folsom Prison in Sacramento with whom I've been corresponding for the past six years. I began writing to him as part of the Zen Center's outreach program, and my role is to support Joel in his Buddhist practice.

To explain the drop-off in my writing to him, I tell Joel about my breakup and my decision to stay in Buenos Aires indefinitely. Now he, the one who's stuck within prison walls of concrete and steel, is supporting me, the one who's bound by the prison of her own making. I'm cautious to keep my letter free of the interactions I had with Evelyn. Heaven forbid he hear about my act of violence and murderous impulses—with me out here walking free. What he sends back to me is a verse from "Anthem," a song by Leonard Cohen, who did time in a Zen monastery. It suggests there's a crack in everything and that that's how the light gets in. I meditate on this passage and think about Joel's wisdom. I'm glad he is in a place enlightened enough to permit him to practice his devotion to Buddhism, just as I am in a place allowing me my devotion to tango.

Another distraction is the simple act of getting out. Here I am in this city that has so much beauty and culture, famous as the "Paris of South America," and yet when I'm not dancing, I'm submerged in a subterranean place, gnawing like a dog with a bone on the ruin I created back home. I begin to feel like a character in the Julio Cortázar story in which the people ride the city's crowded underground—the *subte*—and never come up. Indeed, there is a thriving underground culture in the city's subway—jugglers, child performers, monologuists, musicians, beggars, strolling peddlers of cheap goods. I could easily observe them for hours, or study the vibrant frescolike murals painted on tiles, scenes of the country's gaucho, pioneer, and industrious past. Or stare at the people's hair. I'm in awe of their impossibly thick, dark tresses, almost always long on the women. I can see their Amerindian blood (about half the population has some) in their facial features, their hair, skin, and eyes. And they're absolutely beautiful. It has been said that Argentines are Italians who speak Spanish and think they are French—as reflected in their old architecture. But, on the *subte,* they are not fancy or showy dressers like the French. Their style—simple, plain dress with very little jewelry—is due in part to not wanting to arouse suspicion that they possess any valuables in the aftermath of the financial crisis, during a time when stealing—robbery and petty theft alike—is part of everyday life.

Thankfully, the city has a healthy list of museums in which to escape my scary thoughts. Since my tolerance for museums is about one hour per visit—or my attention deficit gets too large—I map out a "fam tour" (travel-writer-speak for "familiarization tour") of the ones that I'll return to over and over. They include: Museo Nacional de Bellas Artes; the exquisite Museo de Arte Decorativo, with its portico and Corinthian columns; the gauchoesque Museo de Motivos Argentinos J. Hernandez; the steel and glass Museo de Arte Latinoamericano de Buenos Aires, or MALBA; Carlos

Gardel's house, now a compact museum in the Abasto area, where he lived with his single mom, Berthe; the magnificent Palacio de las Aguas Corrientes, one of the city's crown jewels, with turquoise-enameled coral bricks; and, right in my own barrio, the little Museo de Artes Plásticas Eduardo Sivori in a 1912 Bavarian style house.

The Porteños say the city has one hundred barrios. In reality there are only forty-seven, but the exaggeration is purposeful; they say it to highlight the diversity that reigns from the central market of Abasto (Carlos Gardel's hood) to the fabulous old architecture of San Telmo to the crayon-colored tenements of La Boca. Palermo, my barrio, is the city's largest and is divided into Palermo Soho, Palermo Hollywood, Viejo Palermo, and Palermo Chico.

In Palermo Park, a few blocks from my loft, I find a graven image on a pedestal in the rose garden, *La Flor de Juventud* (Flower of Youth), a 1921 bronze by Zonza Briano. The image is that of a woman sitting naked, her shapely legs tucked under her in the camel pose, her face to the sun, her tresses thrown back. The first time I lay eyes on her, John Keats's "Ode on a Grecian Urn" pops into my mind: "Thou still unravished bride of quietness/Thou foster child of silence and slow time." I'll recite them from now on when I visit. But the woman on Keats's urn, like the exteriors of the *superoperados,* can never get old; her fruit can never ripen nor be "ravished" by time or by anyone. I don't envy her. Despite my suffering I don't want to be she who can never enjoy (and suffer) love, liaisons, commitments, never experience the "glories" of death and rebirth, the ups and downs of samsara. I want to think of my Flor as someone like me, someone who ripens and changes with the sunlight. She comes alive for me. I start calling her a ravished un-bride—like me—and leave fallen jacaranda blossoms in her groin before departing.

I walk down crowded Santa Fe Street, a shoppers' haven, sometimes all the way to Belgrano, a barrio I've come to love for its quiet residential streets and much-intact old European architecture. I take side streets past the Cuban embassy; down Baez Street in Las Cañitas, said to have some of the city's liveliest nightlife; past Ray Fahd Islamic Center, a Taj Mahal of a mosque that former president Carlos Menem built. I find the Barrio China, the city's two compact blocks of Chinatown, which is home to a requisite temple, a dragon-themed restaurant, and trinkets from China. In the Once Barrio, where many Jews settled after fleeing persecution in Europe in the early 1900s, I find what I call "the Jewish garment district." The unadorned storefronts and ramshackle clothing shops on the crowded Paso Street are reminiscent of that like-named area in New York City. I visit Plaza Miserere in the Once. There I see some of the poorest people trying to enjoy a bit of open space and dozens of the best-fed and groomed cats living on the monument there. At the square's southwest corner is a sprawling shrine to the 194 victims of the 2004 Cromañon nightclub fire. Dozens of sneakers, those of the dead, dangle from a line over an open shed with candles, rosary beads, handwritten messages, and hundreds of photos of those who were lost. The memorabilia evoke the sadness of lives cut too short, and the suffering, both of those who died and the many family members left behind, is overwhelming.

It's September now, and the evenings are still cold. This would be the warmest time of year back home, but Argentina is coming out of its winter into spring. Off I go prowling for good dance partners at Club Gricel. I enter the warmly lit dance hall, a bit timid of the social scene, but confident in my dance skills. One of the hosts, Patricio, seats me in the women's section—near my power pillar. It's unfortunate that I never got used to contact lenses. I have to keep my glasses on to scan the men's section as I wait for one of them to *cabeceo* me—to make an eye-lock with head nod, the requisite body-language invitation to dance, a venerable custom among many here in Argentina. The *cabeceo* recalls the Zen saying, "Don't just do something, sit there." I love the idea of just sitting here and taking what's offered.

I hear complaints from both men and women about the unfairness of the custom of waiting for the man to nod his head. I don't mind it, though, because the women, in fact, have the power to say no. And we have the option to turn our visage on a man and raise our eyebrows—please *cabeceo* me. No one save the two having done the interaction will know whether he resists. Call it sexist, but for me it is grand theater, one that goes with my tango wardrobe of beaded, frilly, sequined, see-through gossamer and my painted face and nails. It is a chance to partake of this macho culture on its terms and its turf. I never forget that I am a guest in this country.

For the Argentines, who have witnessed terrible human rights abuses, I sense there is a consensus to keep sacred something that is theirs and that is venerable. The *cabeceo* is a ritual that clearly evolved from olden days. It evokes a scene, say, in a La Boca *conventillo*, a man and woman peering at each other across a doorway or a windowsill, using just their eyes to set up a meeting. For me the *cabeceo* is full of *buena onda*—good vibes. And as a nonverbal cue, it is fitting, because, unlike with most other dances, you never talk during tango, which would be redundant, because the dance is a dialogue.

Tonight I am impatient and feeling overlooked and neglected. Tonight it feels as if everyone but me is *cabeceo*ing. The worst recourse is to brood, so I use these moments to follow my breath meditatively and observe these feelings exactly as I would in the *zendo*, sitting on a cushion staring at a wall. Guided depression, I call it. Whether in the *zendo* or the *milonga*, I always meet the same person: various versions of myself.

Invariably, the invitations start coming, and when they do there's a clear moment of transition in which I go from feeling unloved to feeling whole and harmonious with a stranger, with the cosmos. I accept the truth, that there is virtue even in the waiting. It's these moments, in the *milongas*, that I live for. In the *milonga*, a microcosm of larger life, I begin to develop this muscle called waiting, without grasping, anticipating, or judging, and that is something I want to take with me everywhere, every moment. I know the customs well—never say thank you until the end of the *tanda*, as it means you want to sit down. I am on a steep learning curve with the language, Castellano, the branch of Spanish spoken here, and I can make some *charla*, small talk, during the mandatory ten- to twenty-second wait into songs, but little more. If you accept a man's offer to dance, you implicitly agree to dance with him the whole *tanda*. I knew these basic codes before I came, because Christy discussed them in her classes. I can recall chuckling, only half-believing it would really be so. But I see that it is—no one dares leave his or her partner during a *tanda*. As I start to understand how things operate, I realize that I'm falling in love. In the same way you're surprised by the habits and quirks of a new lover, I find myself charmed by the culture and traditions of this country. The immediate familiarity I felt upon arriving in Buenos Aires, because of its similarity to many European cities I love, is beginning to feel more nuanced, more its own, more special and unique and full of potential.

One custom I learned "on the job," so to speak. I was dancing with a man from Uruguay when he invited me to have ice cream. I hesitated in the moment of his invitation simply because I was caught off guard. He stopped dancing abruptly, in the middle of a song, in the middle of the floor, and politely escorted me to my seat. Later I learned the *codigo* (code). His invitation—and most invitations to have coffee or leave the club for some seemingly trivial outing—are invitations to have sex. My friend Ángel had pulled me aside and whispered wildly about the Uruguayan, "Don't trust him!" From his tone, I understood that there was some sort of psychological competition (or "dance") going on and that the Uruguayan must have concluded, erroneously, that I'd said "yes" to coffee with Ángel, with whom I'd danced several tandas. Hence the Uruguayan was quite put out.

His response to my demurral was an unusually egregious and obnoxious one—most men accept "no" and, though they may persist a bit, are respectful of the fact that many women want only to dance. In fact, many men come only to dance and be sociable, too. My friend Michael, who's English, was once invited to coffee by an Argentine woman who came prepared with questions written in English on a piece of paper. "Would you like to take me to bed?" was there among "Where are you from?" and "What do you do?" I didn't ask Michael if he followed up, but his lip-smacking grin suggested that at the very least he savored receiving the brazen invitation.

After the second *cabeceo*, I sit a long time without a man's interest. I'm on the verge of impatience again when I sense a tall well-dressed man steal to a table behind me. I feel his presence, but how to receive his *cabeceo*? If I turn around I'll lose the subtlety of the ritual or, worse, be ignored—I'd die of embarrassment. But then it's a *tanda* by Carlos Di Sarli, one of the most romantic composers. I learned my first steps to Di Sarli. My toes are flexing. Fortunately, the stranger makes it easy by flouting custom and whispering loud enough for me to hear, "*¿Queres bailar?*"

Sí, quiero bailar. I want to dance.

He is tall enough for me to bury my face into the lapel of his beautiful tan cashmere suit. His name is Alberto and he's a clothing designer. I dance with many trolls—a term I use affectionately, as in the dwarves of Scandinavian mythology who hide under bridges. True, I wouldn't look twice at them on the street, but in the *milonga* they lead me where I want to go. They are hunched and short, not at all athletic. Their bellies hang over their belts. It is not unusual to feel a bristly scratching on the right side of my head from their coarse hair. They're clean, but their dress is generally shabby or dated. These are the men I wait for. These are the men I love dancing with. They're gold mines of the old culture, old mannerisms and etiquette. I can feel in their lead that they learned tango by heart, by watching and doing, not in any formal class. This class of *tanguero* is in his body more so than his North American counterpart, generally speaking. How to explain? A thousands pulses in his skin simmer at the temperature of water for yerba maté (which should never be boiled) and these convey messages. It's tango for sure—the flavor and structure are there, but with a *je ne sais quoi* wildness. It's like the difference in flavor between farmed salmon and wild string-caught salmon. They're a disappearing breed, an endangered species, as tango gets quantified, classified, and even technical.

But Alberto is a welcome diversion—and he has a distinct flavor, too. He does a startling *cadencia*, a rock step, in which his right thigh is sandwiched between my two thighs as we rock with the music. In this single move you can see why tango was censored at the turn of the nineteenth century.

"*Me gusta tu estilo de bailar*" ("I like your style of dancing"), I tell Alberto.

He has soft blue eyes. He smiles and says that he's been dancing tango only ten months, but he is a musician and that's why he's picked it up fast. (In fact, while foreigners lament its difficult "technicalities," many of the best Porteño dancers have never taken lessons because they can't afford to.)

Alberto invites me to head over to El Beso, where the dancing might be better. "*Sí, la energia es muy baja aca*" ("The energy is very low here"), I say, wanting to show my command of his tongue.

We walk to his car and he drives us over. He asks if I'm afraid to go with him, a stranger. I gaze out at the damp night through his much-splintered windshield and wonder what sort of violence it suffered. I think briefly that, yes, I should be more careful. But there's absolutely nothing he could do to me that would be worse than what has already happened in my life—my own mistakes, losing Dan, having my world pulled out from under me so suddenly. "*No, no tengo miedo—para nada*" ("I'm not afraid—not for nothing"), I say.

We sit separately at El Beso, an intimate club with a great sound system, so we can dance with others. And then, close to 2 AM, he invites me to his apartment in the Recoleta, not too far from the club. He says something in poor English, of which I catch " . . . just music." Sure, I'm up for the company. I have no interest in sex, and on the way over, as if to assure me that that's not his intention either, he teaches me a new word, *mimos*. He tells me straight out that he would just like some *mimos*—affection.

He shows me a room that has a dozen or so stiff naked torsos. They are the mannequins he uses for his work as a designer. His designs are lovely, and I finger some fabrics and tell him, "*¡Qué lindo!*" I look around and spot several photos of his two sons. He tells me he's been separated from his wife for several years. I sit on his bed against pillows as he plays his guitar and sings songs he wrote. He has a nice voice.

He puts on a DVD of English rock and when an old George Harrison song, "While My Guitar Gently Weeps," comes on, it makes me sad. Dan, who never shared my love of music, began to take piano lessons after he broke up with me. Alberto and I lie together and just rub backs. He has an insatiable need for *mimos*. Whenever I stop, he tells me, "*Más, más*" (More, more). I rub his back, his chest, his head, his legs—nothing between his waist and thighs. I give good *mimos*, he says. I ask, Does that make me *mimosa*? Yes, he says and falls out, sound asleep. And then, I realize what he said back at El Beso was exactly what I thought I heard, *No fucking, just music.*

A few days later on a Saturday evening, I run into Alberto at Plaza Bohemia, a *milonga* known for its cliqueishness and snubbing of foreigners. But now I am an insider, and Alberto gets me out on the floor where he showcases my skills, leading me in crisp *voleos*, which I do shamelessly high. I catch my heel on the hem of my green miniskirt during one of the kicks, pulling it so far down that my one-piece leotard is revealed. This time when Alberto does his rocking *cadencia*, I play with it and add momentum, pushing back, flirting with my body. He smiles with his body, I feel it somehow.

For all this, I do not feel sexually aroused with Alberto. Certainly, the *milonga*, with its close physical contact and this dance that approximates socially acceptable "foreplay," may well be a carnal hotbed of would-be sex partners. Of all the thousands of male bodies I have leaned into and brushed against since starting to dance tango, only two have aroused my sexual senses. And in both instances, the men left profound marks on my life. One of them, Dave, catalyzed the trouble I currently found myself in, and the other I had not yet met.

It's not sexual attraction I feel with Alberto, but something else—the *príncipe azul* syndrome. The *príncipe azul* is the Argentine equivalent of our knight in shining armor. Maybe I'm making up for not having experienced this yearning in my twenties, when my peers were rushing into marriage fairytales that didn't end happily ever after. I tally his attributes—he is tall, handsome, a well-paid professional, intellectually stimulating, exotic in his foreign-ness, and he dances tango well. In my fantasy I conjure up a future in which we start dating outside the *milongas*. I take Alberto to the States, where I show him off to my friends. Mom will like him, I think, and on and on I spin the tale.

Later that week I go home with Alberto a second time, this time from Salon Canning. This time the *mimos* have no limits. He wants sexual touching. He leads with his erection, but we don't know each other well enough and I protest, thinking of my carefully planned scenario in which romance and falling in love play a major role. "We should go to dinner and talk and get better acquainted . . . " I say while struggling playfully, until he realizes that no is no and we fall asleep.

In the morning we have a lively discussion about world politics—the first of many in Argentina, a country in which President Bush is declared, very matter of factly, no less an assassin or satanic than Saddam Hussein, and responsible for at least as much loss of life. Venezuela's president, Hugo Chávez, has just called Bush a devil, and Alberto wonders if the CIA will assassinate him for his outspokenness. The CIA's power to manipulate and control is a household fact, as inevitable as corrupt governments.

I see Alberto again several days later. I have suffered nothing but loneliness, uprootedness, and despair in the days since I went home with him last. I have decided we'll go all the way. Maybe if we have sex he'll be my *novio*. It's a misguided conclusion I recognize on some level, but my cognitive faculties are still skewed. He shows up at Porteño y Bailarin on Riobamba, where the room hums when Danny Flaco, a virtuoso of *milonga*, enters the room. He is a cross between Joey Bishop and Sammy Davis Jr. He sits with his Rat Pack of friends at their table on the edge of the dance floor where they watch and dance very little—in fact, only when a prized (young and beautiful) dancer shows up. They laugh and guffaw a lot. They are the presiding alpha males, and other *milongueros* seem to stop by as if to kiss their rings.

Alberto and I are dancing better than ever, and I wish I could say that was enough. But I find myself transgressing my own precept, "Take what's offered." There is a saying here that if a couple dances three *tandas* or more they're sleeping together. Alberto and I dance half a dozen throughout the night. Finally, I make the overture.

"Let's go to your place."

At three in the morning that's what we do. When we arrive, he says, rather poetically, that we could write a page, a chapter, or a whole book—he doesn't know. As it turns out, it's no epic novel. Despite the subtle sensuality of his dancing, the sex is unrewarding and mechanical, and the conversation afterward is stilted. We lie against pillows, side by side, like a married couple, each reading a book. He is reading an Argentine poet I do not know. I tell him I love Chilean poet Pablo Neruda by way of engaging him in conversation.

"*A mi, no me gusta*," Alberto says. He doesn't like Neruda. All the while he stares through reading glasses at his book. I recall Dan with his TV remote and actually laugh to myself. Guys everywhere read the same manual.

"You would know what the crab in its clawhold of gold holds/And I answer, ocean will say it." Neruda's "Las Enigmas." I memorized the poem when Dan and I were first seeing each other and I was reading (for the third time) Stephen Hawking's *A Brief History of Time*. Dan and I would discuss the origins of the universe for hours and I would pretend to explain quantum physics to him. We started off with the big bang. Not a mere whimper. "You would sift the electrical matter that moves on the tines of the void." I say the lines of this poem etched in my loving heart long ago, softly, a mantra, under my breath. I only know the English version, which would mean nothing to Alberto. It is way too grandiose for this moment anyway.

The already stilted conversation eventually ceases altogether. We sleep until noon. *Y después, nada.* And then, nothing.

He disappears into that black hole where socks and premature lovers go. I write him an email weeks later: "You didn't say anything about a footnote," I write. He writes back effusively, in all caps for emphasis, that I am a warm and good person, that he even loves me, that I should call on him for anything. But he doesn't feel the *fuego,* fire.

But I knew that going into it. And yet how often do we feel that? I think back over the course of my life, the number of men who have aroused that *fuego:* Very few. The mystical fire of transformation that emanates from the solar plexus or third chakra was never ignited with Alberto. What I felt was indigestion. The fourth chakra, the heart—my perpetual heartburn.

Now I just feel shitty.

I feel awkward seeing him for a while after that, but sex with a *milonguero* is like the *cabeceo*—only the two of you have to know about it. In this way, the *milonga,* with its decorum, is a cauldron of affairs, trysts, one-night stands simmering subsurface, about to boil somewhere else.

Over time the awkwardness will lessen, and I realize that the tryst with Alberto did mask my funk briefly, a temporary rescue from my mental routine of gnawing on what can't be undone. But every time I see Alberto with a new woman, obviously pursuing her, rocking her in his unique *cadencia,* I can't help but wonder if she gives good *mimos.*

Chapter 5

Even Gauchos Dance Tango

Adiós, pampa mía!
Me voy, Me voy a tierras extrañas.

Goodbye, my pampa!
I'm leaving, I'm leaving for strange lands.

—*"Adiós, pampa mía," lyrics by Ivo Pelay*

It's a Friday night in late September when I decide to go to the *milonga* at Salon Canning. Every time I sit down after dancing, I feel something like a loving jolt, so intense is the tap on the back I keep getting from a woman I've never seen before. At first, I'm annoyed, since it means I have to turn away from the altar of dance and the potential invitations that await me from men in the wings. I'm still a novice at the art of *cabeceo,* still practicing how to sculpt my facial features just so—to look neither desperate nor dismissive, to project a certain nonchalance mingled with a suspicion of interest. Posture is critical; you keep your chin up, your line of sight constant, and peruse faces at a slow, even pace, ready to stop on a dime. At any moment Mr. Right (for the upcoming *tanda)* could solidify out of the sea of poker-faced *milongueros,* his eyes twitching out in code, *Shall we dance?* Interruptions stall the crucial process of concentration.

But I do get past the abruptness of her affection and we have an immediate rapport. Her name is Patricia Jacovella, and I'm hardly upset by the praise she lavishes upon me. "Wow, you dance beautiful! Your feet hardly touch the ground. My God, how lovely! Where did you learn? How long have you been dancing?"—she doesn't wait for answers—*"¡Qué lindo!"*

Upon discovering I'm from San Francisco, she switches to her impressive Queen's English, peppered with colloquialisms—"In a nutshell, you're the best!" Her voice is rich and unrestrained, pleasantly grainy, her every phrase saturated with laughter and smiles. It's not unusual for Argentine women to stop me to briefly compliment my dancing, a gesture I greatly value. But this woman is over the top. It would have been easy to dismiss such a bubbly person as disingenuous, but we had chemistry. Later I'd realize that I'd been chosen by Patricia, that she'd felt some genuine animal magnetism that I couldn't acknowledge until I was able to stop being dismissive of her attempts to talk to me.

Patricia, recklessly affectionate, invites me on the spot to visit her in San Antonio de Areco, Argentina's gaucho central, two hours away by bus to the northwest of Buenos Aires. "You must see it," she swoons. "Here's my phone and address."

"Sure," I say to Patricia, "some weekend . . . " allowing my voice to trail off, imagining she doesn't expect me to accept her invitation. But I do email her. After all, I barely know anyone. And over the course of the next week Patricia encourages me to call her Pato, and we deepen our acquaintance through emails, studded with many exclamation points. Her friendliness proves as genuine as it is infectious. It's not until getting to know Pato that I realize how sorely I need girlfriends. Besides losing my best male friend, Dan, I've left many close girlfriends behind in Northern California, not to mention that I feel far removed from my five sisters, who all live on the East Coast.

Two Saturdays after meeting Pato, I head to the Retiro bus station to catch a ride to San Antonio de Areco. The Retiro has the vibe and excitation of an airport and evokes the thrill I felt as a kid in New York City's Port Authority and Penn Station. After weeks of struggling to keep my sense of purpose afloat, I'm reminded: I was born to travel. It's a rush to be pulled along by the throngs—families from the provinces and young international globetrotters traveling on the cheap. Give me the roar of the engines, the screech of brakes, the smell of the crowds, and I'm home.

Chorizo-shaped (proper feng shui for a terminal), the station spreads at least a quarter-mile long on two levels with shops, cafés, 206 ticket windows, and double-decker buses coming and going, amazingly near schedule, into more than 75 stalls. Wearing my two-sizes-too-big cargo pants and my JanSport backpack, I squeeze anonymously through packs of people, unemployed and industrious. Orange-vested *policía,* alternately daydreaming or vigilant, mill around New York–style vendor booths that line the sidewalks for several blocks leading up to the station. The vendors sell everything from sequined thongs, workout togs, plastic watches, and kids' cartoon stickers to deodorant, batteries, girlie magazines, and Coney Island hot dogs (called Super Panchos). The air smells of mustard and pizza. There's a shoeshine man and the glass case of a full-service butcher festooned with fat links of sausage and heavy with purple hunks of Argentine beef, organ meats, entrails, and blocks of aged cheeses.

The buses depart along the backside of Retiro, past the *villa miseria,* or slums (similar to Rio de Janeiro's favelas) of dirt-poor people, including some *cartoneros,* scavenger families who pick the city's trash clean of cash-worthy recyclables each evening from six to nine o'clock. As my bus departs, I note many lines of colorful laundry strung from cracked brick-and-concrete balconies and between roofless walls. A dog scarfs up castaway food near one of many rusted, windowless, wheelless autos. Adolescents wearing backpacks walk with purpose down the dirt street.

Soon the bus is rolling along the banks of the Río de la Plata, with ocean-size views to the horizon that remind me of San Francisco's Embarcadero. Fishing poles lean against a stone embankment, their lines cast into the muddy waters by anglers nowhere to be seen. In the span of an hour and a half, as I arrive in San Antonio de Areco, the din of city life seems worlds away.

I wait on the green at the edge of town studying the stone bust of an eternal cowboy, Victorino Nogueira (1895–1971), with his Stetson hat and neckerchief. A line drawing of gauchos on a cattle drive covers a ceramic-tile mural, as simply and naively etched as France's Lascaux cave paintings.

Peering down the grid of streets lined with neat stone, brick, and stucco homes fronted by little gardens, cacti, and black iron gates, I feel the allure of San Antonio. I sniff the unmistakable lure and romance of Argentina's heartland even before I stroll the town park, cut by the lazy Areco River, with its historic Martínez Bridge, Stonehenge-like benches, and gangly *ombú*, which Pato insists "is not a tree, it's an herb—its roots grow aboveground." Tree or herb, it is as iconic to the pampas as the baobab to the African savanna, the organ-pipe cactus to the Sonora desert.

A small red car pulls up to meet me at the curb of the bus station and Pato's vivacious "Hellooo! *¡Bienvenida a San Antonio de Areco!*" breaks my reverie. I hop in.

"So much to show you—La Bamba and Ombú. Oh, and we'll go to the gaucho museum tomorrow. Tonight is a *folklórico* festival at La Peña. Sure you want to go. Let's drop your bag at the hotel."

"*Qué energía*," I laugh, as excited about getting to know Pato better as her turf.

"You must be hungry. We'll have lunch. Surely you like *parrilla*—grass-fed Argentine beef."

"I prefer the blood of vegetables," I tell her, "but I love it if you love it." I say this to warn her that I don't consume animal flesh the way the average Argentine does, but before she can chew on that, we're on Lavalle Street and she's jumping out of the car so we can drop my bag.

"Here's your hotel," she says, already out the door.

El Balcón Colonial, the Andalusian-white hostelry with its three rooms on the second level, all fronted by a terra-cotta-tiled balcony, is so small it looks like a private home. My room is cozy and unadorned but for beige lace curtains. It has a double bed, two single bunks, and a private bathroom. For sixteen bucks a night it's quite a steal.

We drive down the quiet tree-lined streets, with townsfolk cycling on heavy clunkers. At one corner, Pato points to the architecture of two homes, one being more elaborate Italian-style with "gingerbread icing" (stone ornament) and columns, the other more traditionally Spanish. Both are striking, and having been made aware of the architecture of the town, I now note the ubiquity of ironwork and arched windows and doors throughout town.

"San Antonio was established in 1730. You can see dwellings up to two hundred years old still standing," Pato narrates. I love that the town doesn't look renovated beyond its original character. A number of buildings are quite faded, the weathered coral stone etched with spidery cracks.

"And this one here," Pato points to a mottled-pink brick structure skirted with unsightly galvanized steel, "is an original adobe undergoing restoration. It's going to be a pub some day, if it ever gets finished." A few blocks away is the main plaza, Arellano, that fronts the town's namesake church. The pretty San Antonio church was built to honor Saint Anthony of Padua (who supposedly saved the town settlers from the Indians, who are all but gone). The plaza is inviting with its many trees, plant-filled urns, and gazebo. It's near artisan shops with leather and woven textiles and ateliers where silver is hand-forged into some of the finest jewelry, belt buckles, utensils, and maté gourds. We visit the workshop of Gustavo Stagnaro, who has spent the past year making a five-hundred-piece set of silverware and oak and silver glasses—service for forty—for $170,000.

"Such sensitive designs," I note. "How sweetly unmacho."

Pato tells me that her cowboy ex-husband wrote poems. "He was charming but hard," she says. They are still friends. She talks of him as I might of Dan, as if they may get back together in old age. Since her divorce, she has been teaching English and Spanish. Her primary business, though, is a guide operation called Living Your Spanish, and I can't help but think that there's no work she'd be better suited to. She takes me down a long, bumpy country road to Ombú, a fifteen-minute drive outside of San Antonio, where we run into Oscar, an old horse breaker with a whisk-broom mustache, who tells us he's had five fractured bones, mostly ribs. Someone shoots a photo of us, with Oscar huddled between, that I've since labeled "Sisters separated at birth, reunited on the pampas."

Ombú is stunning, with big, old trees and a gracious 1880 colonial mansion where people relax on its wrap-around porch. Guests enjoy the tranquility amid hundreds of quiet hectares of green pasture where cattle or sheep graze. "They can pitch in with the stock-rearing activities," says Pato—just like at dude ranches in the States—"milking or driving cattle to harness, ear-tagging, and branding."

We drive another fifteen minutes and visit the equally pastoral La Bamba, which dates to 1830 when its Spanish colonial building was a post house on the Camino Real that joined Buenos Aires with the north of Argentina. I recognize La Bamba's arcaded terra-cotta mansion from the 1984 movie *Camila,* which was filmed here. An acclaimed Oscar nominee, the film is based on a true story of an Argentine socialite in the 1800s, Camila O'Gorman, whose short intelligent life lasted only from 1828 to 1848. She was born into an aristocratic family of Irish, Spanish, and French blood. In those days, it was either the convent or marriage to a man of similar social and economic standing. But Camila defied those constraints. She read foreign literature (that a girl!) and valued love over forced marriage.

In the film, as in life, Camila falls for a man of the cloth, the Jesuit Ladislao Gutiérrez. It is she who boldly teaches him to rethink the rigid boundary between what is profane and sacred. Eventually, their prohibited love affair is discovered and they are condemned to die, without a trial. They are scapegoats of the church, the state, and a calcified patriarchy. Camila fueled the scandal by rejecting the claims of her family that she was kidnapped and raped, asserting that the affair was her idea (as it seems it was). Camila and Ladislao were executed by firing squad. She was barely twenty years old, and eight months pregnant.

Camila is often the first reference cited by my dance partners upon hearing my name, which, as names go, happens to be associated with tragedy (my own current tragicomedy aside): Greta Garbo's Camille, who dies beautifully of consumption as the gallant Robert Taylor watches, and Rodin's lover, Camille Claudel, an artist who was sent away to an insane asylum.

By the time I see *Camila*, here in Buenos Aires, I am so identified with the character that I am furious with Argentina for having this unspeakable crime of church and state. History gives me a tiny recompense in knowing that an eventual international uproar over Camila's execution contributed to the demise of then-dictator Juan Manuel de Rosas.

꧁ꆂꆃꆂ꧂

As Pato leads me toward her favorite *parrilla*, Rancho el Tata, which takes us twenty kilometers north along Highway 8, I see how San Antonio might be likened to the patently quaint gold rush towns in California's Sierra foothills along Highway 49. Except those towns were born of a commerce that is now less influential than the tourism its romance nurtures—as gold mining has ground to a near halt.

Blessed with some of the world's richest grazing lands, Argentina still boasts beef as its prime industry, though other types of agriculture also flourish around San Antonio. Pato, who speaks as fluently with her hands as her voice, even while driving, urges me to turn my head to admire the landscape. "Look at these lush prairie lands! Look why Buenos Aires Province is the cradle of gaucho culture!" Her enthusiasm is as contagious as always. "The soil is deep, rich, so full of nutrients. You could eat it straight!"

We are driving through the humid pampas, a Quechua word for "plain." I can see tufts of the obstinate pampas grass that we try so hard to discourage in Northern California. Farther west will be the semiarid pampas, nearly featureless lowlands.

"About 70 percent of the cattle ranches around San Antonio have gone to crops—soy, wheat, corn," Pato laments. "They are proving about 40 percent more profitable than beef."

"That's good, no?" I question. "At least in the case of soy, which is better for soil than cattle. Right?" I start talking about how cattle is a protein machine in reverse; how it takes about five to ten pounds of soy to make one pound of beef. While I'm amazed at my own capacity to retrieve these facts that have been stored in my memory vault for twenty-plus years (I wrote a cookbook on tofu and other soy products for Rodale Press in 1983), my notions of soy are outdated. Unfortunately, the soy that has become Argentina's number one export is genetically modified to include its own herbicide and has become a monoculture that depletes the soil and drives down the price of this legume. Expanding cultivation of this crop is at the expense of livestock—as well as traditional crops such as maize, wheat, cotton, lentils, and potatoes.

Pato looks at me with an edge of cynicism, catching me for the city slicker I am.

"Yeah," she says wistfully, "but the beef has history . . . "

"You're sweet on meat," I say with a smile.

"It's what it does for the landscape. It's something deeper, unique here . . . " she trails off.

"Cowboys are your weakness," I say, poking fun at her a little bit. But I stop when I see the look on her face. I realize, somewhat embarrassed, that I'm treading on her national identity.

The pampas are the sacred ground of legend, song, and culture of the gaucho. There is even a tango ballad to them, "Adiós Pampa Mía." They spread from the Atlantic to the Andes, stretching to Uruguay and Brazil. South America's "oceans of grass" conjure up a similar feeling in the psyche of Argentines as the western United States, with its red rock country and mesquite- and creosote-covered Sonora and Mojave deserts, does in the psyche of Americans. Every Argentine schoolchild has read the epic 1873 poem "Martin Fierro," by José Hernández, a seminal work about the plight of the gaucho that's likened to *El Cid, Song of Roland,* and *The Iliad.*

"The Argentine cowboy roamed the open range working for cattle ranchers," says Pato. "He never owned land because he valued his independence. His spirit was so given to the wild—he owned the birds, grass, skies, leaves, the trees themselves!" I can tell by the way she's speaking that she doesn't hold my comment against me. Her love for the gaucho is earnest and true, and it moves me to a nostalgic space. I am seeing the landscape through Pato's eyes now.

Pato has earned her right to wax rhapsodic. She's had organic bonding with the pampas through her years with the man who broke horses. Ironically, born and bred in Buenos Aires, he longed for the rural life—and it must've been soul-deep because he since found another wife to share his love with him. Pato says that she loved living rustically on a ranch with no electricity early on in her life. "I'd spend two hours ironing his shirts, with their many pleats, and scarves. I loved it all. We raised three children—all boys—and hens, ducks, calves, sheep, and vegetables. We collected ten liters of milk a day. I made cheese, ice cream, and *dulce de leche* on a wood-burning stove."

Then, as the kids got older, she grew tired of being stranded when it rained and the road to and from their ranch became an impassable river of mud. She longed for movies, theater, and dancing. "He was happy with beef, bread, and maté," she tells me.

We reach Rancho el Tata, an undistinguished structure set back from the two-lane highway on a thick lawn with outdoor seating for warm weather. Pato stops at every table to hug or chat with friends, introducing me as her American friend. She presents me to Iris, the petite, pretty, unprepossessing owner, who kisses us both. We sit on the heated, plastic-enclosed terrace in view of the open brick *parrilla*. Although the barbecue looks industrial in strength, it resembles those in the homes of many Argentine families for whom *asado* is an indispensable weekly ritual, often on Sundays.

A cook emerges with his long tongs in hand to add wood fuel to the barbecue from a nearby stockpile. I watch as he tends to the sizzling meat, momentarily thrilled to observe the red-hot embers flare up with an occasional flame. I recognize the slabs of beef and ribs, but the *chinchulenes* (or chitlins), the offal (or intestines) of a calf, are a new delicacy. I do not try them, but I do eat heartily from every other grass-fed part Iris lays before us. This is my first *parrilla* and I'm not disappointed.

Pato expresses gusto with a passion that adds its own flavor. "I love my *morcilla*," she moans, stabbing the blood pudding in its casing with her fork. I do the same and try not to think of "cooked animal blood," or about how horrified my numerous vegetarian friends back home might be.

We partake of tender *lomo* (sirloin) on a brochette, and what the Argentines call *bife chorizo* (just to confuse foreigners, I've decided), the best cut of meat closest to the bone on the side of the cow's back. It's tastier than any beef I've ever eaten, with a pleasant hint of game, the kind I love in venison. I keep taking generous tastes of a pale meat, like veal, but a thicker cut that's moister and sweet. When I ask Pato what it is, she tells me it's a gland.

"Thymus, or is it marrow?" I ask.

"*Sesos*," she says, a little too tentatively.

"Point to this gland," I say suspiciously.

She points to her skull.

"I'm eating brains!" The look of disbelief brings a smile to her face. Which makes them taste even better.

I always thought brains would be fluid, something that could leak out of your ears, I tell her, as I cut off another big slice of the gray matter with bravado. I can see she approves and perhaps foresees a day when we'll regularly sit side by side, she eating her cooked animal blood and I, my grilled brains.

We also eat Iris's signature meat empanadas, lightly sweet, almost Mediterranean spiced, in crispy fried dough. (This is one of two types of empanada crust; the other is a puff pastry dough called *hojaldre.*) We top off our meal with espresso and a delicious bread pudding dessert in a coulis of burnt sugar.

"Sharing this juicy red meat gives new meaning to 'blood sisters,'" I tell Pato.

"You like it?"

"*Sí, sí.* It's enough to stave off iron deficiency for the rest of my life."

"*Come, mi hermana de sangre,* I'll show you more *gauchesco* culture. That'll make a meat lover out of you."

We drive back to town, a quiet interlude, perhaps due to being comatosely stuffed. We rest at Pato's little cottage, where she lives with her sons, border collie, cat, and garden. She has painted one wall in the living room sangria red, a color that suits her personality. She is wearing the same color top with her black leather, knee-high riding boots. I shoot a lovely photo of her slim figure against the wall.

We sit in front of the fireplace and look at *Los Gauchos,* by Aldo Sessa, a hefty coffeetable book whose photos are romantically cast with pancho-clad gauchos strumming guitars atop horses amid much golden light pouring down on the pampas or around glowing fires. One gaucho picks his teeth with a silver dagger. There are more graphic photos, too—a whole skinned cow being carved; a group of gauchos with sharp knives pinning down a horse with blood and cartilage flying.

"Why are they amputating that horse's leg?" I ask in disgust.

"*Querida,* that is a gelding—they are castrating him."

But of course.

"Never mind that," she tells me as if humoring a child. "Look at this photo of my clients from Kansas a few months ago. It's taken at the gaucho museum." The men in the photo are gorgeous. They have that polished all-American look that I like but that never matches up with men I have anything in common with.

"I'll take the dark one," I laugh, pointing to the Rock Hudson lookalike.

She likes the blond one (think Steve McQueen). "But we can bloody forget it. They're all gay."

I hold the photo to my breast and recite, "Why can't I quit you?"

"Eh?" Pato questions, looking at me with raised eyebrows.

"It's a line from *Brokeback Mountain,*" I tell her. "You know? About two gay cowboys who fall in love."

Pato recalls the movie but moves along without much recognition for something that's still romantically tragic to me. She continues to stare at the photo, perhaps wondering if these men might be married back home, indulging in a gay tryst down in Argentina where no one would be any wiser.

The Argentine gauchos stroll around in their soft, billowy clothing, further blurring the fixed ideas of how a macho man should present himself. *Bombachas,* the name for their loose white pantaloon, is also the word for women's undies. Their unabashedly feminine esthetic allowed the early gauchos to embroider their shirts and pants with delicate French lace. They wore colorful, flowing handwoven panchos and headscarves that looked like babushkas tied under their chins and around their necks. They cinched their waists sensually with wide pigskin belts. On their feet they wore almost dainty slipperlike horse-skin boots made by removing the animal's hide from its leg in one piece. Their saddles, underlain by several pliable layers of woven textiles, are still made of pillow-soft *carpincho* leather, the suede like hide of a water pig. The gauchos carry no guns. Their only weapon, the knife, is a tool of work and survival (and teeth-cleaning). In early nineteenth-century gaucho portraits by Cesáreo Bernaldo de Quirós I've seen at Buenos Aires's Museum of Fine Arts, the gaucho is depicted as darkly handsome, with Moorish features. He stands in sharp contrast to Clint Eastwood with his WASPish good looks.

The gaucho's paraphernalia would be considered too effeminate for the likes of the Wild West cowboy, whose signature pose, perhaps branded too indelibly in my mind by the hot iron of myth, is an isosceles triangle. His denim-clad legs form the sides, spread-eagle on a base of dirt. The negative space, always a distant long shot, is pregnant with the pending duel. The vortex is his tightly packed crotch fittingly on a plane with his hip-slung holster holding his two extended "penises" ever ready to discharge and kill.

Gauchos didn't dance tango in the 1920s, but that didn't stop Hollywood from dressing Rudolph Valentino in chaps and *bombachas* to perform the dance in *The Four Horsemen of the Apocalypse* in 1921. Tango fever was not only turned up a few notches worldwide after the release of that film, but the luxurious scene on the pampas ("The Scent of a Cowboy," it might have been titled if it were released today) solidified the anachronism, generating even more movies with tango-dancing gauchos.

However, the gauchos who were naturally given to song and dance have influenced tango's evolution, most notably with their *zapateo,* percussive footwork, including the *repique,* a move that involves striking the floor with a spurred heel, which shows up in the steps of the leaders as *taconeos.* The leader digs the floor with his heels to the beat of the music. The leader's and follower's fast-twitch *adornos* would seem to stem from the gaucho's *floreos,* rapid decorative movements.

The evening following the *parrilla,* I sit mesmerized for four hours as I observe the gaucho influence in villagers' feet as they dance *folklórico* at La Peña (the town's community center). Despite too much smoke and consumption of beer, wine, empanadas, and *pastelitas,* I manage to keep focused on one man with charcoal black hair, sculpted beard, sideburns, and chiseled features. He could be right off the pages of Pato's *Los Gauchos.* He wears fluid black *pantalónes,* a belt laden with silver coins, a vest, bolero, kerchief, beret, and boots. His feet are more limber than Michael Jackson's, his soles grazing the floor, his ankles pliable as rubber as his foot bends at a nintey-degree angle to the leg.

I find the *folklórico* dances life-affirming. The best-known one in Argentina, the *chacarera*, done at *milongas*, always hits my tribal nerve as men and women collectively act out eternal rites of flirting and gallantry. The men stomp in sync with each other. The walls tremble, and so do I, as I feel the depth of time. The dancers are no longer men in suits or women in cocktail tango dresses; they morph into couples on the pampas in the old west of Argentina right before my eyes, and I'm swept up by the romanticism of the moment.

The following day, Pato and I cross the historic Martínez Bridge that separates the village from the Museum of the Gaucho, a collection of buildings on ninety serene hectares. The complex incorporates the original *pulpería*, called La Blanqueada, which is more than 150 years old. Its publike interior is staged with lifelike wax figures of gauchos in full regalia, sitting at tables and sipping maté. The museum was built in 1938 to honor Ricardo Güiraldes, author of *Don Segundo Sombra*, a popular work—which sometimes paints the gaucho as a noble savage—that's been translated into twenty-six languages. Güiraldes, a writer, poet, and high-society playboy with F. Scott Fitzgerald flair, is as much the protagonist here as the gaucho. He hobnobbed with artists and writers, like Borges.

Güiraldes is said to have helped spread tango to Europe, where he visited in 1910. He portrays an outmoded vision of tango, with this unflattering reference to women—and men: "The all-absorbing love of a tyrant, jealously guarding his dominion, over women who have surrendered submissively, like obedient beasts."

Soon it's time to part. I'm due back at the bus station, and Pato and I have to say our goodbyes, which last for a good twenty minutes as we enumerate many plans for the future, here and back in Buenos Aires. We've packed so much into a short weekend—sightseeing, gauchos, *folklórico, parrilla,* not to mention the start of a treasured friendship with a woman who, like me, can be swept away by the sudden romanticism of a moment. And to think I almost let those loving jolts go unnoticed in the dance hall, clinging to a fixed idea of tango requirements. Never, ever, cling to fixed ideas on anything, my Zen teachers have told me over and over. I think about all of this as I watch two young gauchos in clean white pleated shirts and red berets clomp by on their horse.

Chapter 6

Sex, Lies, and Tango

El tango es un pensamiento triste que se puede bailar.

Tango is a sad thought that can be danced.

—*Enrique Santos Discépolo, early twentieth-century tango lyricist*

Buenos Aires straddles the thirty-fifth parallel, the same latitude as San Francisco, California, but below the equator. It's strange to think of the many ways these two cities—the city in which I've chosen to live out my exile and the city I adopted as home more than thirty years ago—mirror each other. Like California, Argentina is long and narrow and similarly framed by an ocean and range, the Atlantic and the rugged Andes. Just as the Golden State boasts the highest and lowest points on the continental United States (Mount Whitney and Death Valley), Argentina contains South America's two most extreme elevations: Mount Aconcagua at 22,834 feet and Laguna del Carbón at 344 feet below sea level.

This Latin city, which sits on the world's widest river, Río de la Plata (a few miles from the Atlantic), doesn't possess the same level of natural beauty as San Francisco (few cities do), but it is unequivocally pretty with its parks and plazas, and it shares a similarly stimulating persona with its wonderful European Renaissance architecture, artists, intellectuals, and free spirits. It never dozes. Back home my circadian rhythms would be adjusting to winter right now, but they have no trouble accepting a second spring this year.

I'm still grieving regularly. Sometimes, just to get to the next breath sanely, I meditate or do yoga. But I am beginning to feel connected to this place. Spring makes me feel more alive than half-dead. My death-march dreams have subsided. Dan often appears in my sleeping state, a silent witness I can't reach, and Evelyn does, too, a sort of rag doll presence. As long as I have these radioactive feelings toward her, I know I still have work to do.

I read Pema Chödrön's *Start Where You Are* and try her practice of "flashing" on what she calls *bodhicitta,* or awakened heart, the soft vulnerable spot we all have buried in us. But when I sit still and try to flash, next thing I know I am vividly reliving—with perverse relish—the moment I yanked Evelyn's hair with blind fury. I'm hopeless.

But I'm a full-fledged *milonguera* now, and I slip into dance halls with ease. I'm often taken for a Porteña, until I speak. I mentally line up my regular partners, the ones I want to *cabeceo* me, in a certain order. There's a saying that the Buddha killed his first three students; likewise, in the event that I "kill" my first three partners, I line up certain men I'd rather use as warm-ups, saving my best for after that. My Porteño partners are finally starting to believe that I am staying here in their city indefinitely. They are used to foreigners pouring in and out monthly. When one of us actually stays beyond a few weeks, they feel honored and want to know if we intend to see more of their country's diversity. "Oh, yes, I will," I tell them.

I have just returned home from a morning visit to my temple-park across the fourteen-lane Libertador, the Champs-Élysées of Buenos Aires. The jacaranda trees have burst into blossom, aglow in lavender. I find solace from my morning blues amid the park's soaring fountains, a pergola that drips grapevines like my tears, and a prolific rose garden where I perform "rose-storative" therapy, vying with bees to smell the heady rainbow of blooms.

I am at home in my well-lighted loft waiting for Johnny Charles, a name I've affectionately given to Juan Carlos, a tango teacher I first began to notice at a few of the matinee *milongas* that I frequent. The first time he led me in *vals*, or the tango waltz, he stood out like a prince among commoners. I felt like the *plumita* (little feather), a term of endearment that *tangueros* use when they're complimenting good followers.

Juan Carlos and I have a special connection. More than likely I am among a harem of followers who feel the same way. But since the clock stops when I dance tango, it doesn't matter what happens before the *salida*. He is about six foot one, lean, with a barrel chest that is perfectly configured to motor mine, which is small and compact.

"You must be a teacher," I said to Juan Carlos during our first *charla*. He humbly admitted he was and gave me his card, featuring a full-body pose of himself and one of his dance partners. I was still enthralled with my *príncipe azul* when I first meet Juan Carlos, so I didn't call right away. I was taking *nuevo* tango classes at Tango Brujo, but there were plenty of times when Juan Carlos was my sole reason for showing up at a *milonga*. It was well worth suffering the less adept leaders to have just one *tanda* with him, master of the light touch, during which he'd move me like a cloud scudding across the sky.

Although I usually go to his studio on Avenida Santa Fe, I have invited Juan Carlos to give me today's lesson in my loft, with its shining wood floor. Later I learn that I've failed to heed yet another *codigo*—summoning a man to my home means I'm plainly interested in sex.

But Juan Carlos is an unlikely romantic partner for me. He is streetwise but not formally educated. He is earthy; his face is handsome, almost indigenous looking, but weathered with deep lines, making him appear older than his forty-six years. He wears a thin braided gold chain and his silver-streaked dark hair back in a ponytail. His black eyes are the sort that can suck the light right out of a room, especially when he gets angry, which I hear he's quite capable of though I have yet to witness it firsthand.

When Juan Carlos comes through the door and kisses me hello on the cheek, as all teachers and students do here, I am enveloped in his distinct scent—a mix of musk, cloves, and orange. He wears jeans and, like most Argentines, is extremely well groomed.

I wonder immediately if he'll notice the bowl of apples on my table, which I've assembled, jokingly, for his benefit. He has teased me that my *colita* (literally "little tail") is just like a *manzana*.

Do I realize I'm sticking my "ap-pull" out so far? he wants to know. It's true my hyperflexibility permits me to tilt my tailbone, which houses the chakra of sexual desire, so that it's nearly parallel to the floor. But I only push it out as far as is needed to help shape and balance the *carpa*, or tent, that describes the inward lean of two heads making one.

"The men," he says, "they sit like this . . . " he cranes his neck and opens his eyes wide, " . . . and stare at your *colita*." He laughs.

"That's *chamuyo*," I declare, using a *lunfardo*, or slang, word that means exaggeration. I'm fifty-five years old, so what can I do but laugh, too? I'm not one to rebuff flattery. "Maybe I will become known as La Colita de la Milonga," I say, "kind of like Toulouse-Lautrec's famous Montmartre cancan dancer, La Goulue." Her real name was Louise Weber, after all, but she earned this nickname for the gluttonous habit of picking up men's glasses at the cabaret and imbibing the last drops (or *gouttes)* of their drinks.

"Yes, I like the sound of that," Juan Carlos says. "People will say, 'Ah, look, there goes La Colita," I laugh out loud when I think of the literal translation in English: "There goes The Little Tail." Although

I suppose it would be more accurately translated as "Little Ass," which doesn't have the ring I like.

I laugh too hard, and a lot more than Juan Carlos, who looks ready to get serious. So I get serious, too, and explain to him that I have unusually long femurs, so my knees bump the leader's if I don't push my lower spine back. Juan Carlos could care less about facts and technicalities. He teaches from the heart, not the head. He simply shapes and leads me with his body. He has no names for patterns and moves, as we, who've imported tango, do.

"Not two, one!" Juan Carlos can often be heard exclaiming to his male students. He wants them to forget themselves and focus on the follower as the center of their world. The follower's only admonition is to *not* think. Juan Carlos is a passionate *tanguero* who's never taken a dance lesson in his life. He's unaware of the way he echoes Suzuki Roshi, one of my dharma teachers whose version was "not two, not one"—which was meant to keep us aware of not counting our elusive Self as a separate unit.

Although I have prided myself on never clinging, as many students do, to any one teacher, Juan Carlos is about to become my Zen master.

We work hard and dance to classics like Carlos Di Sarli's "Bahía Blanca" and Francisco Canaro's "Desde el Alma" and "Corazón de Oro." This last song recalls Dave. We danced regularly to this song, and the memory of it only pushes me back into the space of guilt and anger that is part of this lurid journey that is my fall from grace.

Juan Carlos works with me to clean up some of my habits—he corrects my forward *ochos* so that I use more of my upper body against his torso to "communicate deeply." He gets me to slowly, sensually swivel my ribcage against his chest so he can better feel my footwork.

"*¡Eso!*" ("That's it!") He praises me when I get it.

When we're done, Juan Carlos makes an advance. He wants to take a bite out of my apple—and I don't mean the fruit in the bowl on the counter. While I'm clear that I'm not interested in anything sexual, I did flout the *codigo*. I laugh as I shake my head, *No, we're not going there,* and pull his hand off of my skirt. Then he wants to pet my upper body, patting the gold and blue beadwork of the mandala on my stretchy top. I realize that I should have seen this coming, and, well, I can't blame a guy for trying; I'll have to assert my boundaries.

"Listen," I explain, in a fit of giddy self-assessment that seems appropriate for the moment, "if my tail is a *manzana,* these are only *frambuesas* [raspberries]," I tell him. "Not for you."

He leaves peaceably and I smile to myself, not at all displeased with our dance session, which lasted three hours.

But, I think, *no way I'm getting involved with this one.*

A few nights later, I find myself at Club Español, one of the most elegant, well-maintained dance salons in downtown Buenos Aires. A restaurant on the ground floor offers white linen service and delicious seafood dishes. The elevator is a gilded cage—gold-painted woven cast iron—with a red velvet seat in it. A broad, plush red-carpeted staircase with railings of intricately carved rose marble leads to the salon. Marble columns with cherubs and caryatids soar majestically. The wooden floor and bar, as well as the crystal chandeliers, are quintessential old, opulent Argentina. The dance hall with its French provincial panels and gilding looks like a room in Chateau Versailles.

I've arrived for the Thursday *milonga* at about 8 PM. The place is packed. I have to stand in the doorway and await the *cortina*—the short piece of music that signals the end of a *tanda*—so the host can know which, if any, seats are free for me to sit in. I catch sight of Juan Carlos dancing with one of his young students. I love this about him—many teachers will not dance with their students in public. But I feel a twinge of something. *Celos?* Can it be? Jealousy.

At last I hear the *cortina*, which is always the same at Español, an urgent rendition of Ástor Piazzolla's "Libertango" from *Forever Tango*, the Broadway hit. It is a sight to see the floor packed with stylishly clad dancers suddenly empty as they hurry double-time to their seats. Swirls of tango's trademark scalloped gossamer and silken dresses flutter and stream behind the women, who are breathlessly eager to sit calmly at the edge of their seats to prepare for the next *cabeceo*.

I like Español not just for its elegance, but because it attracts many good young and old dancers, and I seldom sit out a *tanda*. But now I am distracted and no doubt missing the eyes of men who want to invite me to dance—which can have consequences in the long run. I sit only fifteen feet from Juan Carlos but he has yet to look my way. I pull up my usual pithy bromides: Stay close and do nothing; just show up and take what's offered. I watch my breathing the way I do in meditation, as a way to focus on the moment as it is, not as I want it to be. But as the clock ticks and Juan's eyes are everywhere but on mine, the dreaded brood starts to ink out even the pretty blue sparkles I've sprinkled over myself.

I pick up a flyer for another *milonga* and write on it the following rather overt message: APPLE WANTS TO DANCE. I leave it on his table where he'll see it when he returns. When he finally reads it and looks my way, I feel a little silly. I've been watching him, waiting, and though he's smiling, it feels a bit too smirky, I decide. But he gives me the nod, an invitation to dance the next *tanda,* a tango-*milonga,* or six step. It's very get-down, with its percussive music and knee breaks, unlike traditional tango themes. It lets me make good use of my wayward tail.

After the first song in the *tanda,* Juan Carlos looks sternly at my face, neck, bodice, and says, "That's no good. Do not do that." At first I think he is criticizing my strapless dress, but then I realize he means the glitter.

"Why?" I ask. I wonder if he's worried that they present dangers to my partners' eyes.

"Because men have to go home to their wives," he says. "The wife will know where he was." He says this as if I'm a card-carrying *tanguera* who should know better. "It's okay with me, but not other men," he adds. I hesitate, trying to figure out if he's trying to tell me something. Although I know he has a grown son, he's specifically told me he does not have a wife or girlfriend.

I recall how I've witnessed men and women arriving after work at Confitería Ideal, an afternoon *milonga,* and changing into dance attire in the restroom.

"Okay, Juan," I say. "I'll never again wear sparkles." But his black eyes look so damning, I tremble a bit. I still don't know Juan Carlos well enough to know his dark brooding side.

We turn back to dancing, and I'm again lost in the weightlessness I feel with Juan Carlos. It's divine. There is a style here among old *milongueros,* most of whom are a head shorter than I, in which they hold you really tight (Jack the Gripper, I call them). They push you downward (Pile Drivers), driving you into the floor, and lead with their hand tapping commands into your lower back. I've tried to cure some of them of the rib digging, but most cannot change their old habits. The balls of my feet, my metatarsals, begin to burn and bruise after an hour of dancing with such leaders.

But when I dance with Juan Carlos, all that pain and discomfort instantly dissolves. It's astonishing. It's what I imagine the physical and mental experience of being filled with light to feel like, in the religious sense, being the Catholic-raised Italian-bred woman I am. Only it's not out of the body. It is so fully in the body. This is the God experience right here, right now—not in some mythological afterlife.

For our next practice session, I go to Juan Carlos's bright studio. We dance a whole song chest to chest without arms. It is a difficult exercise, often given to advanced beginners so they can stop leading with arms and hands and actually feel where tango comes from. But for Juan Carlos and me it's easy.

"*¿Cansada?*" he asks after an hour and a half.

"No," I answer, energized. Dancing doesn't make me tired; it recharges my battery.

He hugs me affectionately and then romantically. This time my beaded top peels off easily, as does my skirt. Like skin off a grape.

I had told Juan Carlos and myself that I wasn't interested. But apparently, that conviction is out the window. Now I recall the conversation during a flirtation in which I said that I needed to be sure he didn't have a *novia* and that I don't share my men with other women. He had assured me he had no one else. Though that conversation happened a while ago, prior to the heat of this moment, it feels reassuring now, since we had proceeded to talk about STDs, and he went so far as to offer to get his certificate of clean health, just conferred upon him two months ago by his doctor.

Now, seeing that all my defenses are just about down, he asks me if I want to see that certificate. I pull him down into me—his body language is convincing enough.

My breathing is yogic in nature, but I know this is all about the flesh, not the spirit. In tantric sex, you and your partner consciously work to open all seven chakras—even if it takes hours, or days, or a lifetime—before you both climax amid laser beams of kundalini (Hindu for the invisible force that harmonizes our relationship with the cosmos) you've generated.

Juan Carlos and I generate vials of sweat and heat—and a few steamy orgasms—in the space of an hour. It is very physically satisfying.

And then, boom, I fall into my usual trap of fantasizing about our future together. We will go back to San Francisco together—I will help him get a visa. We'll open a business teaching tango. He'll be the real deal—a native Porteño—and he'll draw the crowds from far and near. My friends will stand aside and shake their heads, amazed but pleased that I have found my soul mate. Clearly, I don't know how to be casual about sex.

Juan Carlos does not change his behavior one iota after we sleep together. We have agreed to be discreet in public and act as if *nada* has passed between us. We continue to dance together, and he dances with his many other *alumnas* (students) as he always has. One afternoon we are out dancing a *milonga* to "Tango Negro," a song with an Afro-Caribbean rhythm. The drums pound and he guides me around the dance floor, at one point sans arms, just torsos. During the percussion, we stand in place and do the move that will become ours alone. It is a beautifully synchronized full-body bump and grind, recalling primal and tribal ritual. It is done in time with the drums and the lub-dub of heart-pumping blood.

"*¿Mojada?*" Juan Carlos asks salaciously. I search to place the word. *"Piso mojado"* jumps to mind, one of the few Spanish phrases I knew before coming here, having read it on yellow sandwich boards sprawled across public restrooms to notify people to tread carefully.

But Juan Carlos is not asking me if the floor is wet. "Yes," I reply. I am turned on. The charge in the room could power the world's energy needs.

It's dances like these that prompt us to return to his studio several more times for lovemaking sessions. It's been a long time since I've regularly worn a postorgasmic flush.

Several days later, longing to just visit, sit, and talk, I ring his bell unannounced. After a long while he comes down barefoot, his dark eyes intense on his somber face.

"*¿Qué tal?*" he asks shortly, as if I'm an encyclopedia salesperson.

I confess that I'm feeling a little homesick and that I'm hoping for a visit.

Juan Carlos demurs. He has a student coming soon and must prepare. Which is odd, because he often invites me to help him teach his students. But I can sense he wants me to leave, so I do, crestfallen.

The next time I see Juan Carlos for a practice session, he is overly critical of every move I make. At first, I listen and try to correct my steps, even when I think he's off base. But when he gives conflicting feedback—first I'm stepping too wide, then too long—I argue back. This raises his hackles. He closes his thumb and forefinger together and passes them across his pursed lips. Zip it up. We don't need Spanish or English to communicate that. "Too much *hablar*. Quiet, please." I begin to feel exhaustion rather than the uplifting, energizing workout we usually have, so I plop myself on the couch and feel the blood rushing through my veins and head.

"What's the matter?" he asks cuttingly. Without waiting for me to answer he says. "I'll tell you what it is. You don't want to change. You don't listen."

I look straight into his eyes. "I don't mind criticism, but it's the way in which it's given."

I've apparently given him the ammunition he wants because he presses on even more forcefully than before. "So you don't like *mi manera* [my way]. That's it! I'm done with teaching you. We can dance in the *milonga*, but no more sessions."

I'm upset. My heart is thumping with fear more than anything else. I can sense his anger rising, and I can see, his reasons aside, that this distancing act is for real and that I shouldn't get in the way.

"Johnny Charles," I say, changing my tone, trying to find the calm behind his raised temper. "It's fine, whatever, but sit here, let's be friends. I am a stranger in a strange land. I need all the friends I can get. Don't stay mad at me." He sits next to me and his ire wears down. We are quiet and then I hold his hand like a friend.

He hangs his head and says, "I bad man."

"No, Juan, you are not bad."

"Yes. I lie."

"About what?" *Oh my God, he's HIV-positive*, I think.

"I have wife."

Relief spreads over me. "Why didn't you tell me?" I ask.

"Because then you will not . . . "

"You're right, I wouldn't have." I shake my head, gazing at our linked hands.

"I bad."

"No, you're not bad. But we have to stop now. I understand."

"I sorry."

"Me too."

We sit, and in the silence I feel a weight lifted. I take down the shingle I'd hung out for a life back in San Francisco with Juan Carlos. And because I don't want to leave him on a negative note, I suggest we dance a *milonga*, which we do so well together.

He puts on "Tango Negro," and the pounding drums fill my ears and body. I even feel my *bodhicitta* open, that soft spot I cannot flash upon at will at home alone. For me this is more than enough compensation—we'll always have *milonga*.

But apparently it's not enough for Juan. He shamelessly makes an attempt for one last bite of my ap-pull. I feel disappointed with him, irritated that he can't sink into this moment the way I do. I keep all my fruit to myself.

We continue to dance at *milongas* and in his studio over the following months. It takes me a while to harness my libido and think of him as just a friend. I realize that thing that I couldn't recognize in his dark forbidding eyes had everything to do with my father, who died just two years ago. My father, who could be deeply affectionate and loving, full of song and dance and joie de vivre, and then darkly enraged, brooding, distant, abusive; my father, whom I had to share with five sisters, four brothers, and one mother.

In Juan Carlos's torso is my father complex. Dancing tango is not the first experience that's brought me up against this fear of my father. I've encountered it over the years in intimate relationships. But there's something unnerving about experiencing it here, with my father now gone, in a dance that I hold divine.

When Juan Carlos yells at me to correct something, I shake with the same fear and anticipation of disappointing someone I held dear as a child. But his torso also holds my Heaven and God experience, too, and so I confront the conflict head-on, just as I did long ago with my father, who could be the most charismatic, loving man on earth and then the father from Hell when he went dark and directed the dissatisfaction he felt within onto his sons and daughters and his wife. I am lucky to have had my father live long enough to have said to his entire family, "I'm sorry"—for his excessive toughness, providing my first major opportunity to feel what forgiveness is in this life.

So I am able to stay with the very old fear that rears its head and even recall how my father loved to dance with my mother and all of his daughters. A musician in his youth, he and my mother would improvise their beat dancing to big band music. I know now that my dad had the potential for tango rapture in his body (as does my mother). And perhaps that, the Tao of tango, was what allowed him to die the death of a rock-bottom drunk and resurrect, a renewed and better person, who lived another twenty-five years, making friends wherever he and my mother traveled in their big Lincoln Continental (few eighty-four-year-olds have close to two hundred people travel from far and near to their wake). Thus, through the grace of having done it before, I get through this small-potatoes rough period with Juan Carlos.

It doesn't matter that Juan Carlos will never be able to comprehend the degree to which my interactions with him are the working through of my residual Oedipus complex. It is grueling to stick with it, but eventually rewarding. I get over my fear, which, like my father's own fears, is a projection from within. When I no longer shroud Juan Carlos in the dark side of my father, we are able to develop a friendship—even as I watch him flirt with every new *alumna* who passes through. But I am also penetrating the delusion, which is one of three great obstacles to pure practice, and the one which undoubtedly led to my involvement with him in the first place. I wonder if I'm one of the few women—maybe the only one— he lets help out in his studio. "Not two, one!" he commands, and I follow his lead, urging the other followers to heed his instruction: *No hablar y no pensar* (no talking and no thinking), just dance.

Chapter 7

Abandon All Hope,
You Who Enter Here

Yo soy el alma misma de mi tango
Cargado de rancor y desengaños.

I am the soul of my tango
Loaded with anger and disillusion

—*"Con Alma de Tango," 1959*

In a good week, I am pressing up against sixty to seventy male
bodices, specimens ranging from the prime of life to just this side
of the coffin. I inhale every nuance of male essence. I have an acute
sense of smell, and I can interpret that warm envelope each man
arrives in the way some people read auras: He's just been at a fish

restaurant . . . lives in a musty apartment . . . uses overly chlorinated water . . . stored his jacket in mothballs too long . . . didn't shower after sex. My nose simply reports to my brain, but this reflex takes a backseat to dancing. *"¡Qué rico olor!"* is what I say if I like his cologne, which I often do.

I'm careful not to give in to my olfactory senses too much. I've been seduced already twice, and it's hard for me to dismiss the role smell might have played in those two brief sexual ventures. They've been like vaccinations against further carnal complicity. I slip easily into celibacy, more by default than choice, driven by blind body wisdom. The postorgasmic flush I'd gotten used to with Juan Carlos gives way to tango's tantric flush. There is no doubt that the physical act of dancing tango alters my physique from sheer physical exertion. Every one of my muscles hugs to the bone, showing definition and cutting through my thin clothing. At times I become acutely aware of my abs, glutes, intercostal muscles, and spine the way I have been taught to do in yoga classes.

It's my yoga practice that allows me to motor from my core and that affords me visible levity, as if I am about to take off and fly. My given guy of the minute serves as an anchor, keeping me grounded as we as engage in something akin to cell fusion.

Dorothy Parker once quipped, "Of course beauty is skin deep. Who ever heard of a cute pancreas?" Ah, but she is wrong. I have no doubt that tango dancers' organs are purified and cleansed of toxins. They should have a special niche in the ever-growing donor market.

I'm often impressed by how good I look at two or three in the morning after dancing for hours, my skin pulled tightly back. I sometimes hate to put that face to bed. Tango gives me a temporary facelift, here in the world's cosmetic surgery capital, where tour packages include consultations with "estheticians" and where I've seen a few too many sculpted noses and perky breasts as I casually stroll through my favorite barrios.

Experiencing every inch of my physique in this new, intense way, I begin to see through the blur of my wounded feelings to the richness around me, even in the mundane. I follow—what else?—my nose. The lavender-painted Laundromat, for example, exudes a warm, perfumey detergent scent that makes me want to stand and sniff for long minutes. As does the empanada-pizza factory whose yeasty doughs wrap the spiced beef, *calabaza* (squash), *humita* (corn mashed into a béchamel sauce), Roquefort, chard, ham, and mushrooms that fill my refrigerator. Sweet jasmine wafts from the bushes around the corner while the ambiguous two-tone musk of those decadent ladies across the street laces the air in front of the *otelo,* or sex hotel.

I make a practice of paying attention to the music—composers, lyrics, song titles, singers. I flood my loft with local sound waves when I return from my walk each morning. I live for Todo Tango, which not only plays tango music, but also features talk shows on famous lyricists and composers. On the day that Julio Sosa, a lesser-known singer from the 1950s, is featured, I use the information I gather to impress one of my dance partners later on that night: "Oh, that Sosa, he was just a less tender imitation of Gardel," I say, showboating. He gives me a big smile and says, "*¡Bárbaro!* You know more than us Porteños." *Yes!* I think, giddy with self-congratulatory sentiments. The Argentines are so proud of their composers, some of whose music has endured close to a hundred years, that it's rewarding to actually impress them.

I swoon with delight when I make out the opening notes of Roberto Goyeneche singing Aníbal Troilo's "Toda Mi Vida." It is a crowd-pleasing rhythmic tango often played in *milongas*. "Ah, but you have to hear Francisco Fiorentino sing it," my partner tells me. I take this suggestion as a compliment, since it leads me to believe that my partner sees my true and deep appreciation for the music as well as the dance.

I learn to recognize Ángel Vargas and Raúl Béron, who sings the iconic "Malena" so beautifully. Malena is the Mona Lisa of tango personae. No one is sure exactly whose real-life portrait she embodies, and there has been almost as much conjecture about her real-life inspiration as there has been for Da Vinci's *Gioconda*. Perhaps she's a composite of different women—one can only speculate. What's sure is that she's a classic brooding archetype. But as the lyrics purport, Malena sings tango *como ninguna* (like no one else). She pours her broken heart and soul into song. She has the voice of a lark, we're told, but some back-alley darkness acquired in the poor barrio of her youth gives it a choking quality. Malena drinks too much. She has the very blood of the *bandoneón* in her veins. Whoever Malena was, her story often brings me to tears.

But then, so does "Desde el Alma," one of the most romantic, upbeat melodies that's played so frequently it's described as "a synonym for waltz in Argentina." This hugely popular song was written in 1911 by a fourteen-year-old girl named Rosita Melo. The notes, she said, rose from her soul; hence the song's name, which translates as "From the Soul."

Apart from the music that so moves me, Todo Tango has a penchant for repeatedly broadcasting public service announcements that serve as reminders that I'm living in a country that, though now democratic, was in the iron grip of cold-blooded dictators not long ago. Argentina has a long history of alternating between military juntas (1955–'73 and 1974–'83) and radical governments (such as that of Perón, 1946–'55 and 1973–'74). The current democracy was only restored in 1983. One ad is an appeal to anyone having information on the whereabouts of Juan Julio Lopez, a seventy-seven-year-old bricklayer who vanished in September after testifying against Miguel Etchecolatz, a police official from the 1970s dictatorship, which was responsible for the "disappearance" of thousands of citizens.

Ricardo, a *milonguero* friend, turns out to be a good teacher on things political in Argentina. When I meet him at Plaza Bohemia, known locally by its address, Maipu 444, he says to me, proudly, that he is, and always has been, a member of the Communist Party. He tells me that he's lucky to be alive, because he could easily have been among the 1970s "disappeared" for his political activities. He's a slight but energetic man with thin white hair. I put him in his seventies.

Ricardo is a retired architect who now makes jewelry that he sells at *milonga* Niño Bien. We first spend time together outside the *milonga* when he invites me to visit his workshop one day. As I watch him mold silver, gold, and semiprecious stones into rings and necklaces, I extend an invitation, asking him if he would accompany me to the small Evita Museum on Lafinur Street. I've been there before, I tell him, but I'd appreciate his homegrown take on some of the exhibits.

Though the Recoleta Cemetery holds her mortal remains, the museum, housed in a handsome nineteenth-century former mansion that once sheltered single moms, seems to hold her mythic remains. It promises "the truth with historical rigor," but the warmly lit official portraits of Juan and Eva Perón that greet visitors upon entry could not be more airbrushed. First lady Eva Perón, born Eva Maria Duarte in 1919 of humble origins, appears decked in furs at every turn, even as audio clips resound with her disavowal of riches, her love for the humble, and her hate of wealthy oligarchs. There are perhaps a few too many copies of her autobiography, *The Reason for My Life*, on display. Lining the walls are her glass-encased personal effects, including her fine clothing, jewelry, perfume, eyeglasses, prayer book, diploma, and even the hypodermic syringe that must have administered her morphine on her deathbed.

I enjoyed seeing Evita as a brunet cover girl on a 1945 issue of *Sintonía* magazine in a modest one-piece bathing suit. She poses demurely, her hands positioned rather self-consciously behind her head. It wasn't too long after that when Evita decided to go eternally blond, not unlike her near-contemporary Norma Jean. But unlike the woman who would become Marilyn Monroe, Evita was indisputably the maker of her own persona—and of Perón's. She was an ambitious and well-paid radio and film performer when she met Colonel Juan Perón in 1944. They married just one year later, and as first lady, Eva Perón spent millions of Argentina's pesos on homes, shelters, and schools for the poor and dispossessed. She was a friend to the rank and file, to single mothers, and to orphans.

She kissed lepers, created healthcare for citizens, and invited the working class, *descamisados* (shirtless ones), into her office. She founded the Female Perónist Party and secured the vote for women in 1947. When she died in 1952, at the young age of thirty-three, thousands petitioned the Pope to canonize her.

Ricardo sits uncharacteristically silent, his jewelry strewn to the side while he patiently listens to me recount my impressions of the museum. And then, much to my surprise, he launches into a dark diatribe about how much he hated Eva Perón.

"My mother hated her, my father hated her. Do you know what she was?" he demands.

"No," I say, shocked to be witnessing this degree of rancor from a man who's usually so self-possessed.

"She was a whore." As I listen to his rant, I am consumed by the embarrassment I feel at my own obtuseness—of not understanding the more nuanced image Evita has here in her home country. I feel a bit like the blundering Ugly American, insensitively blurting my cultural spin before waiting to hear what the locals think. I sheepishly retract my invitation as he winds down and returns to a state of relative calm.

I know that I'm susceptible to Evita mystique thanks to Andrew Lloyd Webber's Broadway musical and Alan Parker's 1996 movie version staring Madonna as Eva. But the impression of her here wasn't so easily derailed by Hollywood glamour, and I have since been reminded over and over that she didn't so much love the poor as abhor the rich. I learn that Perónism is now blamed for everything that is wrong in Argentina, much in the way Lyndon B. Johnson's Great Society was blamed (mostly by Republicans) for every social ill of the 1990s, forcing Democrats to punish en masse welfare recipients.

I learn to keep Evita to myself like a secret guilty pleasure. I admire her bronze likeness on the Plaza Evita on Libertador, where I note that she is sculpted with her tail sticking out just like mine does when I dance tango. I shoot a digital photo of it and label the file "Evita's Colita" to share with friends and fellow *tangueros* who remark on my protruding tail.

⚜

On the dance floor I'd only witnessed Ricardo's soft center and gentle demeanor, but outside the *milonga* I learn to appreciate his acerbic wit and many strong opinions. When I assert that he must not celebrate Christmas because of his Russian Jewish heritage, he's quick to set me in my place: "Oh, yes I do! I am Argentine!" He offers unsolicited advice on everything from repositioning my *colita* to wearing a light perfume to not eating garlic.

"I'll take it under advisement," I say, using one of Dan's lawyerly deflections, which I adopted not too long into our relationship. Notwithstanding his quaint charm-school advice, I like Ricardo a lot. I believe he has my best interest at heart—although I stick to my own ideas about my *colita*, perfume, and garlic.

Because I've taken an interest in Ricardo's passion around local politics, he invites me to accompany him to a demonstration on Avenida de Mayo, where angry citizens are gathering to urge the government to find Lopez—and find him alive. I call on Ricardo at his attractive twelfth-floor apartment on Perón Street, where he lives with his wife. Their apartment shimmers with the reflections of their colored glass-bottle collection that lines nearly every shelf in their main room, catching the early spring late-day sun. Ricardo points out the artsy black-and-white headshots of Adriana that they've hung over the mantle. She has the baby-face cuteness of Shirley Temple mixed with the intelligent beauty of Loretta Young. He seems mesmerized by her image there, and I feel grateful for the possibility of a platonic relationship with a fellow *tanguero*.

We walk along Callao to the Congreso and turn down Avenida de Mayo. As I watch the people pouring onto the streets, I feel the lull before a storm. I also feel a sense of hopelessness. Ubiquitous posters have made Juan Lopez's harmless and aged face familiar everywhere—on subways, on TV, in store windows. I even receive a text message (on the cell phone provided with my loft rental) from the government expressing its commitment to help find Juan Julio Lopez. But I'm sure he's gone the route of Jimmy Hoffa. I see many young people and union workers, dressed modestly, cleanly, sporting T-shirts that state their work or party affiliation. They line up peacefully in cadres along the street as the police stand around looking as harmless as school patrols. Ricardo stops to chat with many people who know him.

Like everything in Argentina, it seems, the *manifestación* reminds me of Dan. He and I marched fervently one Saturday in 2003 against the U.S. invasion of Iraq. The peace march was loaded with masses of people of every age group and social milieu. It was middle-class strong, and I was sure that the Bush administration would be persuaded by our efforts. I had no idea then the extent to which the thirst for oil dollars, bolstered by our fanatic religious right, was already forming a perfect storm for an illegitimate war. I feel that familiar feeling of helplessness for the Argentines, who are so earnestly trying to bring the Dirty War culprits to justice. But the unseen forces still loom, flexing their muscle by "disappearing" Lopez.

Ricardo must note my distraction because he suddenly suggests a little detour.

"Come on," he gestures, "let me show you something." We step inside the magnificent Palacio Barolo, a 1923 building with ornate marble balconies full of references to *The Divine Comedy*. Mario Palanti, the Italian architect hired to design it, loved Dante. Its twenty-two stories are divided into Hell (basement and ground floor), Purgatory (one to fourteen), and Heaven (fifteen to twenty-two). Each of its one hundred meters of height represents one of Dante's cantos.

"It's one of Buenos Aires's architectural masterpieces," Ricardo tells me as we enter the grand lobby. "From its roof you get one of the best views of the cupolas of Buenos Aires." I think of Dante's famous *Inferno* caveat emptor at the Gate of Hell, *"Lasciate ogne speranza, voi ch'intrate"* (Abandon all hope, you who enter here). Many times since tango made my life take a U-turn, this phrase has occurred to me as I stood on the edge of the invisible threshold between stillness and dance.

As we head back down the avenue toward the presidential Pink House, Ricardo tells me I can come back any Thursday evening to see the regular silent demonstration of the Mothers of the Plaza de Mayo. These mothers and grandmothers, many bent and white-haired, lost their young-adult children (among more than twenty-two thousand by some estimates) during the Dirty War and have never found a trace of them. They had to fight for the right to demonstrate. There was a time when they were not allowed to talk while they demonstrated. Their ranks are thinning, but some still show up and wear the white scarves that symbolize the diapers or tender age of their lost children. Some of the abducted women were pregnant and kept alive to deliver their babies before they were tortured and killed. Military men kept and raised the babies, who are now adults—another ongoing sordid chapter.

How, I ask myself, *could this have happened in the same culture that gave me tango?* It's similar to the question I asked myself when the United States went to war with Iraq: *How could my country—so fiercely protective of democracy—wage a preemptive war against a sovereign nation?*

My own broken heart feels so trivial in comparison to the unfathomable suffering of others. As Ricardo and I stroll away from the Plaza de Mayo, the drums start pounding and sabers start rattling, and I feel the thrill of rising up against injustice in the air, but for me it is now a distant urge, second to the work of not slipping into self-pity.

I decide not to stay for the march. I take leave of Ricardo and board the Subte D back to my barrio. En route, dwellers from *la villa miseria* step into cars to make a peso, selling cheap items—pens, pads, hairclips, sewing needles—or performing. A beautiful little girl who can't be older than nine performs an astounding juggling act. She juggles three and four balls, balancing herself in a skateboarder's stance as the rocking train car jostles underneath us. She wears a soiled and torn colorful clown suit, but she is clean and beautiful with thick black wavy tresses neatly pulled back. I cannot bear the thought that she must return to *la villa miseria,* where who knows what perversions have already chipped away at her innocence. But all I can do is what all the other attentive passengers do, applaud heartily and offer a few pesos. I'm crushed by the blankness in her dark eyes as she collects what's offered and moves swiftly on to her next gig. I know that blankness to be our collective powerlessness, or our penchant for always blaming something dead and past— Perónism, the Great Society, the other woman.

At home I feel my aloneness and *miseria* as the dark night spreads before me. I can go to sleep early and risk bad dreams, or I can put on a spaghetti-strap top, fishnet stockings, and a short, tight black skirt with a slit on its side.

I choose to get dressed and go out. I walk out into the cool night and nod warmly to the transvestites—one shapely blond bombshell, one zaftig caramel babe. I long to strike up a conversation with them about their work, but I'm too shy with my language skills. I have a perverse fascination with them. Shameless, flamboyant, holding their heads up high, they're so out there. No matter what you do, "you should burn yourself completely, like a good bonfire," said the late great Suzuki Roshi. "Leave no trace of yourself," he repeatedly told us. I think of that now when I see the *travestis* out there, putting on the Ritz. Give yourself fully, wholeheartedly, to every moment. Not even an ash should be left. Whether you're suffering, selling sex, demonstrating, or dancing, just do it. Do it fully.

As I pass by in my tiny outfit, they take scant notice of me. I leave a trail in my wake—half-burned embers of shame, guilt, regret, remorse, resentment—and it's not until I arrive at the *milonga* and step across the threshold that I stop leaving any trace of Self.

Chapter 8

Falling Down and
Getting Back Up Again

Lo que a muchos averguenza, a otros hacer gozar.

What shames many, gives joy to others.

> —*Caption to a tiled mural that features tango dancers,*
> *Retiro subway station*

Michael Wenger is a deceptively low-key guy whose quiet dharma talks kindle with a slow-burning passion. Dharma is a word that means "truth as it is moment to moment" and not as our egos would spin it. Early on he gave me one of my favorite Zen sayings, "You're perfect the way you are." He was fond of pausing, catching you in a moment of complacent contentment, before adding, "And you can use a little improvement."

Michael once gave a dharma talk at the San Francisco Zen Center, which I often think of now, on the art of falling down and getting up again. If you're not falling down (and getting up) your practice is not being oxygenated, he explained. It's in a stuffy box. "The dharma cannot be realized by just standing up," he said. He gave this lecture because Zennites tend to be idealistic and hard on ourselves. (A disproportionate number of us are or were Catholics and Jews who have redirected the guilt and suffering into different packaging.) And for those of us who thought we might be beyond all that he added, "Furthermore, if you're not falling down, make yourself fall down. Fall down a thousand times a day."

I hear you now, brother, I think to myself. I have the impulse to yell out, in a very un-Zen manner, "Yay, God!"

First Alberto, then Juan Carlos. I could take myself to task bigtime for major lapses in judgment, but I pick myself up instead. And now I vow not to get back in the race. And I'm lucky, too, because instead of another lover, I find a wise new girlfriend in Carmen Iglesias. I like how her first name is a Spanish version of mine and that her surname means church. It turns out that her sister's name is Graciela and my closest sister is Grace. We were both born in our grandmothers' houses surrounded by their gardens, which we both grew up to love.

"My grandmother lived in a *chorizo* apartment," Carmen tells me on the night we compare our stories.

"Mine lived in a railroad flat," I say.

"My grandmother grew something called a Perfect rose, and I loved to look at them."

"Mine grew herbs and vegetables, and I loved to eat them."

Carmen dances tango like a flame on a breeze—or maybe sometimes she's the breeze on the flame. She's alternately dominated by passion or reason, and sometimes a fluctuating mix of both. I found her by following a paper trail. How could I not have been intrigued by her flyer, which announced DANCING YOGA FOR TANGO DANCERS? Since it's my own conviction that tango is yoga, there was no way I could ignore the possibility of seeking out the person who'd made the same connection. Yoga is a discipline that sensitizes the body for subliminal messages (exchanged in tango) and greases the mechanical and energetic machinery at play like nothing else. It thrills me to an irreverent degree that my yoga feet stretch out from the balls (or metatarsals), not the toes, exactly like feet dancing in spike heels.

Many teachers pronounce ballet as an obvious supporting discipline for tango. But ballet, born among nobles and aristocracy during the Renaissance, is more focused on exhibition than either tango or yoga, both of which originated in humble milieus. While ballet developed to please the eye of observers, tango and yoga both developed from within, as nonverbal dialogues between opposing forces.

When I first call Carmen I'm pleased to find her English is much better than my budding Spanish. We set up a meeting at Confitería Ideal's Friday-afternoon *milonga*. I find her sitting in the women's section, looking nothing like I expected. Taller and slimmer than me, she is my photo positive, light where I'm dark. She has striking glass-blue eyes and a massive bouquet of tawny locks. My own board-straight hair was long for years until I got back into dancing. After much deliberation, I cropped it, the dead weight falling away like snake skin whose shedding was long overdue.

She tells me how she is often mistaken for a foreigner. I laugh and say, "And I'm often taken for a Porteña." Which is something that delights me.

She tells me how she started tango just four years ago at Viejo Correo, a small neighborhood *milonga* in what appears to be an old family-style Italian restaurant with a grottolike interior of limestone-white walls, red tablecloths, and wrought-iron fixtures. The place makes me hanker for big plates of spaghetti and meatballs and Chianti that comes in those basket-cradled bottles.

Carmen says, "I looked around, and instead of seeing other *tangueros* enjoying this sensual dance, I saw a lot of people aching. It's my profession to help people manage pain, so I knew I could teach dancers to conserve rather than lose energy while dancing, and to relax emotionally and psychically."

Carmen tells me she works with men and women for whom embracing can be intimidating, and even traumatizing. It's the first time I consider that not all Argentines have a natural affinity for hugging complete strangers. Having come from a family where people hug and kiss even after a huge fight, I know that I'm personally inured to this trauma.

Carmen has the kind of healing practice you wouldn't expect from an attractive Argentine who dresses almost exclusively in sporty attire. She started practicing yoga when she was seventeen, some thirty years ago, and claims it's helped her overcome hepatitis. She studied art and worked as a fashion model. Then, while working as a marketing manager for Pepsi-Cola, she fell ill from all the stress. She had severe anemia, but the doctors couldn't treat it. "They gave me iron, but it did nothing. I couldn't get out of bed. I was twenty-five. I died and my consciousness was opened."

Carmen pauses and I hold her gaze for a few seconds, as if we are both letting the ghost of her past Self wander fleetingly through the room. "*I can't keep doing this,* I said to myself. I recovered, and I stuck with yoga."

She continued in a traditional apprenticeship for twelve years with her teacher, an Argentine woman who was a disciple of a German lama who worked for German intelligence in World War I, and then studied in India before coming to live anonymously in Buenos Aires.

When I watch Carmen dance I see the way her lanky limbs display a graceful Isadora Duncan style of yoga. By contrast, my Iyengar training is more isometric, akin to slow break dancing, whereby you actively shape and pull your muscles to create resistance within your own body. Both styles of yoga can support tango's fluidity, or liquid balance, as well as its *quebradas,* or breaks in the standing body's line, such as when the hips sway, or the spine torques laterally or vertically. And because yoga trains you to breathe calmly, even under stress, thus reducing your body's natural propensity to sweat, it strongly complements a tango practice that requires a dancer to meet the moment with balance, flexibility, and spontaneity. Carmen and I talk for hours about all of this and more. We are like two zealots, ready to start our own church of yoga and convert the whole world.

"The human body is a miniature universe in itself," writes yoga master B. K. S. Iyengar in his book *Light on Yoga.* I think about this a week later as I sit focusing on my inhaling and exhaling. Carmen has invited me to one of her workshops, and she's asking us to consider our breath and how delicate our sense of smell is. "There's a tiny hole in the nasal passage," she explains, "and if you suck in

too hard, you lose the aroma of the rose." I consider this notion of
not being able to hold the rose's scent, and how the one thing in this
universe that I'd want to hoard, my breath, I cannot. Breathing is
an autonomous "letting-go" system. You cannot keep it, sorry; you
have to give it back. And then I think of how easy my breath comes
and goes when I dance tango.

Carmen has six of us little human "universes" sitting silently
on the floor in a turn-of-the-century building on Venezuela in the
Balvanera, a barrio where Carlos Gardel once lived. She directs us
to breathe in for four counts and out for two. Carmen's workshop
works soothingly with the subtle body and doesn't involve any
of my pretzel poses. As we sit comfortably on our mats, Carmen
describes the locus of the seven chakras from the base of the spine
(the one embodying sexual desire) to the pinnacle of the skull
(unity with the divine), symbolized beautifully in Eastern art by the
thousand-petaled lotus. The chakras, says Iyengar, correspond to
glands, gonads, and organs, and "regulate the body mechanism as
fly-wheels regulate an engine."

So much ancient wisdom lies along the spine. For Hindus, the
spine is the channel for kundalini, represented by a circular serpent,
its tail in its mouth. Kundalini, says Iyengar, is "latent energy that
has to be aroused and made to go up the spine, piercing the chakras."
You can think of this as an allegory, he says, "for the tremendous
vitality, especially sexual" attained with yogic practice. The serpent
materializes when yogic breathing, called *pranayama*, opens the
chakras. Such is my tango rapture, when my breath is so deep and
big, I *am* the universe. My prowess, skill, and strength are not just
sexual, but valiant—I want nothing less than this same vitality I feel
for every being in the cosmos.

Bold and stouthearted, I imagine the kundalini serpent we've just generated swaying with us in the next segment. Carmen has us stand and dance freeform—moving our hands and fingers as in flamenco. "The hands are very important to move energy around and inside us so that we never get tired," she says. And with her hands like twirling butterflies, she moves her whole upper body like fire in a breeze, her legs rooted to the earth like an *ombú* tree. For all the dancing I've done, including ballet, jazz, and tap, I've never worked with my fingers. I try it and feel the surge of something new.

With this we begin to dance to *milonga* music. We work on a common contrabody movement (CBM) that requires gentle torsion of the spine, often called "body disassociation," a phrase that I find distastefully reminiscent of a psychological disorder.

Carmen helps each participant to correctly execute the CBM, using the breathing techniques we have just practiced. The three-hour workshop winds down with everybody's favorite pose, *savasana*, or corpse pose. We lay on our backs, breathing, zoning out, and Carmen makes soothing hands-on adjustments to our "dead" bodies.

When we come back to life, Carmen introduces us to each other. I'm pleased to meet Cecilia Gonzales, a teacher who dances with Cacho Dante, a *milonguero* locally renowned for his exceptional musicality. One of the men is Carmen's friend, Ed Waller, from Santa Cruz, California, who has kind eyes, as blue and sparkly as Carmen's. He pays me a great compliment in telling me that he's watched me dance at Club Español and wanted to dance with me. *How could I have overlooked such a sweet countenance?* I wonder. "Well, let's, next time," I say. Ed also shares my attraction to Zen, meditating regularly at Shobogenjii Temple in the Palermo. I know I will want to see more of a person who, like me, regularly navigates the overlapping paths of tango, Zen, and yoga.

ᏬᎧᎦᎧᏬ

I invite Carmen to come by my loft to talk about the possibility of my doing an article on her for *Yoga Journal.* I've been looking for subjects to write about, and I think she'd be perfect. When she arrives, I share with her a story I wrote on yoga studios in New Orleans, post–Hurricane Katrina. Carmen has already told me that she has never been drawn to my style of yoga because of the way Iyengar focuses mostly on the physical end of the practice.

It had come out as an apology, but how could I take offense? I'm often hard-pressed to sift the physical out of the spiritual. I entered yoga from a purely physical motivation. Having developed limberness early on from acrobatics classes, I took to yoga easily. I began a regular practice with a book by Yogi Vithaldis in 1973. Even then, yoga—an exotic Eastern art elsewhere—was in the air like San Francisco's fog. In 1984, I spent a weekend at Kripalu Institute, an ashram in a former seminary in the Berkshires of Massachusetts. I loved the experience—the rustic lakeside scenery and rainbow of fresh vegan food—but I was turned off by the bowing to Hindu gurus, mostly men, or, more accurately, to their images. When I came to Zen Buddhism, I understood that the frequent bowing and prostrations were paying homage, not to any person, but to our collective enlightenment. And I loved the way we collapsed the body to touch our forehead to the ground, a dramatic act of surrender to the universe that appealed to the dancer in me.

When Carmen is done reading, she timidly takes out a package. I watch her thin-boned fingers, those of a Galician princess, undo the brown paper to reveal two substantial pieces of cake layered thickly with *dulce de leche.*

This custardlike confection is an Argentine invention that reminds me of tango in how delightful it is with just its bare essential ingredients. The cook combines nothing more than milk (four liters) and sugar (one kilogram), and a bit of vanilla if desired. You need a patient stirring arm, but it's the *fuego muy fuerte* (very high flame) that caramelizes and thickens, transforming the mixture into a heavenly custard greater than the sum of its parts.

"It's from Confitería La Burdalesa on Sante Fe," Carmen tells me. I give her a look that tells her I haven't heard of it. "You haven't been there yet?" Her eyes are wide and incredulous.

I boil water for linden leaf tea and we sit like ladies of leisure at a yoga church social, ready to indulge. When I put the first forkful of tender *dulce de leche*–laced cake on my tongue, I taste a surefire friend. "*¡Qué rico!*" I exclaim, using that favorite four-letter word of mine that I use to describe a sensory spectrum that ranges from rich and delicious food to the divine scent of a man.

I try to take it in as slowly as Carmen, but I get way ahead of her as she talks—about men, husbands, kids. She's just returned from Port Townsend, Washington, where she taught workshops to the small tango community and stayed with her American boy-friend, Francis.

"But we've decided we should now be just friends," she says matter-of-factly. Like a good girlfriend does, I detect the underlying disappointment and stoicism and respect it. She proudly tells me that she's never been married and has never wanted children. "I never felt the need to recreate myself." I like her unequivocal tone, the way that it rings so true without being a sideways criticism of those who choose to have children. Rather it's her shorthand way of letting me know she is (like me) among women who have not labored long and hard over our "biological fate." No doubt we've had our share of anguish, though, over other ideals, destinies, dreams, dragons, demons, men, all the other good stuff that can consume women.

Her stance on marriage and children is particularly rare in this Latin country. The number of melon-shaped bellies on young women in Buenos Aires is remarkable—as is the divorce rate. Nearly every man over forty whom I meet in the *milongas* either has two grown kids and is separated or divorced, or never married the mother of his children in the first place. Subway seats and parking places display icons reserving them for pregnant women.

I give Carmen a few dismal sound bites on Dan. Oh, yes, I had this guy, had to cut him loose, ho-hum. I use her same matter-of-fact, stoic tone, not wanting to get drawn into the details just yet, and having exhausted myself with a good morning cry earlier that morning. As for kids, I tell her, I adore them. But I relish my balancing act, in the spirit of zero population growth, for my siblings, who, so far (bless them), have given me three dozen nieces and nephews at last quarter's count. Some of them are "greats," though I can't keep them straight because of the way some of the greats are older than the previous generation. If Carmen had been weaned on the glass teat of American TV, I'd have told her how my family could have written the old Pillsbury jingle: *Nothin' says lovin' like somethin' from the oven.*

I confide in her that Dan and I had visited the option of having a child much more optimistically than we ever visited the idea of marriage. We were already of "advanced age" repro-wise by the time we seriously started these conversations, but fertility ran rabidly high in our families and I know we could have, would have, maybe should have if we really wanted one. Somehow we didn't, though. We let it drop, our busy lives pulling us places, filling our days.

And then came tango.

Although I've only known Carmen a short time, I notice that she often appears distant and sad. Other times her eyes sizzle like a Fourth of July sparkler—like when she talks of wandering farther down a spiritual path than she had ever imagined from her days as a rep for a Fortune 500 company. In 1996, she attended the University of Yoga in Brazil, where, she says, she "got in touch with the most ancient form of yoga, Swasthya, where you dance the asanas." She tells me that Swasthya originated in northern India and that flamenco, too, had seeds there—something I never would have guessed.

"I thought it developed in Andalusia, " I say.

"Yes, but five thousand years before that, in northern India, all yoga was tantric, which involves powerful rituals of body and mind, including mantras and mudras with the hands." Her hands suddenly levitate and flutter in arclike swirls as she demonstrates the *mariposas*, or butterflies, she showed us in class. I see the flamenco in her wheeling hands. I look at the backs of my brownish hands, coarse-knuckled with large nail beds, too big for my body, and sit on top of them.

"Well, when the Aryan hordes invaded northern India, they forbade the tantra practices because they bring about a very balanced sex life, and you don't want to go to war—"

"I've been thinking this about tango," I interrupt. "If more people danced it, I think we'd have a long period of world peace." I don't tell her that in my wildest imaginings, tango dancers form cells like al-Qaeda, kidnapping terrorists and state-sanctioned war makers and getting them all to dance tango. I recognize that it's magical thinking, but in my reveries tango becomes the rehab of choice in drug clinics and prisons, for sex offenders and wayward heads of state.

"So," she continues, either ignoring me or humoring me, "there was a diaspora from India. Some people went to China, where they influenced Chinese medicine, which uses mudras, too. Some went to other parts of India, where Patanjali and Vedanta yoga for health blossomed. And others went to the south of Spain, where the mudras eventually manifested in flamenco."

What a deep archaeological dig it is, I think, to dissect tango's roots and influences. You scrape away at successive layers beyond Argentina and find Italy, Spain, Cuba, Africa, and now India. Tantra, an ancient form of spiritual eroticism (or erotic spiritualism), surfaces in flamenco, which surfaces in tango. I love the idea of excavating the dance's sexuality down to a spiritual grounding.

I think how after a mere two months here, with two ill-advised liaisons under my belt, I have profaned two things I held sacred: tango and sex. Falling down at this rate, I'd be picking myself up from twelve bum adventures per year. I take no solace in the knowledge that this is *not* what Michael Wenger meant.

You might think that tango has a frying-pan-into-the-fire danger for someone who's interested in healing from intimacy gone awry; that the ashram, temple, *zendo,* or convent would have been the better choice. But no, the *fuego* is right where I belong.

As Carmen and I talk, the realization of what I need to do begins to take root: I need to heal by holding off from the act of sex rather than indulging my every infatuation. At least for a while.

I show Carmen two books I have on tantric yoga. I've been curious about tantra, whose Sanskrit root "tan" means "to stretch"— as if it might be the missing link between tango and yoga. I do not hold the misconception of many Westerners that tantric yoga was a Kama Sutra solely focused on physical pleasure and the Big O—achieving unbelievable long-lasting chains of godly orgasms. Instead, tantra and Tao sex are much more about the great discipline of delaying orgasm. (Men, you'll have to read the book to believe me when I say that it is in fact incredibly gratifying.)

Carmen pulls out of her bag an even more detailed book to read, *Healing Love Through the Tao,* by Mantak Chia. It's dog-eared and underlined. She says that in looking for an alternative to the kind of yogic celibacy that simply promotes "saving" your sex drive, she came upon the tantric option, which "recycles" sexual energy and desire. I simply have to spend time with the book, she says.

"Good luck finding a guy who will do all of this," she tells me.

"I'll break him in slowly," I say. "I won't tell him right off the bat that a man's test of his sexual prowess is his ability to imbibe a glass of wine through his penis and then release it back into the glass—proving his ability to control release of semen, thus valuable energy."

"No I wouldn't bring that up on the first date," Carmen says, laughing. And then she gives me one of her pearls. "If you look for the spiritual, you will find pleasure, but if you look for just pleasure, it's unlikely you will find either."

"I'll remember that," I promise.

❧

I find a copy of the book in English later that week. It confirms what I'd been thinking about my capacity to be rapturously celibate and still make right use of my sexual energy. And I am not talking about masturbation (although it could be incorporated, according to the book).

I have been accustomed to thinking of my yogic practice as ridding me of stuff—waste products, negative energy—but reading along reframes my practice: It's also a way to create healing power. I can channel sexual energy from my "ovarian palace" (the area below the naval and above the pubis) and up the spine. I read about how to channel my energy, using breathing techniques and visualization, past the "sacral pump," the "jade pillow" (cervical vertebra), and the "cranial pump," then down the frontal body. (Pass GO, collect $200.) What started out as a garden-variety sex drive then becomes a sort of refined, higher energy as it passes all these points. It's a gross oversimplification, like telling you to take I-80 from my sister Grace's house in Hoboken, New Jersey, to my house in San

Francisco, but you get the drift. Even those who live in the subtle body, either through yoga or similar practices, will find that the techniques require a good measure of imagination, not to mention profound body awareness.

After finishing the book I decide once and for all that it's time to lock the "palace" door for a while. Little do I know I will be entering the longest period of celibacy since my uneventful deflowering at age twenty. (And don't for one minute think that the palace doors aren't regularly met up against temptation and opportunity.) Entertaining the idea of indulging my sexual urgency in a wholesome way is thrilling, actually. I'm looking forward to riding the warm thermals of arousal, sending sexual chi up my spine toward the divine pinnacle chakra of my skull where, someday, it will cascade out as a thousand-petal lotus. Someday.

I think of how the next guy, if and when, will not be getting the keys to the palace until he bones up (sorry) on tantra tango and sex. I imagine how fun it could be with the essential oils, incense, poses, special foods, and buddy-breathing techniques.

I begin to understand the premiums this brand of celibacy offers when I meet my next infatuation, Pablo. He's a happy-go-lucky *tanguero* with the glow of fireflies in his black eyes. He always seeks me out to dance and always mentions how I must come meet his parents, who will cook fine Italian fare for us. He's such a wholesome sort of guy whom everybody likes and trusts that it's easy to fool myself momentarily. The more we dance in his snug-as-a-glove body-to-body style with those seductive *cadencias,* I find my mind spinning and weaving a tapestry of places Pablo and I could go . . . but I do none of the routine follow-up as I did with Alberto and Juan Carlos. On the dance floor, or at home where I sit, I just breathe and focus that delicious energy of attraction and surprise up my spine, cleaning out all seven chakras. And every time my sex urge passes GO, I collect way more than $200. I collect stamina, power, balance to stay on my axis; in the moment, I'm whole and true to my commitment.

Chapter 9

The Language of Tango

Dance! As if the world is watching, but you don't know it.

—*Anonymous Zen saying*

Imagine one North American city preserving the stomping grounds of Glenn Miller, Duke Ellington, Count Basie, and the dozens of other great big band leaders. Imagine that this city keeps the swing scene thriving in old clubs wherein the maestros actually played, as well as in many new ones. Picture constant waves of new generations of orchestras, DJs who know the recordings like their own family trees, and public radio and TV stations whose sole purpose is to send that music out to the masses, keeping it alive and thriving. Finally, imagine crowds of all ages coming from all over the world to dance to that music—in clubs, in hole-in-the-wall venues, and on the streets.

Such is the tango scene here in Buenos Aires—like Heaven on earth.

The only thing that might have approximated Buenos Aires's *milonga* scene would have been New Orleans's jazz scene prior to Hurricane Katrina. Swing music's endurance seems marginal when compared with that of tango, which has weathered much, including a dictatorship that forbade assembling in public. There is an embarrassment of riches in Buenos Aires. The fire of passion burns like it was just lit. It's not hard to imagine tango's forebears smiling on their descendants, who are still kicking ass as the form evolves.

It's heady being among today's ferment on all things tango. In dance schools, music studios, and tango publications there is hot, hot debate, strident banter, and hairsplitting over current styles. Did Fabian Salas and Gustavo Naveira profane or elevate the sacred *milonguero* style with their *nuevo* moves? Does Pugliese deserve all the merit for his dramatic compositions, or did he just copy Gobi, his predecessor? Every other *taxista* has an opinion, as he swerves to avoid collisions at the countless intersections with no traffic lights or stop signs. He's likely to feel hip and sophisticated when he tells you that he adores Ástor Piazzola, the Stravinsky of tango, who had his heyday in the 1950s and whose primary goal was that people should listen and not dance to his dissonant riffs.

In the *milonga* there is just the language of tango. Some say the word "tango" is a corruption of the word "tambor," meaning drum, an instrument whose prevalence in the dance's Afro-Cuban roots can't be understated. My favorite theory is that tango comes from the Latin *tangere*, to touch. Every night—or afternoon—of the week, one can touch and be touched. What better medicine to cure any ailment you might have?

⁂

One afternoon, I'm on my way to Confitería Ideal in search of this very cure. I'm walking with my friend Arthur from San Francisco who is visiting Buenos Aires. He says, "Just imagine what it must've been like in the late 1930s—to be walking down Corrientes Street and hear Biagi's live music coming out of one of the clubs!"

"Yeah," I say, recalling how a Porteño friend told me that trumpet player Dizzy Gillespie just showed up and started playing one day in 1956 at composer Osvaldo Fresedo's concert (that live recording is now highly treasured). It didn't seem at all far-fetched, or like something equally brilliant couldn't happen now. Even though in 1956 I was a five-year-old back in New Jersey, it's as if I've been able to appropriate that memory. I feel some sense of having *been there*.

I'm pleased at how Arthur's understanding of the music is rubbing off on me. At La Ideal we dance to Biagi's waltz, "Viejo Portón," during which Arthur schools my ear, "Listen how the violins scream higher and higher, reaching a crescendo so lofty you can't believe they'll go higher." And they do, just before they cascade down.

"I had never noticed that before," I say. And now, any time I hear it, I'm all chills and goose bumps.

Arthur and I became good friends on the dance floors of San Francisco before eventually becoming cycling buddies. I was grateful for his companionship when I first felt so shut out by Dan. I attribute Arthur's mastery of the oral tradition to his having grown up in a small village in the Scottish highlands without TV, and I was comforted by the long stories he'd recount as we cycled the hills and small mountains along the San Francisco Bay.

Seeing him here in the birthplace of tango, indulging and expressing his passion, is a treat. He abandons himself to classes in dance and Spanish with his trademark gregariousness. He scopes out his favorite followers in the *milongas*. He makes friends with La Ideal's DJ, Marcelo Roja, who, he explains, has the mark of a good DJ because of his understanding of the crowd's taste in *La Guardia Vieja* (Old Guard), Golden Era, and modern tango.

As I've noted before, many *tangueros* are techies by profession— and Arthur is no exception. When we take a class together with Luciana Valle, his deconstruction of the dance mechanics and the music reminds me that there is a whole other universe to tango I've yet to explore—that is, from the male or leader's perspective. There is always a new horizon in tango.

A new horizon comes to me with the introduction to a man named Peter. Peter is German by birth, but he's lived in the States and in Buenos Aires for many years. I marvel at his earthy emotions as he gushes freely to our mutual friend about the connection he just had with a dancer, a French woman. I'm accustomed to the swooning and exclaiming among the women, but it's a novelty to hear men emote, especially this tall, silver-haired, elegant man whom I'd expected to be so very collected.

As they chat, I wonder if the French woman is "luscious," the standard adjective that I often hear used to describe a sensual follower. My mouth waters, as I can think of nothing but a juicy, meltingly ripe piece of fruit. I'm sure the term originated with men, enraptured with fleshy, full women, but women use the word, too. Luscious would certainly apply to Dave, with his plush barrel chest; likewise to Juan Carlos and a few other men I've danced with. I like the term and don't think I'd mind it at all if my partners referred to me as ripe, juicy, meltable, dee-licious—and luscious. Such are the feelings that consume me as I consider my newfound strength and sense of purpose. Luscious sensuality at every turn.

As I get to know Peter and his partner, Inge, I find he is no exception to the rule that *no one takes tango casually.* During my first dance with him, I find myself hoping that I'm measuring up to the French woman. We have a nice smooth connection, and he invites me again at other *milongas.* I feel honored when Peter offers to share an essay he wrote in which he considers one of the most simmering debates—that between the *milonguero* and *nuevo* styles. *Milonguero* is the close-embrace style that developed of necessity on the crowded dance floors; *nuevo,* danced to the same music, employs an open embrace and more fancy (some would say "exhibitionist") foot- and leg work that requires more space.

Even before I read his essay, I know that Peter prefers the *milonguero* style—he transmits palpable signals through his gentle embrace. Peter is generally quiet, reserved, soft-spoken, and so I'm moved when I read his impassioned prose. He invokes Proust's "exquisite pleasure" at tasting the madeleine, when, as the French author put it, "the vicissitudes of life had become indifferent . . . its disasters innocuous, its brevity illusory." I feel a kindred spirit in Peter, as this piece affirms tango's Zenlike experience for him.

Most important to me, though, is how his essay enlightens me on an aspect of the leader's perspective that I, as a follower with closed eyes, never have to think about: what the dance floor looks like as the leader navigates. Peter asserts that "this feeling of oneness with partner and music, oneness with all there is, this feeling of moving 'in a zone' is afforded most readily in the *milonguero* embrace . . . [because] the dance patterns are as much determined by the movement of the other dancers as by the individual's wishes . . . all dancers on the floor become part of, and move like a big organism to, the music."

Now when I dance with Peter I'm even more attuned to the urgency he brings to the dance with his heightened concentration. No one has yet told me that I'm "luscious," but in my mind, at least, I feel myself ripening to that state when I dance with Peter.

The next Saturday night at a *milonga* called Los Consagrados, I dance with Enrique, a regular partner, who tells me how, when he was five years old, he met Carlos Di Sarli, creator of the utterly romantic "Bahía Blanca," at the composer's home. Impressed, I ask to touch the hem of Enrique's pants. I revere these singers and composers as I do the Dalai Lama or Mother Teresa. Di Sarli's romance is visceral and untiring, the way Hoagy Carmichael's "Stardust Melody" is. I feel a similar religiosity about Osvaldo Pugliese, a composer who upped the passion in tango in the 1950s when no one thought that was possible.

Contemporary musicians attribute mystical powers to the very names of musicians. Saying "Pugliese" is thought to bring good luck. A whole monumental caricature of him and his orchestra stands in his barrio, Villa Crespo, although it's tragically vandalized now. Pugliese, who gave his band members the same cut of pay as he took for himself, did jail time for his Communist beliefs.

There are songs that make my breath catch like a sudden squeeze of the *bandoneón* when I hear their first notes. "Todo te Nombra," by Francisco Canaro (who was Uruguayan) and "Toda Mi Vida," by Aníbal Troilo, affectionately called Pichuco, make me anxiously await the man who will lead me through these tunes from tango's Mount Olympus.

One Friday afternoon in mid-October, I join Carol, a tourist from Australia, for coffee between one *milonga* and the next. She tells me she's taken some private lessons with Juan Carlos Copes for $100 an hour. "It was a splurge," she says, "but he's no spring chicken, and when will I be in Buenos Aires again?"

Juan Carlos, who will turn seventy-six in May 2007, is a pioneer with Maria Nieves (his dance partner for forty years). They met in 1948 and became the Astaire/Rogers of tango. They continued to rev tango fever around the world as stars in the show *Tango Argentina,* which made its Broadway debut in 1985.

I feel a distinctive pang of envy, but then, I am dancing regularly with the unheralded peers and elders of Copes. My reverence for Copes is enormous, and because my home away from home is the *milonga,* I feel I have danced with him and other greats by contact, by transference of their energy up through my soles, through palm-to-palm, heart-to-heart sweat and blood transfusions.

Carol tells me that she's going to the Abasto district to see Copes's show at Esquina Carlos Gardel. I go to the *milonga* at Maipu 444 and dance with a regular there who is Copes's senior by three years. I call him Mr. Frumpy for his dress, which alternates between cotton checkered shirts, orange tie, and pants and sky blue suit and powder blue suede shoes. His dancing is pure Golden Age—very smooth and fluid, not marked by the digital feel or jerkiness of hothouse dancers who count in their heads. He sits out most *tandas,* "talking" to me across the room with his eyes or nods of the head: *I'm saving you, for the waltz,* his look says. He crowns me with many *piropos,* my favorite being, "You dance like the *tangueras* of the 1940s."

The privilege of dancing with men like Mr. Frumpy can't be measured, nor can the joy of being seen with them, national treasures that they are. When I'm dancing and notice that the seats are empty of spectators, I feel a certain lack of validity, like the tree in the Zen koan that makes no sound when it falls because no one's around to hear it. Like one-handed clapping. A sign at the Zen Center reads, DANCE AS IF NO ONE IS WATCHING. But I'd be lying if I said I didn't dance in part for the thrill of being seen. I always wanted to sneak in during off hours and alter it to, DANCE AS IF

THE WORLD IS WATCHING, BUT YOU DON'T KNOW IT. It's my own homegrown koan.

"Tango es un vicio" is a common phrase I hear as my fellow dancers start to recognize that I've become a fixture at *milongas*. I nod my head, agreeing that it is a "vicious cycle." It was weeks into hearing this that I bothered to check the dictionary to find out that *vicio* means "vice," at which point I start to counter this assessment: "No," I say, *"Tango es un vertud."* It's a virtue to me, to be sure. "Tango saved my life," I sometimes share.

On this hallowed ground, I am dancing thousands of circles, a geometric figure with spiritual significance—for Sufi dancers, for ancient Hawaiians, for Native Americans. In Jungian psychology, the circle, a mandala, is a symbol representing the effort to reunify the self. We go to *milonga* the way we go to church or market, places that nourish body and soul. I find on the web a story called "The Church of Tango," by Cherie Magnus, depicting the dim churchlike lighting of melting candles and hushed aura of a funky *milonga* aptly named Catedral in the Almagro barrio. I like that others feel the spirituality in the dance.

Away from the *milonga*, my idle mind is the devil's playground. I try to think of Evelyn, my avowed poison, as a form of medicine. Homeopathic medicine. I try to connect with her. But this is still way too difficult since I still find myself occasionally lulling myself asleep by reliving the pulling of her hair. I know I have work to do to acknowledge the seventh precept: realizing Self and Other as one. I know she is me and I am she. I am still at battle with myself.

My mind will not meditate on forgiveness; it prefers Dante's nine circles of Hell. With each progressively worse sin, each concentric circle gets closer to Satan at the center. Circle Nine is betrayal, and its punishment is being cemented in a lake of ice from the waist down. *Not harsh enough!* I think. I can't help but recall my Sicilian heritage when I visualize being cemented. I want for my traitor the searing with flames, the basting with human excrement, the maggots that suck blood and tears in the circles of lesser sins. *But wait,* I think, *she is you.* And then I push the thought out of my mind.

I have a book that instructs not to deny or push away this part of me that is roaring angry. It's called *Start Where You Are,* by Pema Chödrön, an American Buddhist. It was in a box of my giveaway books when it slipped out. I picked it up and it fell open of its own accord to the passage that reads: "Suppose that . . . every time you think of a particular person you get furious." I felt a chill. "Breathe it in," is her instruction. To develop sympathy for my own confusion. To not blame the person or myself, just acknowledge that there is fury and rage. "[H]ot, black, and heavy," writes Chödrön. I can tell you this: It is exhausting to experience pure hatred, even without fixating or acting on it.

Just when I think it might wear itself down, what with the space and time (six thousand miles and nearly two months), Evelyn sends me an email: "Are you still experiencing the anger you had for me, or is that getting somewhat better?"

My anger, she'd told me before I left, was causing her great distress. Before I left, I'd composed and sent several written apologies in the hopes of preventing her from filing a restraining order. But now a significant amount of time has passed, and receiving this email knocks me off my game. Coincidentally (or not?), I've received an email from Dan, asking how I am, less than twenty-four hours before hers, reinforcing my paranoia. This throws me into a royal funk and starts me on an unshakably dark trajectory of endless speculation: *She's taking my temperature because she's moving in with Dan/They're getting married and want to make sure I'm out of their way for good/Here I am sitting in the dark channeling my chi while they're having great sex, conjugal bliss, the whole empanada, everything I wasn't good enough to achieve.*

A slew of choice responses runs through my mind, but I think of Pema Chödrön and I breathe them in. I have been trying hard, since arriving here, to consider a koan: where my bottomless anger toward Evelyn originates. I actually envied her in the unhesitating way she stepped into my role with Dan, something I could never have done if the situation were reversed, having too many years of training to wait in line for my needs to be met. It's a certain lack of self-importance that I can trace somewhat to years of growing up among my many siblings. Perhaps the start of my not liking to be *pushed out of the way* goes back to when I was only a year and four days old and my mother came home with my new baby sister Grace—she says I was pissed and wouldn't go to her. Maybe it goes back to when I was three months and she got pregnant again. Who knows? All this is intellectual speculation, home-cooked analysis, and I have yet to convince my emotions to swallow it.

I don't respond to Evelyn and I cut off communication with Dan completely out of self-preservation, not wanting to hear or know about their happy plans, if any, while I'm trying to move forward and mend the tear in my soul. But the more I think about not emailing Dan back, the more I long to hear from him.

A couplet from Pedro Laurenz's tango "Como Dos Extraños" comes to mind: *Angustia de saber muertas ya/la ilusión y la fe.* (Anguish of knowing hope and faith were already dead.) It is ridiculous to suffer what is dying. Let it go. But just as only San Francisco, with its Heaven-sent fog, has the *lactobacillus sanfranciscensis* needed to make the one true sourdough, humid Buenos Aires has a unique organism in its air conducive to *angustia,* a pervasive, sticky mixture of anguish and anxiety. *Angustia argentinensis* is the name I come up with to describe the "organism" that inoculates my feelings and creates chronic suffering just when I think I might be on the verge of serenity.

Get thee to a milonga, I tell my *angustia, so that you might be leavened by song and dance in the round.* Only in the *milonga* do I experience a safe haven from the chaos and splintering that has the power to stop me in my tracks, to keep me in bed all day. The knowledge that I'll be set free upon entering the round is what keeps me going back night after night. The irony of my tango solace does not escape me. The dance has been bound up with violence from its very start. Apache tango, a rough style, originated in Paris in the early 1900s. In the archetypal fight over the woman, usually a beautiful prostitute, two tango roughs challenge each other with knives and eye-popping foot patterns and figures (think *West Side Story*). One magazine described these early *tangueros* as going "fly to fly" as they challenged each other with early tango patterns.

But I have a tall and nonviolent order for tango. It must fill a gaping hole—the way form fills emptiness. I must keep it pure and untrammeled like the dharma and not allow it to drive me into triviality, clinging, or aversion. In the *milonga*, I keep to my tango precepts (show up, accept what's offered, be present, be kind).

More or less.

It's easy to remain good and righteous after being greeted so warmly with hugs, kisses, and sincere inquiries after my well-being as I become familiar to the many organizers whose labor of love puts so many different *milongas* on the map. At Le Gricel, Adriana is always decked out in tango finery, and when I compliment her she gives me a 10 percent discount coupon to her supplier. At La Ideal, Alicia whispers in my ear when a great new leader appears on the scene—to make sure I dance with him. Graciela and Blas at La Milonguita treat me like a relative who just dropped by for a drink. They seat me at the best table available. Chiche and Marta, who teach a class at Torcuato Tasso (in a restaurant in San Telmo where *milongas* were held secretly during the military junta years), remind me of my parents in their younger days. Chiche leads me in the pattern he's showing the class, and I feel my father, the angelic side of Dad that adored dance.

Walking into a *milonga* is like opening an oven door. The sound and vibes envelop you like a wave of heat. Often, there is nothing special on the outside to mark that something's cooking on the inside. *Milongas* are all over the city in safe and sketchy hoods and residential spaces alike; as often in commercial areas as downtown ones. Four Greek columns mark the entrance to Salon Canning, which celebrated fifty years in 2006. A few blocks away, there is the weird feng shui of La Viruta. Underground, chorizo-shaped La Viruta is not given to the free flow of chi, that elusive unifier of the cosmos. Still, it's wildly attractive to many dancers.

One warm Saturday night in late October, I start *milonga*-hopping early. I climb the stairs of La Nacional, where numerous plaques are on display to remind visitors that this is an old Italian American club. The neglect extends to the bare yellowed walls of the high-ceilinged dance hall on the second floor, where unadorned lightbulbs beg for shades.

A man, shorter than me by a head, invites me to dance. Everything goes smoothly until he half trips me. He begins to yell at me loudly and pronounces me in need of his classes as he hands me his flyer. I tell him to buzz off and to never, ever yell at me again. Anywhere. But especially in front of people. This elicits a weird whimpering behavior as he whines in accented English, "Sorry, sorry, I sorry." I later learn that he pulls this stunt on foreigners regularly, and that he often succeeds in getting beginners who believe they need his lessons.

I return to my seat and wait.

A tiny old man, shorter than me by two heads this time, who must be ninety, looks pleadingly at me to dance. Not an auspicious start, but it's early—barely midnight—so I accept. He has a lemon-size lump on his balding head. He is so bad that I take the lead from him, which provokes some applause. He is an elfin clown looking for a straight man. I am it.

Again I return to my seat. I collect myself, sit, and wait.

The host seats a six-foot-tall blond next to me. *Competition,* I think. But she opens her mouth to speak, and I see that she's a man. She introduces herself as Raquel and tells me she's from Southern California. She wears a strapless black dress with a slit up one side. As I try to square her Kim Novak features with her deep voice, she whispers into my ear.

"Oh, now he's a good ride," she nods toward a Porteño. She gives me her card. She works in an esthetic surgery office.

"He's a good ride" is whispered in my ear many more times—occasionally modified to "He's a rough ride." She gets more invitations to dance than I do.

Another attractive blond dances by us. Her back is bare from neck to waist. A broad swath of her tummy shows above and below her belly button. Her top is skimpy, a mere bib over her very full breasts, which show seductively at the sides. "Oh, she's some famous actress," Raquel feels compelled to inform me, "on the *telenovelas* [soaps]." I'm mildly intrigued, though I feel content to leave it at that. But Raquel continues, "She was in a horrible car accident, didn't think she'd live. Doctors sewed her back together."

"She dances beautifully," I say. I enjoy watching her, but I also wish to deflect Raquel's *chisme.*

"She's sixty—older than me!" says Raquel. "Oh, there's my future husband." She points to a man I have danced with who looks very smiley and conventional. "He's number five," she adds.

"Five? What happened to the other four?"

"I got tired of them. We're all friends still—we take ski trips together." It dawns on me that Raquel is not a transvestite but a transsexual. As Mr. Smiley Conventional drops by to kiss her hello,

I wonder how he got in line to be her next husband. But who am I to judge?

This is my first visit to La Nacional and the tone is set. I know to bring air kisses and sport my best costume to such venues as Niño Bien, or to wear a strong *cabeceo* and not act foreign at places like Lo de Celia. At La Nacional I will forever harbor a sense of being on a set created by Fellini or David Lynch. At Ideal, I expect to see the Old Snow Lion, a big, lumbering, genteel man with a drift of white hair. He has seen his day and now he follows me and other women around, prowling catlike, harmlessly but annoyingly sneaking up from behind. When I accept his invitation I know I've made his day. His face breaks into a dumb grin and he leads me over and over in the same monotonous forward *ocho* like a happy cat playing with the mouse he is too infirm to catch. Once he sensed my impatience, and I couldn't bear the look of pain that spread over his face. He went and sat next to a column, looking like Charles Laughton as Quasimodo saying to the pillar, "Why wasn't I made of stone like thee?" Oh, I hated myself.

I accept a dance with my friend Ángel, who whispers in my ear, "How could you dance with that Juan? He can't even follow the music." I say nothing, smiling to myself, because during the waltz Juan had whispered in my ear, "What has Ángel got to teach? He does the same three steps over and over." Though a softer version of the early *tangueros* battling "fly to fly," typical *milonguero chisme*, it's still a form of violence.

This harmful speech feels disappointing at times. I expect higher standards from tango aficionados. I know the *chisme* is part of the *milonga* culture, and I don't want to stonewall people with a holier-than-thou air. I'm not in a position to do that, or to preach or try to convert people to my camp. What drew me to Zen was its lack of PR, its teach-by-being approach. Besides, I'm battling my own harmful feelings. So all I can do is try to practice nonviolent listening, a stance I've probably internalized from my good therapist, accepting the person's agitated feelings behind his gossipy banter without judging him nor encouraging.

It's a challenge to listen nonjudgmentally, but I recall my touchstone for the precepts, my *rakusu* with my name sewn into the silken back: INNER FLAME, PEACEFUL HEART, and the Japanese character that looks like two tango dancers. This garment is now also a touchstone for my tango precepts, and I imagine that I could dance in it if I sewed strings along the sides of it. It would be just like the sexy bib the stitched-together actress wears—a tribute to the gradual and inevitable converging of my two formerly separate practices.

Chapter 10

You Man, I Woman

When dancers transcend being dancers, there is a dance.

—Reb Anderson, from his 2004 lecture "Exploring the Dance of Buddha"

Part of what I love about Buenos Aires is that it rivals Paris with its numerous cafés and bar-cafés. The temptation to become the professional café-sitter I once was is great. But I have Ángel's apartment instead, a small studio where he teaches tango amid bright, retro decor. It's a clearinghouse for the cultural exchange I once sought in cafés.

"¿Comes la carne?" ("Do you eat meat?") Ángel yells from his kitchen where he's preparing lunch, now that his last student, Claude, has left. Ángel spends as much time as I do dancing and dreaming of tango. It wasn't long before I started seeing him regularly at his favorite *milongas*, Confitería Ideal and Club Español. I couldn't help but be flattered by the way he sat out several *tandas* to study the followers before he finally invited one—me—to dance.

"*¡Como todo!*" I yell back, thinking how the meat that used to weigh in like a mere condiment in my diet is tipping the balance of the legumes and grains these days. He tramps across the wooden floorboards on his sock-covered dance shoes into the dining-dance area, where I await the lunch he's preparing me. The practice of covering one's shoes is done to reduce the noise, and it's important in Buenos Aires, where so many people live in apartments with downstairs neighbors. He comes bearing a fork-impaled slice of *morcilla*. I grab the dark-chocolate brown slab off the fork with my fingers and bite into it with exaggerated gusto.

"Yummm, *muy rico!*" I say as I chew, mashing the soft meat— the coagulated blood of bovine product—against the roof of my mouth. I like the mild clovelike spice flavor, but I push the thought of what it actually is out of my head. I don't tell Ángel that I don't love the "mouth feel"—you don't need teeth to eat this. You can just gum it up. I even prefer cow brains, with their chewy texture, grilled to juicy perfection. But having watched Argentines, like my friend Pato, feast on *morcilla* with a reverence I reserve for my mother's creamy-cheesey cannoli, I'm persuaded to try it more often.

"It's rich in iron," Ángel tells me. He inflates his upper body and sticks out his chest like a *compadrito*. He goes on to kvetch about one of his students, Lola, who won't eat meat. He's convinced that this is why she can't dance right. I just smile and let it wash over me, since just a few days ago I had listened to Lola's side of this little border skirmish. She was near tears, telling me how Ángel hated her. I have seen Ángel lose patience with her and berate her mercifully, but I've also seen her challenge his style of explaining things. That gets to him on a cellular level—since he lives and breathes for tango.

Ángel comes off as stereotypically macho in the way he hates to be questioned. And though he can be frustrating for this very reason, I can't help but admire him for having once said that he liked Eva Perón for the simple reason that she secured women the right to vote. He proclaims himself a feminist, something few of his peers would do. He is a refined descendant of tango's early *compadritos*, zoot suiters who strutted and battled each other through tango steps. Ángel would never fight, though. He is the Pope of La Ideal. And now Ángel and I have established our preference to dance with one another to such a degree that other *milongueros* know to humbly wait until we've had a first dance before inviting me to the floor. One night a week a table at La Ideal is automatically reserved with the sign ÁNGEL Y AMIGAS, and I often make a point of being there.

I once even skunked a world-famous dancer, Omar Vega, a faux pas that happened so fast I couldn't undo it. Omar had invited me to dance a second before Ángel nodded at me to accept the next dance. I reacted so instinctively to my desire to dance with Ángel that I turned on my heel, ignoring Omar even as he rose to meet me. When the *milonga* was over I apologized profusely, explaining that Ángel was my friend and teacher.

"Ángel is your teacher?" Omar asked, rolling his eyes and making the sign of the cross across his chest. "*Está bien*," he said before swaggering away, as if to say, *I won't kill ya this time, but this goes on your résumé.*

It was a Tony Soprano moment. Omar even looks like James Gandolfini. I wanted to yell after him, "Hey, I've stuck up for you when people blabbed about your skirt chasing!" (It was true—I had told more than one person that I wasn't interested in hearing about Omar's legendary sex life so long as he taught well.) But the thought of saying it reminded me of the dumb old New Jersey joke that goes: People say you eat shit sandwiches but I tell them it can't be true because you don't eat sandwiches. I expected he'd never invite me to dance again.

I like meeting Ángel's adoring students, mostly women, whom he gets solely by word of mouth, from Seattle to Stockholm, Australia to Austria. Generally we dance for pleasure, but I've come to know him well enough now that I occasionally assist him. He charges students the equivalent of twenty U.S. dollars for an hour and a half. He adores them all, with the rare exception of Lola. There's a saying in tango that "the woman dances her own dance," and although I've tried to convince Lola that Ángel loves her, she's locked in her own mysterious embrace with him.

I have just finished assisting Ángel with a lesson with Claude, who's from Belgium. Ángel and I have worked up an appetite showing Claude how to execute a *cadena*, or chain of turns, that looks particularly impressive on the floor. There is an attractive symmetry to the chain—he goes, she goes, he goes, she goes. The lead and follow footwork is done in what is called normal or parallel system—the leader steps left while the follower steps right or vice versa. (In the cross system, leader and follower step on their left or right feet at the same time—footwork unique to tango. The smooth switching back and forth between normal and cross systems is an art form, and it's one of the things that makes just walking in tango so phenomenally eye-catching.)

With good partners the *cadena* becomes an accord between two opposing forces—so sweet because you can't tell who's leading and who's following. All that spectators see is one motion. The impetus of the move, the centrifugal force, is shared between the pair. Claude, like most non-Argentine *tangueros,* was still too much in his head on how the move works, and so I found myself, over the past hour and a half, pushing him harder than I should, stealing the lead. I so wanted to show him how to be in his body rather than his head. I wanted to show him how to *not* think, but it was energy draining, and I've now come to terms with the fact that it's not something one can show. It's something Claude must learn by feeling. He was getting dizzy just thinking about the move, and I'd burned so many calories by the time he left that I could eat everything that Ángel brings out of the kitchen, twice.

Since I downed the *morcilla* with Argentine-like gusto, Ángel next places in front of me a steaming plate piled with braised red cabbage, a bed of brown rice, and a big piece of *milanesa,* thin breaded and fried veal that's considered to be the comfort food of Argentina. There's even a restaurant in Buenos Aires that makes large pizzas with heaping amounts of mozzarella and sauce on a crust of *milanesa.* Ángel sprinkles a spoonful of Virgin-brand beer yeast on top of the whole meal to add flavor—"and many B vitamins," he tells me.

I tell Ángel I like Claude, that he's a sweet man, and clean—but his breath! "So overpowering!" I say. I feel the need to explain why I'd been craning my neck to one side during the lesson.

Ángel makes a face and confirms, "Yes, *aliento*." Halitosis. "And it's everywhere—*el pelo, la ropa* [the hair, the clothes] . . ."

Ángel, like many Argentines, carries a portable atomizer to *milongas* and sprays himself hourly. He sucks mints every fifteen minutes. Time after time, Argentine men and women tell me how Europeans, French in particular, do not shower enough and have bad BO. I'm pleased that we can share our feelings with each other about such occupational hazards.

I clean my plate, along with two wheat rolls, and then down a container of *dulce de leche* for dessert. Ángel is amazed, like everyone else, that I eat so much. I've had dance partners ask me repeatedly if I'm anorexic, a serious problem among girls in image-obsessed Argentina.

"*Soy Siciliana*," I tell them proudly. "*Me gusta la comida.*" I inherited my venturesome palate from my parents.

We sit in silence, digesting. I admire the jungle of green plants that catch sunlight on his open second-floor terrace. I am delighted and thankful to be here. To be invited into a *milonguero's* life outside the *milonga* venue is truly something to treasure. Ángel's apartment is warm and reminiscent of the one Grandma Cusumano and Aunts Mary and Jenny and two cousins crowded into in Linden, New Jersey, for many years. Like theirs, it's filled with kitschy knickknacks and framed photos—of him and his wife and other family members. Ángel has two grown daughters with a woman he was never married to. His favorite photo is one in which he poses alongside his current wife (whom he calls his "girlfriend"), and Sally Potter, the director of the film *The Tango Lesson.*

"How does she dance?" I ask, pointing to Sally. He brushes the question away with his hand and a facial expression that I know well enough to take as a compliment. *Not like you,* it says. What a friend.

After we've eaten, we dance a little, socks over our shoes. Ángel reminds me of Juan Carlos for his nice motoring torso. He is solid and stocky like a bear. It's said that when you strip a bear of his skin he looks like a man—like Ángel, who is big and thick-boned. His lead is gentle but firm and clear. His floor craft is impeccable. He is one of a few leaders who can negotiate a crowded floor and never bump into other dancers.

"You man, I woman," Ángel's fond of saying, indicating that we're reversing our lead and follow so he can show me what he wants me to do. Often when he says to his male students, "You woman, I man," they get a worried look on their faces that never fails to crack me up. Ángel is irrevocably, maddeningly heterosexual. I watch him get infatuated with student after student. There is always the *alumna* of the week whom he's mentoring. "I give them confidence to dance," he boasts. Paternalist though it be, it seems to be true.

We don't have any set schedule. I just call him up when the mood hits and ask, "When can we dance?" and he finds a slot for me. His number one criticism of me is that I am always *apurada,* too much in a hurry.

Sometimes he shouts like he's scolding a child, though he softens his approach after seeing my reaction. *Just wait till I master good quips in his tongue,* I think. "You my number one student," he responds when I won't take his reprimands.

I know he's right. I tend to speed up with the emotion of the dance. When I do that I'm not hovering in my Not Think Zone. This is what's called grasping at pleasure, Buddhism's second of the Four Noble Truths and major cause of suffering. I need to execute my step, enjoy, and let it go; to wait without thought or word or anticipation. *Nothing to it,* I think. But often I'm right back to that grasping-at-pleasure place.

Ángel helps me clean up other habits, too. He shows me nice *adornos* to add to my repertoire. But he can be full of himself, showing me a step that's already mine. *Hey!* I'm dying to say, *you plagiarized me! You can't teach me a step that already belongs to me!* A step I performed with Libertango at Candlestick Park at halftime during a San Francisco 49ers game. A step I'm certified to teach, having gotten certified through Christy Cote's training course—at the bronze and silver level. But I stand still and just breathe and listen. I let him go on.

Reb Anderson appears on my shoulder: "If tango teachers realize they don't know anything about tango . . . something more important than their being a teacher will occur. Tango will occur. And the world will be a better place. Because there's dancing."

I take a deep breath and think about the beauty of the dance and all that it holds for me. The curlicue move I thought he plagiarized is only about my ego.

❧

When I assist Ángel, he often likes to sip his favorite mix of diet Coke and Fernet Branca, a coffee-brown liqueur my grandparents drank to keep them regular, out of a beer mug. He serves his students only purified water ("twice filtered," he boasts) and three different types of mints. The women who arrive in spike heels are first ordered to sink into his white sofa and cover the spikes with rubber caps. Everyone, even the men, wears Ángel's fluffy blue or red socks over their shoes. Pugliese, Di Sarli, or Canaro blossom in the background from his iPod. The *charla* is always tango related, and Ángel usually has a standard question. This week's is "Who's going to see Los Reyes de Tango this Thursday?" For anyone who expresses interest, Ángel scratches one initial on the back of the flyer and hands it over—a free pass from the Pope.

Sometimes I videotape Ángel with his students. One mirrored wall makes the small place feel bigger than it actually is. There's always warmth and friendliness here. I've made many acquaintances— Nancy from upstate New York, Julia from Manhattan, Elena from Austria, Naoko from Seattle, and Eleanor Anchorena, a high-society woman whose grandfather was an important city father who gave his name to the street where Ángel's studio is.

I also met one of my best girlfriends, Marcela, through Ángel. We sit next to each other at La Ideal and she gives me flash reports on the men who are either good or bad. When she asks me for reports on the ones I've danced with, I test her patience if I don't give them thumbs up or thumbs down. I've watched her full glossy red lips countless times as she's been amazed by my reluctance to do this. "What do you mean he was neither good nor bad? I don't understand this." We speak only Castellano, so I flail in my desire to tell her we need a third, maybe fourth, category for men who should not be cast off totally but given a second chance.

Marcela probably wouldn't go for this gray zone, though. The ambiguity might grate on her nerves. But many men fall between *fantástico* and *boludo atomico* (atomic asshole). If a *milonga* is dead, Marcela calls it *una porquería,* a nasty piece of rubbish. She's a stately woman, her boyish hips always gracefully outlined in tango black. She wears her thick wavy hair pulled back tightly to reveal Nefertiti-high cheekbones and a firm jaw. Woe betide the man who smells bad. *¡Qué olor fatal!* is a phrase she taught me, and though it means "What a disgusting smell," to hear her say it implies that the fate of the man from whom the *olor fatal* is being emitted is sealed. Judging from the frequency with which we discuss *olores fatales,* she, Ángel, and I may have the most frequently assailed noses in town.

She spoils me, assaults me really, with her homemade empanadas, apple cake, and flan swimming in caramel sauce. I strike back by inviting her to a fiesta, where I serve my oven-roasted peppers, an array of Argentine cheeses and breads, and avocado-tomato salad drenched in lusty local olive oil. She invites me for a Sunday afternoon of good Mendoza wine at her house. She says, "I see you've lost weight," and she proceeds to serve chocolate-pudding torte and moist mandarin cake made with an orange liquor. I mount a counterattack a couple weeks later at my place with lemon-chili chicken, sausage and beans, and tricolored pasta al pesto. (Of course, she comes armed with her tender cream scones and more flan.) When a mutual *milonguero* friend tells me she makes the world's best sabayon, I corner her and tease, "What's this about sabayon? You have denied me!"

Marcela is eight years younger than I am, but more maternal. By the time we met, I was becoming more accustomed to meeting women like her, who look to be in their early thirties, telling me they had grown children. Marcela has three daughters in their twenties who look like her sisters rather than her children. They all live in New York City and the oldest teaches tango. Marcela was married at sixteen to a diplomat and has lived around the world. She's been divorced a long time, though, and now lives full-time in San Telmo, where she is renovating an old building into her humble chateau.

We call a truce on the "dueling fiestas" and decide that we'll throw a party in her new home when it's ready. It will be the likes of which this town hasn't seen since before the financial crisis. It's amazing to me that it's been four weeks since I first spotted this classy looking *amiga* at Ángel's table. And now we are planning to join forces around food, which we both well know is our way of deepening a promising friendship.

Marcela is one of a few people who gets me to go off my dedication to no harmful speech. "*¿Qué es con él?*" I blurt into the phone to her. "What is it with him?" Gossip slips out so easily in Castellano, perhaps because it doesn't feel like real speech in my mouth just yet. Or perhaps because it's so fun to have a girlfriend like Marcela, who lives for the juicy details and makes me feel like a teenager again. Omar Vega (everyone's favorite target) has come up again, and I seriously want to know what the deal is. After my accidental snub, he did invite me to dance again, but it went horribly. Tango's primary precept for leaders is: Thou shalt know at every moment upon which foot thy follower is. (The corollary for the follower is: Thou shalt never have weight on more than one foot at a time.) These are as fundamental as the first and second laws of thermodynamics. Or like Thou shalt love thy neighbor as thyself, the one great commandment from which all other laws flow. Omar and I never did get our feet in sync. It's obvious that he doesn't fall into Marcela's *fantástico* category. But rather than skewer Omar, she heaps praise on me and my dancing. I'm humbled because I already know enough about her to know she does not do this wantonly.

In "Exploring the Dance of Buddha," Reb Anderson said, "I must not keep standing where I have skill." I am starting to run up against the fact that I'm going to have to eventually move out of the comfort zone I'm in with my dance. I've been content being the dancer in the plain brown wrapper—a generically good *milonguera*, sometimes better than the fancy packaged "brand name" goods. My confidence has grown immensely. I dance tall on the balls of my feet. I only drop my heels to walk to and from my seat. I keep my axis. My legions of anonymous soldiers on the floors around town aid and abet this. My sensitivity gets sharper all the time. I refine my ranks of leaders. I've weeded out those who engage in the old style of leading whereby the man pokes and prods the follower's back with his fingers. It feels like they're tapping out Morse code, and it's distracting from the heart-connection lead, not to mention irritating. At first I try talking nice. "*Señor, por favor, no me gusta este tipo de marca*" ("Sir, I don't like that type of lead"). I'd say I have a 50 percent success rate. I avoid those who don't get it.

I drop leaders who embody the obnoxious view of Ricardo Güiraldes that women are "obedient beasts" who submit. This is passé violence. Such perverted views of my powerful receptive female energy demand that I drop leaders who emit any energy like this, not because they are bad or I don't like them, but because the dance asks me to. I am a faceless warrior in its defense. As the embodiment of the feminine energy that receives and gives back to the male impetus, I feel sovereign. It is not a passive role.

I aim to dance tango without borders, but not without discrimination. Rodolfo is a man who remains a friend whom I hug and kiss warmly when we see each other, but whom I will not dance with because of his whipping lead. He lost six apartments in the 2001 financial crisis and is full of sadness and disillusion, but I'm not dissuaded from my decision. Another man in a class means to compliment me when he says, "You obey well." I laugh sardonically, but he's a nonnative English speaker, so I let him get away with the perhaps unintended insult. A male friend who's a good dancer says to me, meaning to praise a woman he dances with, "She was great, she went everywhere I put her." When he is ready to hear it, I would like to tell him that when he exchanges "put" for "invited," I'll know he's moving toward greatness.

And then there are *los fantásticos*. Or the *divinos milongueros*—like Rufino. At Salon Canning, Rufino steals up behind me. It must have been his smile beating on my back like sunshine that made me turn. It was a *tanda* by Juan D'Arienzo, a composer with a lot of *compás*, or rhythmic beat, which Rufino likes. As we dance, he says, "¡*Qué espectacular!*" several times. He tells me he's been watching and waiting for me to be available. He looks like a young Richard Gere, only more handsome and tender. A contractor who's been renovating an old building in Palermo, Rufino has a lean and athletic body. I'm not being modest when I say that if he saw me sitting in a café, he wouldn't look twice. But he loves the way I move. Like me, he adores the dance. He tells me that he dances with emotion and excitement, and that I know how to respond to him. Another dancer bumps us. Rufino stops, stands still, and enfolds his arms and hands gently around me as if protecting a bouquet of fresh flowers. *How life-affirming is this?* I think to myself. Deeply so. These are the moments I feel I have not lost anything.

I have no need to be Rufino's one and only. (The "palace" door is locked anyway, closed for renovation.) He is free to say everything he says to me to others. I don't try to imagine that he doesn't, and actually I hope he does. Tonight, however, I notice that he leaves the *milonga* after having danced with only me.

Visiting gringos ask whom I'm studying with. They seem to be surprised by the fact that, being surrounded as I am by brand-name teachers, I have not glommed on to one biggie. One reason is because I'm a monkey-see, monkey-do dancer—I learn by watching. And there's plenty to watch in the Garden of Tango Paradise. I seem to disappoint or baffle these foreigners when I won't make recommendations. During my first visit to Buenos Aires, I had asked a Porteño dancer for teacher recommendations. He demurred and said, "The liking of a teacher is such a personal thing as selecting a partner or a friend."

Contrary to what even I would have expected, I have no interest in the high-profile teacher. I don't avoid them, though. In fact, because Alicia Pons is a revered name, I dropped in at her class in a small, warmly lit theater on Cabrera. It was nice and added new awareness, as have group classes with other notables like Jorge

Firpo, Daniel Lapadula, Luciana Valle, and even that prince of darkness Omar Vega.

I still have Juan Carlos Copes, Cacho Dante Gustavo Naveira, and Fabian Salas to try. My erstwhile practice partner Dave and I were crazy about Fabian. We would study a video of him and Carolina del Rivero dancing. I'm committed to taking classes with some of these teachers before I leave Argentina. But there's a syndrome down here that I call the Ivory Tower syndrome, whereby name teachers who perform beautiful choreographed tango onstage cannot for the life of them dance well in *milongas*. They simply aren't used to the tight space and extemporaneous improv. The Argentines know this syndrome well and are much less pressed to dance with famous teachers than are foreigners.

For me, though, the classes are not where it's at. Prowling the *milongas* is much harder work than showing up at any class. I'm hooked on fishing for the surprises among the common man, the man in a plain brown wrapper who takes me around the world in a *colgado* to rival Fabian Salas's, or the one who does a unique pattern with alterations in the usual *molinete* phrasing that wakes me up like Buddha come down from his Nirvana perch. I'm hooked on the rank and file: the Rufinos who turn up invariably, the low-key ambience at Ángel's, and also being my own taskmaster.

The more I refine my dancing, the bigger the intervals between these surprises become. It's now usually every one hundred *tandas* or so that I really experience that old feeling that I used to get every time I went to a *milonga*. But because the surprises are less frequent, they take on a new meaning for me.

Just as I'm feeling that Club Español (where I first danced with Rodolfo the Whip) is fished out, along comes an astonishing dancer.

Tall, lanky, and younger than the other men at Español, he beckons me onto the floor. I look behind me to make sure he isn't inviting some young Porteña. I feel as weightless as an artist's paintbrush in his arms. He paints big, beautiful, and intricate designs on the floor. I am a pendulum marking time. If it sounds passive, bear in mind I have to be actively present to receive the blissful ride, to contribute to the gravity-defying synergy. Greg and I click instantly.

The biggest surprise of the night, though, is not the stranger's dancing but rather that he's not Porteño. Greg is from Seattle. (He got his riveting style, he tells me, from Alex Krebs, a well-known teacher from Canada.) I meet up with Greg a few days later at the Caseron Porteño in Palermo Hollywood.

After that, we check in daily about which venue will be the *milonga* du jour. I eagerly await my turn to dance with him. Besides being one of the top five best leaders I've ever danced with, bar none, Greg is modest, kind, and outgoing, thus popular with everyone, local and foreign.

He is planning a trip to Uruguay, and I offer to go with him and split expenses. It's a chance for me to satisfy tourist visa requirements—that I leave the country every three months. Besides, I want to at least set foot on the other land of tango's birth. Buenos Aires grabs the limelight, but Montevideo shared in the evolution of the dance, too. Tango's most celebrated song, "La Cumparsita," the one that ritualistically closes every *milonga*, day and night, was written by a seventeen-year-old architect student, Gerardo Matos Rodríguez, in a café called La Giralda in Montevideo.

A couple of weeks after we first dance, in November, Greg and I meet in Puerto Madero to catch the early Buquebus, the hydrofoil that gets you across in an hour's time. It crosses the muddy Río de la Plata to Colonia del Sacramento. In the 1700s, Colonia, alternately under Spain or Portugal, was an important port on a trade route prior to the rise of Buenos Aires. Today it's a UNESCO World Heritage Site. Artsy and slow moving, with its boutiques, little museums, and outdoor café–sitting under sycamore shade, Colonia reminds me of what Sausalito is to San Francisco, a restful getaway across water worth a day or weekend trip. Greg shoots photos of the restored lighthouse on a windy bluff over the river, and we roam the cobbled streets of its Barrio Histórico and explore its seventeenth-century ruins. Then we catch a bus, a three-hour ride, to Montevideo.

We've booked a room with twin beds at Hotel Europa in the Ciudad Vieja, the Old City, that was once fortified by a wall. It's a small area, about twenty blocks long and three blocks wide, but it's rich in gloried architecture including classical mansions and art deco edifices. In the taxi from the bus terminal to our hotel, we pass a tall 1746 remnant of the fortress wall, called La Puerta de la Ciudadela, and the enchanting facades on or near the main drag, July Eighteenth Avenue—theaters, museums, churches, banks, and old ornate palaces converted to apartments. There are boutiques, galleries, antique shops, and plazas—attractions to rival those of Buenos Aires. We plan to visit it all the next day. It's pretty late, so we relax over dinner at a good seafood restaurant.

As I lie down on my bed to sleep, I sense a profound fatigue in my bones from the dance schedule I've forced myself to keep. I fall asleep to the feeling of sinking so deep into the bed that I imagine a print of my body will stay the next day long after I've left. In just a few hours, however, I'm awake with a knife turning in my stomach. A bad headache and nausea ensue.

Greg isn't sick, so we have to assume it isn't food poisoning since we ate the same things. He gives me some black carbon pills—they're supposed to absorb the poison, the bugs attacking my innards. They don't stay down. I can't get out of the bed (or wander too far from the bathroom). I sense Greg is the kind of person who would sacrifice his sightseeing and stay with me if I asked. But I need to suffer, perhaps die, alone, and bid him go. I lie there listening to traffic and the odd clomp-clomp of horses drawing carts outside the window. They belong to the hardworking poor who, like Buenos Aires's *cartoneros*, rummage through the trash at night for recyclables.

At 3 PM, Greg returns, his camera loaded with artful shots of the city. He brings me some herbal tea, a simple infusion of chamomile. It does the trick. I'm drained but ready to move.

I conclude that my sudden bout with such a short-lived but traumatic illness was a buildup of nearly six months (since the day Dan gave me the bad news) of poisonous feelings that needed a purge. I'm too weak now to hate anyone. I crave sugar and caffeine. On our hotel's recommendation, we go to La Flaca, where I order a lemon custard tart and double espresso. Fortified, I am able to accompany Greg to Punta del Este, a touristy town on the end of the peninsula outside the city. It's a ritzy beach area on the Atlantic, a getaway for stars and wealthy Argentines. This crisp, breezy day the sandy beach and high-rise hotels are fairly empty of visitors, recalling the Jersey shore of my youth, which used to turn into a ghost town right after Labor Day. We enjoy hiking around the green hilly parkland above the sandy beaches.

At night we take a cab over to a tango venue called Fun Fun, but it is Dead Dead. Apparently we need to come back on a weekend night. Our feet are itching to get back to Buenos Aires, where it's easier to count the few hours when tango is not happening. The next morning we go to a shoe store where I buy a pair of black heels with fake rhinestones and long ankle strap ties with what Greg teases me is a "come hither" look.

The shoes prove their mettle the following Saturday night at El Beso. A lot of men come hither to dance with me, though it might be due more to how luscious Greg makes me look while dancing with him—so supple, pliable, like a plume you want to dip in paint and design the floor with.

When the dancing feels this exalted I think of how necessary it is for teachers, as well as followers and leaders, to do as Reb suggested—forget what they know, so that something bigger, more important than any of us can occur: tango. And the world is a better place. Because there is dancing.

Chapter 11

Deep Tango

Que le habran hecho mis manos?

What have my hands done?

—*"Milonga Triste" (1936)*

One of my favorite stories is from Paul Reps's *Zen Flesh, Zen Bones.*
It's the story of two brothers who are running a temple in Japan.
The elder brother is smart, the younger one, who has only one eye,
isn't so bright. One night, a wandering monk drops in to ask the
brothers for lodging. Per the local custom, the monk requests the
brothers debate him on the dharma teachings. If he wins, he stays,
but if he loses he must move on. The smarter brother, worn out,

leaves his younger brother to debate the monk. "But be sure to do it in silence," he advises.

After some time, the monk gets up to leave. On his way out, he tells the elder brother that he's failed to match wits with his impressively eloquent younger sibling. The shocked brother asks for a recounting, to which the monk replies, "I held up one finger for Buddha. Your brother replied with two fingers, for Buddha and his teaching. I then showed three fingers—for Buddha, his teaching, and his followers. Your brother held up his fist, countering that all three emanate from one realization."

As the monk rounds the corner, out of sight, the dim-witted brother comes looking for him.

"He's gone. You won the debate," said the older brother.

"Won? What do you mean? He held up one finger mocking my eye. I came back with two fingers, congratulating him for having two. He then held up three fingers insinuating that between us, we have three eyes. I balled up my fist to threaten him, and he took off."

The spirit of this story is a reminder that you can find wisdom even in a dullard or fool, if left to your own interpretation. So although people—expats and Argentines alike—are fond of cluing me in that the country, as well as the *milongas,* are full of swindlers and con artists I ought to be wary of, I have yet to share their negative views. Nearly every encounter with Argentines brings me face to face with affirmative experiences.

Still, I realize that it is imperative to dissolve the language barrier to go deeper into tango and the culture. I run through two teachers before I find the perfect fit in soft-spoken, patient Mariel Altobello. Her surname is Italian, which I find comforting. Also, she's an Aquarius, left-handed, and a tango dancer—all defining characteristics of mine as well. She has some Spanish blood, too, and a tad of Amerindian, which render her a portrait of creamy, lineless skin, dark penetrating eyes, and big, soft waves of ebony hair.

As an Aquarius, Mariel can become sullen and brooding without long stretches of solitude. Once she lost all her books to a flood, and even now, upon recalling it, she likens it to losing a close friend. She's a soul mate in numerous ways. As our relationship develops, we share books on spiritual growth. She practices Nichiren Shoshu Buddhism and chants daily. We are both equally at ease explaining things through the metaphysical world as through the physical one. Mariel and I believe in the power of intention and the power of healing. After only a few classes she feels like one of my friends.

She comes to my loft twice a week, and because she is a friend and mentor (though nearly twenty years my junior), I feel motivated in a way I haven't, in the two months since I arrived, to speak her language.

My first big challenge comes with Spanish's two verbs for "to be": *ser* and *estar*. The first is reserved for states of being not easily changed; the latter reflects the impermanence of phenomenon, a verb custom-made for Zen Buddhists—further evidence for me that I'm meant to be here. After dancing tango for hours, *estoy cansada,* but it's impermanent (I hope). *Soy cansada* not only is incorrect, but would imply that my state of tiredness is eternal and unchanging, though it's something I've felt might be possible at times over the past few months.

It startles me to think that native Spanish speakers, no matter how young or old, bright or dull, intimately grasp this difficult concept—when being is fleeting or when being is existential or being precedes essence—through their everyday interpretation of the people and things around them. (To me, this is no different from being born into a culture where you have a guarantee of instantly grasping Sartre and Nietzsche once you learn to speak.) It also means that there's a lot of conviction behind someone's assertion that a guy is (es rather than está) un boludo atomico. Spanish speakers don't hesitate about which verb to choose.

I flounder and misstep more often than I care to admit with this one singular concept. I am like the monk going off into the night dazzled by those otherwise less adept than I.

Argentines speak Castilian, or Castellano—the most widely spoken dialect of Spain, with far many more speakers than its other three dialects, which are Catalan, Basque, and Galician. But leave it to the Argentines—or rather their melting pot of immigrants—to add creative twists and turns to the tongue that you'll never get from your years of high school or college Spanish. Most noticeable is the way the "y" and "ll" are pronounced with a "sh" sound. So, me llamo (my name is) is pronounced "may shah-mo." The word tuyo (yours) is not pronounced "too-yo" as in Mexico and Spain, but "too-sho." When my dance partners ask how I keep fit, I tell them I do "shoga."

Argentine Castellano (cah-stay-SHAH-no) is pleasantly lubricated with lots of soft "sh" sounds. The accent, claims a study from the University of Toronto, is closest in sound and tonality to the Italian dialect spoken around Napoli. After Castellano, Italian is the most widely spoken tongue in Argentina.

Argentines also use the word chau—a lot; it is pronounced like the Italian ciao, but used here only to mean goodbye (not "hello," too, as in Italy). Words like laburo (for trabajo or job) filter in from the Italian *(lavoro); aggiornado,* meaning "updated," comes from *giorno,* the Italian word for day. *Dále* means "let's go," but my grandmother used to say it all the time when she wanted my mother to look at something. *Che,* which you'll hear a hundred times in an hour here, is like our English "hey," and I suspect it comes from the homonymic *c'é,* Italian for "that's," but there are other theories, too. Argentina's most famous revolutionary, Ernesto Guevara, was christened with his pseudonym Che by the Cubans who were amused by his constant uttering of *che, che, che.*

Lunfardo, Argentina's slang, is spoken across classes here and is a fragrant compost heap of words from many sources. It's studied by Spanish-language experts and even has an academy, the Buenos Aires Lunfardo Academy, that's been dedicated to the study of its continual evolution since 1962. When I joked with a woman in an elevator that I was *"casi Porteña,"* almost a Porteña, she replied somewhat proudly that Porteños have *"bocas sucias"* (dirty mouths). And part of this has to do with *lunfardo,* which takes any old dirty word and uses it casually. *¡Qué quilombo!,* for example, is *lunfardo* for "what a mess!" though the word *quilombo* literally means "whorehouse." A spaced-out person is one who *vive en una nube de pedos,* or "lives in a cloud of farts." *Boludos* translates to "big balls," but is never a compliment. A lot of Argentine slang comes from the *milonga* milieu, and lots of *lunfardo* has made its way into tango lyrics.

If you're familiar with Spanish you'll know that there are very few countries that use *vosotros,* which is a plural informal tense, as opposed to a singular informal or plural formal. Only in Argentina will you hear people using *vos sos* instead of *tu eres* or *ustedes son* (or *vosotros sois*—used only in Spain), all of which mean "you are" in various forms. This Rioplatense Spanish, which includes Uruguay, is unique to this region. I find it telling that until recently, Argentine grammar-school children were taught the grammar used in Spain even though it wasn't spoken anywhere— at home or in public or in the media. It would be the equivalent to American kids learning British English in school. Today they learn their peculiar grammar forms and pronunciation—a much-needed national self-validation.

Pronunciation challenges me mercilessly as I am forced to use formerly static parts of my mouth. Even after years, my French "r" is only a reasonable facsimile. I worry that I'm doomed to never get the drumroll "rr" of Spanish. After all, my tongue was hardwired in a New Jersey barrio. I think of the Rs as being like the tussocks in Alaska's Far North whose uneven mounds trip me on every step.

At my lowest points, my U.S. imperialist self materializes and wants to recolonize the language and make Castellano easier for my mouth to handle. Mariel shows me where to place my tongue on the palate to lessen the impact of my Ds. *(What's wrong with our damn Yankee "d"?* I think but would never dare say.) She teaches me shadow reading, *lectura sombra.* I start reading a piece of Spanish writing a second's delay after her, so that my ear first hears the pronunciation, then my tongue mimics it. The improvement in my pronunciation after one shadow reading is impressive, about 40 percent better, she says.

After months of listening so raptly, my head hurts; there are little hidden springs built into the Argentine tongue. Forget about asking them to speak *despacito,* slowly. And I cannot speak too quickly or my words invariably come out like a little kid trying in English to say ask (aks) or breakfast (brekist). Or worse, my brain gets behind on Spanish's built-in gender check—their masculine and feminine articles—and I ask a straight man if he has a boyfriend *(novio)* instead of a girlfriend *(novia).*

Some four hundred million people speak Spanish throughout the world and that number is on the rise. It's predicted that the United States, which currently has thirty-two million Spanish speakers, will be the country with the highest number of Spanish-speaking citizens by 2050. It is a good tongue to master.

To do so I have to do something novel—start talking a lot. Me, the kid who didn't speak for years, the contemplative who welcomed email as God-sent deliverance from the dreaded phone, the writer who fiercely protects her solitude. Everyone in this city of three million—butcher, baker, grocer, *taxista, tanguero*—is a potential teacher. I keep telemarketers on the line until they hang up on me. I make friends with bus drivers. I annoy plenty of people and provide comic relief to others.

Not only do I talk, I sing. Alone in my loft I spend hours with classic tango songs, such as "Malena," "El Choclo," and "Cafetín de Buenos Aires," lip-synching the lyrics rapidly to help me sound

Porteña. I attack lyrics that are like *trabalenguas,* or tongue twisters. The 1936 "Milonga Triste" has me walking in circles in my loft, singing out loud about what my hands have done to leave in my chest so much pain.

Que le habran hecho mis manos?
Que le habran hecho
Para dejarme en el pecho
Tanto dolor?

I'm so possessed that one night, against my better judgment, I sing in public. My friends, Steve and Linda, from Santa Cruz, California, are renovating a 1920s home in the Belgrano barrio and invite over a crowd on Saturday, which turns into what I call the Woodstock of *asados.* All the Argentines there play guitar or sing. Poet and award-winning tango lyricist Marta Pizzo, who has a lark's voice, starts to sing "Pedacito de Cielo" and "Cafetín de Buenos Aires." Before I realize what I'm doing, I'm standing and singing along with her. No one else is. My voice is as loud as hers, my hands motioning pain, sorrow, heartbreak, and loss. *The years have passed/ terrible, evil/leaving that hope that never arrived.*

Part of me is saying, *Quiet, sit down, you fool, you know you can't sing.* But Marta, another soul sister, is as astounded as I am, encouraging me. Afterward she gives me a signed copy of her book *Alma de Tango.*

I read my sob saga into many of tango's lyrics; I've cried into men's lapels at *milongas* even as they too belt out their favorite songs in my ear. There's that one song, which constantly has me pining over Dan, about two lovers who see each other after a long separation and it's a big mistake. They are changed strangers. The *angustia* kills hope (or *la ilusión,* another word whose meaning has a Zen-like quality in its depiction of that thing you pine for but that, in reality, never holds up to the image you've harbored of it). Tango music, wrote the city's most famous author, Jorge Luis Borges, "reveals a personal past which . . . each of us was unaware of, moving us to lament misfortunes we never suffered and wrongs we did not commit." Oh, but I did suffer misfortune, I did commit wrongs.

Part of training my tongue involves engaging gamely in the mandatory *charla* between songs. I can fashion competing *piropos*. I tell men, "Yes, I fall in love with you every time we dance, *mi amor.*" They tell me on a scale of one to ten I'm an eleven. I tell them, "*Querido,* you should give lessons to all the others." I never outright lie, though, because Argentine *milongueros* are skilled at the art of *chamuyo*.

Occasionally my language complacency goes awry. Juan, a man I enjoy dancing with (and who has an extra amount of springs in his tongue), admires my legs and asks if I do sports. "Yes, I swim, walk, do shoga." He says he really likes my molecular structure. "My molecular structure?" I ask. "Not your *estructura molecular,*" he laughs. "I said your '*musculatura.*' My vision is not that good," he quips.

Patricio, the organizer of Club Gricel, says he knows where my misplaced street shoes are hiding. But first I must give him a peso. I pull a peso out of my bag and hand it to him. He looks at me perplexed and then doubles over with laughter, saying, "I said '*un beso.*'"

Anyone who's ever studied a foreign language has this experience: You breeze through some days feeling nearly fluent, comprehension an easy two-way street with every human interaction.

What follows inevitably are days when you not only can't speak, but you seem to have forgotten what you knew. You don't recognize the simplest words. Learning a language is far beyond the mere accumulation of vocabulary and grammar rules. You need to relax and let that part of the brain that already knows all you need to know take over. Learning tango is just like learning a language, and so it hasn't been so long since I was here before. In both cases, there is a key in the listening, a Rosetta stone. Just as words are empty symbols without the corresponding depth of human experience, in tango the steps mean *nada* unless two people listen with their whole being and respond in kind.

Conversation can go deeper than flirting. Miguel is powerful and philosophical in his lead. Upon our first tanda together, we both feel the frisson of excitement at sharing our fluency in dance. To meld to his tall slim body, I must nimbly arch into him until we become two *media lunas,* spooning crescents. After the first dance, we compliment each other with a breathless *"¡Qué lindo!"* I can see he wants to convey more. "The best communication," he says with conviction that reflects in his furrowed brow, "is acceptance." He says more than I can catch—something about another woman's fear—but I understand that he is deeply grateful that I followed—accepted—his surprising figures.

"Es un gozo para mí también" ("Tango is a joy for me, too") is all I can get out. I couldn't begin to tell him it's the great unifier of my body, mind, spirit, and sex life; my past, present, and future. Or that, as I wrote in my journal, "I was waiting all my life for this dance."

The Buddhists say that form is emptiness, meaning that no part of reality is separate from the rest. It all rises and falls together. In tango, form is emptiness, too. This means that I owe my *gozo* and my flawless following as much to that other's fear as to my parents, who could be the meanest, strictest ones on the block, but who danced with abandon. It means I humbly show up empty of expectation and hope, or *ilusión*. And without fail, even on my most desperate, saddest, aggrieved days, something wonderful and peace-giving shows up in my world—even if only for a fleeting moment. I long to tell Miguel this in turn.

Later that week at La Ideal, a young Argentine man with an altar-boy face, a thick swatch of straight black hair, and steel blue eyes invites me to dance. As we chat between songs, he tells me he is married. He seems to have a higher opinion of his dancing than is warranted, but his silky-smooth skin and cherub-lip innocence are beguiling. Then, as we dance, I feel my energy drop. He is pushing his erect penis into the space just below my belly button. At first I doubt myself, but soon there's no denying what he's doing. I find it curious. I am not in the least aroused—he is dissing the Palace. Instead of stooping to his level with any sort of acknowledgment, I continue to dance eloquently. He's too young and shallow (thirty-three, he tells me, but he looks twenty-four) for deep tango. He has not lost enough in years, time, or love, or gained enough sorrow, to know where the real urgency is. I think of the story of the Japanese brothers in the temple, and this time I consider the value of letting the dull brother win. I am not misinterpreting his motives, but I choose not to engage. Later, I ignore his invitation and return his sheepish look with solemn silence: We both know, *boludo*, what your number is.

I head over to Maipu, two blocks away. I dance a couple of hours with mature, engaging men and wipe away that sullied feeling from the young pervert. It so happens that four of my favorite partners are sitting in a line next to each other. One always kisses one's friends hello and goodbye here, so as I'm ready to leave I have to go down the line and bend and kiss four guys in a row goodnight: Alejandro, who made my regulars list the first week here; Jeff, a businessman from New York who's often in Buenos Aires; Michael, a handsome English expat who was surprised I took no offense when he complimented my "bum"; and Juan, a dark swashbuckling *tanguero* with a long groomed mustache and a flamboyant lead. I look over at my Mr. Frumpy, who is sitting some five seats farther away, a national treasure in his powder-blue suede shoes, and consider making him five. But I throw him an air kiss instead. I chuckle as I head into the night alone, not at all displeased where my developing fluency in Argentina's folk dance and its tongue are taking me.

Chapter 12

Sex and City

If on the great journey of life a man cannot find one who is better or at least as good as himself, let him joyfully travel alone: A fool cannot help him on his journey.

—*The Fool from* The Dhammapada

One sunny November morning, I walk to my favorite Palermo park, Parque Tres de Febrero.

The park is so luxuriantly green and in bloom now, I see Claude Monet–like tableaux everywhere—in its shifting puddles of light, reflections on the lake, the colors oozing from purple jacaranda and coral *palo borracho* (literally "drunken branch") trees. Vines, rose bushes, and other flowering plants are interspersed with sun-dappled gazebos, stone benches, arching bridges, fountains, sculptures, and Andalusian tiles, all worthy of that great Impressionist.

Thinking of Monet evokes a sweet memory of Dan and that spectacular trip to Paris in 1993. We were gluttons for everything that Paris offered. We museum-hopped with the fervor of churchgoers. We stood in silence on a footbridge over a pond of waterlilies at Giverny, Monet's country residence just outside of Paris, to share a perspective of the play of light on the pond. The very next day we stood in awed silence at the Marmotton, a whole museum in Paris dedicated to Monet, and saw that exact floating image captured more than a hundred years earlier by the artist's paintbrush on canvas. Those moments felt like prayer. We were so tight, so connected, stepping in sync like the man and the woman in tango. *How could we have let it go?* I ask the clouds in the water before me now.

I cross a narrow neck of the lake on my "bridge of sighs" and step onto the trellised pergola, which follows the edge of the lake for about two hundred and fifty feet. The pergola holds seventeen stone benches. My Stations of the Cross, I call them. I tried them all before I settled on the last one, my power spot, that shady spot at the very end where I regularly do my yoga and sacrifice part of my split Self.

I'm forever meditating on the split that Gail, my art therapist, found evidence of in my artwork. In one of my last paintings, I uncharacteristically avoided all the colored chalks, pastels, and tempera paints. I splattered only black paint across the white sheet.

As I try to recall the name I gave that drawing, I sit on the arbor's first bench. I recall some optimistic free-associative feelings about it. Then Gail pointed to the inevitable cleft. My heart sank because I didn't want to see that crack then, the place in me where an overbearing father and a submissive mother fail to meet, fail to embrace and dance. But I do want to see it now, so I can bring them together and end my suffering.

I take a seat on the next bench where an old gnarled tree hangs over the lake. A yellow-breasted bird with a white and black mask lands on the tree's deeply grooved puzzle bark. I think of forgiveness—how it's as hard as this cold stone bench, and how it's as indispensable to ending suffering as wings to that bird's flight.

I stroll again, sniff a pink climbing rose, then sit near it, and meditate on a universal conundrum: whether I prefer to love or be loved. Ideally, you get both at the same time. But even between longtime partners, one is always giving more than the other at any said moment. My relationship with Dan taught me that love's equilibrium is dynamic, never static. Like in tango's *cadena*, one partner is always pushing while the other is pulling. If this homeostasis is gone, love is dead. Notwithstanding the current deficit of feeling loved, I can say unequivocally if I have to choose between loving and being loved, I'll choose the former. Every time.

A few benches down, I think of what I'd name that black painting today: *Quebrada*. It's one of my new Spanish words that I love. It translates to "gorge," but it works harder than that in Spanish. It can also refer to the breaks in land we call "canyons" or "streambeds." It refers to the breaks in a torch singer's voice we call "choking," and the breaks in the bodyline when dancing tango. I like this title, *Quebrada*, a lot. It allows me to look at something that might be considered a clinical disorder and call it a work of art.

Back at my loft, Mariel arrives and we proceed to have the strangest conversation, but one that builds my Spanish vocabulary significantly, as I learn that *boliche* means nightclub and *preservativo* is a condom.

In the past few weeks no fewer than ten of Mariel's acquaintances have reported visiting a *boliche* sex club, where everyone is having sex out in the open. I listen, pleased that we are having this conversation almost entirely in Spanish.

She's perplexed about the fact that all these *chicas* and *chicos*, who reported that their participation in free sex was *fantastico*, are psychologically balanced. Some are married, some single, both men and women. When Mariel describes the ecstasy with which they've recounted their experiences—*bárbaro*, fantastic—it sounds comparable to how I feel after a weeklong meditation retreat or after a night at the *milongas*.

Mariel almost forgets I'm not a native speaker. So I have to stop her and ask what a *patovica* is. A bouncer, she says, and all the clubs have one, as well as *preservativos*.

I recall one recent night when, for a change from tango, Carmen and I, along with other friends, went swing dancing. The club was filled with mostly people in their twenties and thirties—Lindy swing is an aerobic workout so you need a strong heart. On the bar I noticed a straw basket filled with what I thought were teabags, but upon reaching for one I quickly realized they were condoms, free for the taking. As we left, I had glimpsed one couple on the couch there. They were only smooching, something I love seeing in young couples all over Buenos Aires since it reminds me of Paris, but now I'm wondering if they might have taken it beyond just smooching after we left.

As Mariel goes on to express her astonishment, I try to recall what was scarier for me at their age—STDs or pregnancy. I'm sure it was the latter, the collateral effect of four years of all-girl Catholic high school, where pregnancy, the dreaded result of one night of pleasure, was a scourge that "disappeared" girls for nine months. And witnessing my own mother's "epidemic" of pregnancies certainly didn't help.

Before I we get on with the lesson, I ask Mariel how to say "to each his own." *A cada uno el suyo*, she says, nodding her head in reluctant agreement.

A few days later, I ask Carmen if she's heard about the phenomenon of sex *boliches*. She says yes, that the dailies do articles on them from time to time and that she'll alert me next time they do. "No need to," I tell her. My only curiosity, which the dailies can't satisfy, is whether this practice is a reflection of a whole or split person. But all I can express to sum up my feelings of the moment is, "*A cada uno el suyo.*"

In the *milongas,* my eyes have seen nothing more graphic than tango undulations (and *quebradas*). Since my self-imposed commitment to be celibate commenced a couple of weeks ago, I have had no dearth of offers to go to bed—mostly subtextual, but a few explicit. Marcel, a Frenchman who dances at many of the same *milongas* as I do, asks me in a straightforward way if we might spend the night together. "No," I tell him, "I'm interested only in dancing," and he accepts that response with no repercussions. What I'm thinking is, Mon chéri, *if I wanted to sleep with you, you would not have to ask, you would know.*

In my early days here, I was like Ulysses, nearly lured to my death by the siren call of unfulfilling sex. My voyage is far from over, but I sail on tranquil seas now. For the time being, my dozen or so daily tango embraces satisfy the need for touching, affectionately or sexually.

The more time I spend in the *milonga,* the more curious a place it becomes, staged with subterranean characters who thrive in the dark and may never see the light of day. There's Lurch—big, gangly, and Frankensteinesque; he's that *Addams Family* character whose walk is nearly robotic, whose size 20 feet and neck-lashing "lurches" are hard to overlook on the dance floor. I don't give him a second chance. There is a man I call Curly, whose hips show some scoliotic unevenness. He looks a bit like the Stooge of that name, adorably so, and he often dances with a trancelike grin, his eyes half-closed. There is Mumbles, a man with a stringy gray ponytail and rimless spectacles who never sits. He nervously strides the *milongas,* his mouth ever moving with gargling sounds. He is the rambling narrative fragment personified, on the Ship of Fools, where everyone is on some would-be hero's journey, everyone's making love, no one is making sense.

There is an enormous amount of play in tango, which, like sex, is improvisational in nature. Sometimes you have to ferret through the many dogmatic *tangueros* to find a fun one. And it's exhilarating.

Take my friend John, for instance. He sits hairless and Buddhalike among the regulars at Club Español, our Thursday haunt. His shaven head is a beige clearing among the forest of dark males. The first time we met on the dance floor I leaned my face into his flannel shirt. The very fact he was wearing flannel should have been a clue, but still I was surprised by his Kiwi accent at the end of the first dance.

"Ee-yeah, that was a raunchy song," he said.

"Oh, but I love Canaro's *vals*," I countered.

"So do I," he said.

"You called it raunchy."

"Raunchy means sexy, gooood."

Now that we're friends I love to tease him and tell him often, "You have a raunchy way of dancing, John!" which he rightfully takes as a high compliment. He started learning tango just six months ago and prior to that had never danced before. His brand of undulations must have been God-given.

"You're a prodigy," I tell him. He's tall and handsome and reminds me of Yul Brynner in *The King and I*. At forty-one, he's my junior by fifteen years. His playful style involves a full-body sway and swivel, unusual in leaders, and many airborne turns with his follower. It's delightful to watch his leg muscles through his silky black pants. He makes an art form of play. Women old and young love him, and many invite him to perform in competitions, which he gracefully declines, because competitions here, like those everywhere, are more political than genuine. But also tango is improvisational, meaning it's born anew with each dance, and competitions kill that freshness, requiring practice and memorizing of choreography. His style is clean—it's a tableau that invites his followers to decorate spontaneously with embellishments like leg wraps and *lustradas* where the woman slowly, flirtatiously slides her foot up the man's pant leg. It's a sort of free association you can't do with most leaders.

John and I are as calibrated as Greenwich Mean Time.

"People keep asking if we've choreographed our dancing," he tells me.

"Tell them 'yes, we've spent months practicing,'" I say. "I don't want them to know how easy you are."

John is one of the most charming and handsome New Zealanders I've ever met, and he gives me back my belly laugh. He tells me he's working on his *traspiés,* a syncopation, which he pronounces "trass-pee-aze." I sense that he would happily choreograph a night in bed, too, but he is a *caballero,* a gentleman, and there's no question in my mind that the overture would have to come from me.

When John learns I'm a writer, he tells me, "I've got *the* book for you to write. Tell ya about it when we're done dancing. It'll be a best-seller!"

Already I'm a little disappointed. My least favorite conversation is the one in which nonwriters have the idea for me that will make me rich. I've stopped telling people that if I wanted to make money I'd give up writing. But John is such a darling that I want to hear him out. It turns out his idea is to write a book about sex. Not just any old sex, but sex among older people.

"Um, excuse me. What is old?"

"Old," he says, "seventies and eighties."

"Whew."

Before he goes any further, I laugh for two reasons. The first is that it's been done. I tell him about the two most recent ones I know about, *Sex and the Seasoned Woman,* by Gail Sheehy, and Joan Price's *Better Than I Ever Expected.* And then I remember how my former writing group had collectively groaned over a *baddd* sex scene I'd written. Thereafter I decided to leave sex scenes to Danielle Steel or the late Jacqueline Susann.

It's not that John seeks out women in their seventies and eighties to sleep with, but that he is such a straight-shooter that he often ends up talking with them about their rewarding sex lives. He reminds me of Flaubert's Frédéric Moreau, that eternal heartthrob who earned his sentimental education from an older woman.

As I get to know John, I like him more and more. I enjoy his Kiwi humor, his no-nonsense take on the *milongas,* and his honest admission that he is always thinking of sex when he dances—and his conviction that all men are thinking of sex when dancing. We have intermittent discourse and perpetual disagreement on this subject.

"A man," he says, holding his bare noggin at an angle of repose, "only invites a woman to dance because he wants to have sex with her. That's why most men are not good dancers, y'see. The skill drops off in proportion to the number of lays they git."

John will not be convinced otherwise. Even as I and other women tell him we are not thinking about sex when we are enjoying a dance. Or that we are not sleeping with the men we dance with . . . well, for the most part. He simply doesn't believe it, and I know he's not alone in his disbelief.

Yet, he gets me thinking: My heart probably weighs about as much as his penis. Engorged, both seem equally vital. There he is as preoccupied with his penis as I am with my heart. *So, I think, two vital organs, two portals to intimacy. Who's to say whether one fixation is healthy or unhealthy? Maybe the orgiastic* boliche-*goers are very together. What's the dif?* I want love, then sex. John wants sex, then love.

I know, though, that John needs and wants love as much as I. It's just that he'd never say it. I watch him shoot from the hip to appease his heart, even as I shoot from the heart, hoping to eventually appease my "hips."

Possibly, what attracts me to John, who seems to be more of a softie than he projects, is that he, like me, prefers loving over being loved. I conclude this as I watch subtle changes in him as he falls for gorgeous young Gina, who emigrated here from Italy and who makes Sophia Loren look ordinary. But Gina's jealousy ultimately drives him away. How could someone as sensual as John not be lured to bed by every woman he dances with? It's a perennial dilemma among couples who both dance tango. She drives him crazy in more ways than one. She is perfectly right and perfectly wrong for him.

John grows wary of Buenos Aires, as if his external environment is the problem. He tells me that it's time to go somewhere else and learn some new dance. He's the type of man who will travel the world looking for happiness outside himself. But I come up equally short with the opposite intention—trying to find the solution inside myself.

The gorgeous Sunday morning before John leaves, I'm sitting in my park contemplating how much this new friend has brought to my life—laughter, intrigue, and lots of platonic talk about sex and love. Now it's Renoir canvases I see everywhere amid the many families that frequent the park on weekends, gliding on the lake in rented boats, laughing together, sharing yerba maté, feeding the ducks and geese. I curl up with my solitude on a stone bench under a spot where jasmine creeps over the top of the pergola. I meditate on the way the trees cooperate, taking turns blooming. The jacarandas are losing their blossoms, but the acacia and mimosa are coming into bud with sorbet-pink and orange flowers. I notice there's a certain pain in being present with this beauty, but I stay with it because this morning, like every other one, I chanted *Great is the matter of birth and death/Life is fleeting/Gone, gone/Awake, awake/Each one/ Don't waste this life.* This is what it means—to soak up what's before me. I'm a modern-day gaucho who wants to own nothing but have everything under the sun and moon. As I sit here, *not wasting this life,* I find it increasingly difficult to do this and prepare for the death, which Zen advises is just a passing phenomenon. Wouldn't it be easier to pass on if I were just leaving behind a wasted life?

Before I can rectify the wrongfulness of this line of thinking, I hear a man's voice: *"¿Queres bailar?"* What a surprise to look up from my reverie and see a man, Alfredo, whom I dance with frequently at Salon Canning. He is out strolling with his wife. He introduces me to her, Clarisa, and tells her that I am one of the people he knows from "church," where for three minutes at a time I'm a very important person to him. She laughs, and there is not a shred of discomfort among us, only warm, cordial feelings. His wife says she dances but very infrequently. I already know this is quite common, that only one spouse is passionate about the dance. I tell them about my Monet and Renoir visions here and point to the color and light. Alfredro says, "I'm sixty-three and have been coming here for most of my life and this is the first time anyone has put Monet's or Renoir's face on this landscape." He looks around proudly yet wistfully, as if he had seen this vision himself all his life but was too humble to say so. I'd like to speak to that sentiment, and say, "You Argentines, you people, you're so busy envying other countries, you don't know what you have right under your noses." Instead we share a bit of conversation about our families and where we're from. Just as they leave, Alfredo asks which church I'm attending this week. Niño Bien, I tell him.

John is out of my life as quickly as he arrived—off to live and tango in France. He soon emails me to tell me that he's "been booked by another tall, slick Italian," which is Kiwi for *in love with another woman.*

Ah, but I see through the hard, dismissive language. *Slick,* my eye—he means juicy, melt-my-heart delectable. Yes, there is that passive voice that betrays a hint of covering his ass: *This booking, should it go wrong, was not my idea, but hers.* A bulletproof vest. But something intangible I had seen in John, perhaps his comfort among and easy rapport with women, is what betrayed a man who, not unlike myself, is happy more with loving than being loved. Why doesn't he just admit it? Why the Kevlar?

And what, I wonder, is there for me to admit? How many of us in the *milongas* are called to tango for this trait; we want to love unconditionally, even if only for three minutes at a time.

I remember a couple of books written years ago about women and men who allegedly "loved too much." I thought then as now, *Ridiculous.* Loving, like eating garlic, dancing tango, and traveling, is something you can't do enough of. I didn't read the books, but I imagine what the author meant was that some women and men, John and I perhaps among them, need to love themselves as much they love their neighbors. The crack, the cleft, the split in our Selves, is simply a work of art begging for acceptance as art. Also known as forgiveness. With that thought I feel my overbearing father and my submissive mother get up and dance.

Chapter 13

Birds of a Feather
Tango Together

There is no defense against an open heart and a supple body in dialogue with wildness.

—*Terry Tempest Williams,* An Unspoken Hunger

"Another fine mess I've gotten us into," I say to my friend, Jan, a visiting San Francisco *tanguero.*

We stand together in uncertainty between some wharf industry and the marshy willow-lined *cortaderas,* or foxtail pampas grass, that spread around four lakes in Reserva Ecológica Costanera Sur, a natural habitat fringing the watery edge of Buenos Aires.

"That taxi driver was in too damn big of a hurry to get rid of us," he complains.

It's true. The driver, unsure of where the entrance to the Reserva was, decided to dump us on an empty road before skidding off. "I should have studied the map better," I say, pulling out my much-loved ragged city map.

It takes a half hour of walking and triangulating before Jan and I eventually find our own way to the entrance. Some two hundred bird species and fifty varieties of butterflies fly and flutter about this urban wilderness. I have accumulated enough miles on dance floors to stretch back to Northern California, and the opportunity to get some mileage out in the wild is long overdue.

It was hard to rise early this morning, a bump in my nocturnal schedule. But as I stand here in my cargo pants, billed cap, and hiking boots, I realize how much I've been missing the joy of mornings and nature. Back home, I'd rise to the sound of the foghorn, gauging from its song how thick the fog would be on my morning bike ride across the Golden Gate Bridge.

Now I'm here with my friend, who shares my sensibilities about wild things. Like most of my other regular favorite dancers in San Francisco, I didn't know much about Jan outside of tango, and I'm excited by the opportunity to get to know him better. We both have experienced a similar loss in the past years: He lost his mom and I lost my dad. We've discussed how grateful we both were to have been near our parents as they passed on. My father, at eighty-five, was in the final throes of congestive heart failure, and he breathed his last breath asleep next to my mother, with six of his kids on beds, couches, and on his bedroom floor. Losing our father, who cast a giant shadow, was so momentous an event that we're still all trying to figure out who we are without him around in the flesh.

Jan, who didn't know Dan or my saga prior to coming down here, listens nonjudgmentally to the unabridged version. As I tell my story again, I recall how sanguine and defiant I'd been in the beginning when people would say that tango would change your life—you'll drop all friends who don't tango.

"No it won't, no I won't," I'd say as I witnessed couples breaking up all around me, often finding new partners in their fellow dancers. All-over tango fever. It wouldn't happen to me. Tango was to be like my Zen practice. Dan had no interest in Zen, but had always fully supported my doing it and would join me many nights at the Zen Center for dinners after meditation. But I had kept the *zafu* and the *zendo* pure. Not so the dance floor.

I have not been surrounded by nature lovers in the tango world. It's been only my persistence that's allowed me to satisfy my curiosity for the names of trees here. Besides the big old sycamores and the violet-blossomed jacarandas, there are many *palos borrachos* with lipstick-pink flowers that fall and carpet the grass beneath them. There's the startling *ombú*, with leathery limblike roots aboveground, that looks like it could be a humanoid ancestor. The gangly one on Plaza San Martín is famous, as is the house-size *gomero,* or rubber tree, its tonnage of limbs supported by planks, found on the terrace of Cafe la Biela.

As Jan and I walk the reserve's dirt road, which borders one of the bird-frequented lakes, we share his binoculars. In the space of three hours he sights a respectable list of feathered friends: snowy egrets, a great egret, a white-faced ibis, possible Brazilian teal, rosy-billed pochard, white-backed stilts, southern lapwing, lesser yellowlegs, a rock pigeon, white-rumped swallow, possible red-crested cardinal, and a house sparrow. This reserve is anything but remote, but while you're lost inside it you have no sense of being footsteps away from a major metropolis.

Jan and I sight one last bird, a roseate spoonbill, which blows my cool. My heart climbs toward my throat and resounds with the urgency of a gong pounding inside my ears. My eyes glaze over and turn inward.

"What's the matter?" Jan asks.

"Nothing," I say.

I hand him back his binoculars.

I am back in San Blas, Mexico, exactly a year ago.

"Dan, look, look, they are as pink as sherbet!" I said, excitedly pointing to the spoonbills out on an offshore isle. We had driven up to San Blas from Puerto Vallarta to see one of my old haunts. We hired a local bird guide, Armando Santiago Navarrete, who took us into the cloud forest, coastal marshland, and mountain jungle of his Pacific Coast village. Within two days under his tutelage we'd logged fifty-seven species, including the showy spoonbills.

"I see only egrets," Dan said soberly.

"Some of them are not egrets—they're about the same size as the white egrets, but flamingo pink. See?"

"No, I don't," he said sternly. I knew the rods and cones of his eyes didn't easily let him inside the red family. I knew if I insisted he had to see them, it would make him angry. It was one of my favorite birds on the trip, though, and it was as if that one bird summed up all the ways in which we didn't see the same world. Dan didn't share my view of spiritual endeavors like Zen or tango, or my desire for us to ceremoniously bless our commitment. And in the end he looked at our relationship as black and white, or *all over,* when I still harbored a rosy view of its continuing. These memories of Dan are always sudden and unexpected. They have the power to take my breath away and I never know what might set them off.

Jan seems to perceive my need to go into myself. He lags behind. I know it's normal to feel remorse—Why didn't I do this or say that? Why did I take things for granted?—so I let myself sink into it without trying to fight it.

Jan catches up with me and reminds me of where I am. "Look, in the hedges—a *rufous hornero*," he says. I peer through the binoculars and see the national bird of Argentina. It's an adobe-nest builder, similar to the *calendria*, another bird Dan and I saw in Mexico, whose nests look like hanging bird tenements. But this one builds a mud and twig home that looks like a little adobe oven, or *hornero*, which is where it gets its name from.

I am able to pull myself out of the past and finish out the day with Jan. It's a joy to have him here, and I'm grateful for his perceptiveness and his ability to read my need for space. These regressions into my past last for shorter and shorter intervals the longer I'm here. I am reminded of a Zen parable Blanche Hartman once told a group of nearly a hundred people sitting cross-legged on the grassy-smelling tatami mats in the lush Buddha Hall of the Zen Center. She spoke of how close Heaven is to Hell. Hell, Blanche said, is a place filled with miles of tables piled with the most delicious food imaginable, bowls and bowls of divine victuals. But people are standing around ravenous, salivating, and dying. The chopsticks with which to eat are three feet long and everyone is starving to death because they cannot bring nourishment to their mouths. Heaven, she said, is the exact same place. But the many people there are sitting around, blissed out, feeding each other with the long chopsticks.

I know that all I have to do is take a baby step to my left or to my right and be done with infernal suffering and clinging to my past life with Dan. Sometimes I accomplish this; other times something holds me back. And all I can do is get a respite with tango or distractions with friends.

As we move toward summer, I notice certain standard-issue wear in the un-air-conditioned *milongas*—lots of lacquered *abanicos*, or hand fans. As I watch my fellow dancers flapping away, I try to tell them what I heard over and over as a kid: "Fanning yourself just makes you hotter from the increased activity." I may as well tell the drivers in Argentina that pedestrians have the right of way. But I suspect that, like much else, the fans are a de rigueur fashion statement.

Jan has other friends here and does a lot of sightseeing with them, or on his own. It's great running into him in the *milongas*—sometimes planned, sometimes serendipitously. I love dancing *vals* with him, because I can feel his excitement and passion as he leads me in long strides, floor space permitting. He's here for just a month—and he deserves to have his own Argentine experience—so I wait until he signals me to dance.

The week after we visit the *reserva*, Jan and I decide to share some time outdoors again. There are free concerts every Sunday in the rose garden of my Palermo park, so we head there to catch a jazz combo. We can hear the music even as we stroll through the garlanded pergola and over the footbridge I call the Bridge of Sighs, under which pedal boats rather than gondolas glide. Afterward we walk over to the nearby stunning Japanese Gardens. Trees, shrubs, ground cover, and plants are all artfully landscaped. Yet, from the tall pines to the water-loving lily foliage, it all fits together like a whim of nature. Paths wind past concrete lanterns, stone art and Buddhas, a gong, and arching bridges over ponds burbling with the hungry "feed me" mouths of koi. Which makes me suddenly realize how hungry I am.

I invite Jan to enjoy a home-cooked meal in my loft. I have doctored the bottled *chimichurri* sauce that I bought a few weeks earlier at the Mataderos street fair. Despite being a mix of red pepper, oregano, onion, and vinegar, this classic meat sauce is not piquant enough for my taste. I have to enliven it with Mendoza extra-virgin olive oil, fresh garlic, shallots, and more hot red pepper, which is very difficult to find in Argentina due to the general preference for mild flavors. I've had the chicken soaking in the marinade for a day. While Jan sits and enjoys the view out my sliding glass doors, I heat the marinade into a sauce with butter, then pour it over the chicken, polenta, and oven-roasted *calabazas*.

We dine like aristocracy, and Jan reminds me that Teatro Colón is about to close for more than a year of renovation, until late May 2008, when it is scheduled to reopen for its one-hundredth anniversary. He suggests that we take a tour.

"Sure," I say, pleased that Jan is getting me to soak up the art and culture outside of the *milonga*.

The following Wednesday, I meet Jan on the plaza across from the seven-story theater, which alone could have given Buenos Aires its sobriquet, "the Paris of the south." Its ornate stone architecture is already swaddled in scaffolding. The theater is laden with twenty-four-karat gilded columns, goldleaf to spare, wall-to-ceiling mirrors, frescos to make the Sistine Chapel jealous, and chandeliers weighted down with some two hundred light bulbs.

From one tier of the gold-crusted balconies, we look down on the plush red velvet chairs and wish we could sit in one.

We'll have to wait until 2008 for that, but Jan has done some research and discovered yet another free concert, this one a performance of Buenos Aires's symphony playing tango compositions. It's being held at much smaller but equally beautiful Teatro Cervantes. That night when we meet there, the first thing I notice is a gallery of the Moorish tiles I've come to admire so much throughout this city. Some of my favorite tiles, copper-embossed cobalt-blue satyrs and centaurs, are in the funkiest of places, subway station Moreno of the C Line.

We sit in the balcony and hear a few pretty good singers perform with the orchestra. When they play the crowd-pleasing "Tango Negro," my heart starts thumping, my feet start moving, and I look over at Jan with a look that says, *C'mon, let's dance in the aisles.* Jan returns a look that says, *Sorry, kid, not today, please calm yourself.*

As I steal glimpses of the other patrons, so dignified and impressively still, I'm reminded that for many people tango is not a dance, but only a genre of music to listen to.

We're pretty pumped up when the concert is over and the night is still young at 10:30 PM. We head to Maipu 444 for the *milonga* there, but as soon as we walk through the door, we both realize we've stumbled upon one of Buenos Aire's few gay venues—the straight milonga at Maipu goes until 10 PM, at which point the gay one starts. I've never been around for the transition that happens here, from a straight to gay clientele, but it's funny to think of it as a curtain call of sorts. The straight cast exits down the same stairs the gay cast ascends. There are mostly men in attendance, and it feels so welcoming and relaxed that we take our seats and then dance a *tanda*. We love it when some of the men break with tango protocol, clapping and hooting for us as we dance. Jan only dances with me, but I get to do some lively spinning with a couple of accomplished young men.

A rather liberal-minded friend once said to me that watching men dance tango with one another did nothing for her. I didn't agree but wasn't sure how to articulate why until I saw Carlos Saura's film *Tango*. It's filled with great dancing, including Juan Carlos Copes doing some simple folksy numbers with his daughter Johanna. It's filmed in one of my favorite haunts, Confitería Ideal. Saura inserts a male fantasy sequence where two women, Cecilia Narova and Mía Maestro, tango and kiss. It's quite sensual, with the two women dancing in 1920s period dress. But for me, the jazzy all-male number choreographed by Teatro Colón's primo ballet dancer (and declared bisexual), Julio Boca, was by far the pinnacle of the movie. It was a pleasure to see the feline frames and postures on the very fit, classically trained men in the film such as you'll seldom see in *milongas,* where that brand of athleticism is scarce.

What I enjoyed about watching those men dance with other men was how it became patently clear to me that tango is not necessarily a dance between a man and a woman, but between male and female energies, which both men and women embody to varying degrees.

Both energies are active, dynamic, and playful, and it's a joy to see this, the Tao of tango, in evidence at Maipu this evening.

A few days before Jan has to leave, he suggests one last outing—going to see a film, *El Último Bandoneón*, with Rodolfo Mederos, the famous *bandoneón* player who lives here in Buenos Aires.

The film is in Spanish but we understand enough to gather that the *bandoneón*, an instrument that found its way with immigrants to Argentina and became the soul and voice of tango, is in danger of extinction. First played by black musicians in the 1800s, the last one, I've been told by locals, was made in 1939 (although certain small artisans are starting to craft them once again). I recall with reverence how I got to run my fingers over one, with its inlay of mother-of-pearl. It's a mysterious instrument, this squeezebox invented by the German Heinrich Band. It looks like an accordion, only it has buttons on each side rather than a keyboard, which allows it to produce different notes upon closing and opening the *bandoneón*. It's like the human lung, emanating sound both as it exhales and inhales, making noises that are an alternating mix of crying, moaning, and laughter.

To convey the message that the *bandoneón* will survive, the film ends with Mederos's orchestra, including several young *bandoneonistas* playing an allegro ma non troppo number. The sound bursting from those squeezeboxes is so electrifying that I feel myself growing taller in my seat. I steal a glimpse at Jan:

C'mon, let's dance in the aisles. Jan's look back to me again says: *Please calm yourself.*

It's a warm night and we need ice cream after the movie. The absolute best in the world comes from Persicco. It's Italian, naturally, and I'm unable to eat just one scoop of Persicco. It's always a double—*dulce de leche* and vanilla filled with big chunks of walnuts. It's a sweet last visit with my friend who has helped me expand my horizon to include nature reserves, art, music, film, cooking, ice cream, and a gay *milonga*—all successful new avenues for getting me out of my funk.

I consider all those avenues when I'm back to the *milongas* alone, watching the compulsive and frantic *abanicos,* like nervous birds flapping all around. The days are getting longer, the weather warmer. People keep warning me that summer will be unbearably hot and humid. I tell them it can't be any worse than in New Jersey, where I was braised alive the first twenty-two summers of my life. And besides, I now know there are wonderful wet and wild places outdoors here where I can cool off—and even key a new avian friend by knocking off an email to Jan for guidance.

Chapter 14

Dance of the "Big Water"

Then Sunrise kissed my Chrysalis
And I stood up—and lived—

—Emily Dickinson

I have to vacate my loft on Juncal Street by November 26, as the owners have promised it to other renters. As I prepare for the move, my second in less than three months, I cry often, reliving the month before I came to Buenos Aires. I'd given half my belongings to Goodwill, indiscriminately stripping my life of possessions as punishment for what I'd done. The remaining half is stuffed into a dark storage room off of Dan's garage along with our fifteen years of photos and whatever memories survived my vicious streak of divestment.

I have come to love this cathedral-ceiling space. I have passed hours being at home with grief, my constant companion. But I've also done hours of yoga and prepped myself for countless *milonga* nights. It's been a good space that's treated me well during this hard time.

Each morning I've stood in the shower and tried to find my "power bars" and my "aging toasters," two energy points on my skull and behind my ears that my good friend Betty had shown me. I can't recall what they're supposed to affect, but I do remember how her touch calmed me. She taught me to chant, *All life comes to me with ease and joy and glory.* Over these past few months, when the image of Evelyn and Dan enjoying conjugal bliss has raised my hackles, I've gritted my teeth and chanted this haiku over and over. I've become my own Gestapo: Life will come to me . . . or else. I've tried Pema Chödrön's Tibetan *tonglen* practice, too: Invite my Gestapo and my hair-pulling selves to tea, sit with them, face to face. I've become a walking encyclopedia of practices to ward off my own evil spirits.

Thanksgiving has arrived, and I have two days before I must be out of the loft. Usually my favorite holiday, this one is the second or third worst day of my life. I have only missed one Thanksgiving with family in my entire life—the first year I moved to San Francisco in 1973. I vowed that wouldn't happen again. I can take or leave Christmas (it was a source of financial hardship for us), but Thanksgiving is an

Italian American holiday in my family. When I was a child, I loved hosting all the relatives, some of them newly arrived from Sicily. We would gather in our cellar, close to fifty of us, sitting at several long tables feasting on dishes from the Old World and the New. It was the last happy day of the year before my parents, my father especially, plummeted into stress over Christmas.

If I were home, I'd be splitting the day between my brother's home outside of San Francisco and Dan's big clan, my second family, in Saratoga. This year, some forty members of my blood family are feasting together on the usual homemade raviolis, sausage, spareribs, and meatballs, followed by turkey, stuffing, stuffed mushrooms, and dozens of special side dishes—plus Mom's and everyone's pies, plus Tom's tiramisu and holy cannoli, our trademark Sicilian pastry made from scratch. Almost everyone, including four new nieces and nephews I've met only through email photos, is together at my sister Terry's house, down the shore in Belmar, New Jersey.

I don't dare call. I don't want to hear the chaos in the background—that familiar cacophony of voices that I grew up with that sounds like we're fighting with each other when really we're having one of our calm discussions. That would be torture rather than comfort now. I can imagine the call going out—"Who wants to talk to Camille?!"—followed by each one of my loved ones scrambling to get to the phone.

"She still down in Rio?" one of them would inevitably ask.

"Not Rio—the other place . . . whatchamacallit . . . Bwaynoze Ears."

I'd be forgotten for long minutes as the phone was left lying on the table or on a staircase. I play out the whole scenario: listening to cooing babies, brother-in-law Dan coaxing Cole Porter from the piano, conversations about the great family reunion in Sicily last July (the pleasure of which was dampened for me by my and Dan's imbroglio). I'd have to yell everything twice for my hard-of-hearing mother, to whom I've been incapable of divulging the news about Cam and Dan having gone south. Mom always liked him, but when she found he could make martinis the way she loved (heavy on the Stoli vodka), and after he bought her a special martini glass, he became her golden boy for life.

I am a bubbling ferment of *angustia* all day long. I mope. I do nothing to cheer myself up. As the hours pass slowly, desperately miserable and unhappy, I do something I seldom do. I call a friend, Florencia, to complain.

"Hi, sweetie, what's up?" It's medicine, just hearing her voice.

I have only just recently met Flo and Dee, friends from Los Angeles, through a mutual friend. I call them the Sunshine Girls because the dance floor lights up whenever flaxen-haired Flo, who dresses in bright colors—never in tango black—is dancing. She's a whirling dervish, with ribbons and banners of silky blues, pinks, yellows, and greens flowing in her wake. I tell her, "Every time I see you, you look like you just got religion." She tells me it's her sixteenth trip to Buenos Aires.

Both Dee and Flo wear the smiles of euphoria that make outsiders say, "I want whatever she's having." I know the pair have left a trail of throbbing hearts in their wake and fallen in love, like me, with Argentines by droves. I know they're older than me, but I nearly fell off my chair when Dee told me she has a daughter who's forty-eight. And Flo, too, has three kids, including a son a few years younger than I.

They quickly fall into the roles of surrogate moms and sisters for me. Last time the three of us were together was in the backseat of a taxi. The driver couldn't keep his incredulous eyes on the road and off the flailing limbs in his rearview mirror—mainly Flo's legs, which are Hanes's gold standard. Dee and I have pretty legs, but thin-boned Flo seems to have inherited hers from the likes of Betty Grable. Luckily, it was too dark to see that our skirts had hiked up to our waist as the three of us stretched bare legs up, one at a time, to buckle our strappy spikes. We would hit the deck dancing. It's always great to be with *tangueras* on a mission, with their take-no-prisoners *cabeceos*. Tango is no mere recreation. *Let no* tanda *go undanced* is our motto.

Flo and I dish the dirt for an hour or so on the phone, and then she tells me a wonderfully inspiring story about her own mother. Flo's dad had died very young, leaving her mom to raise young Flo and her little brother alone. Her mom struggled but wouldn't remarry for years. Then, at age sixty, she met "the love of her life," a man fifteen years her senior. They had fifteen of the best years of their lives together—he died at age ninety, leaving Flo's mom quite bereaved. I recall the relentless pressures to get married, to have a kid before I hit the old age of thirty, then forty . . . Flo makes me feel the way I want to feel until the day I die. What's the hurry? I'm just a kid, life has some surprises up ahead.

We hang up and I feel much better. My eyes are dry and clear. I look around the loft, and although I don't see a hundred noisy people and platters of steaming Italian food before me, I feel nourished. It's as if someone from afar is feeding me with long chopsticks. Blanche appears over my shoulder, and I have an image of her giving a lecture in front of the golden statue of Avalokiteshvara, deity of compassion, in the Zen Center's Buddha Hall. She's telling another of my favorite parables. This one is about a man who rode donkeys over a mountain pass weekly only to be stopped each time by border police looking for what he was smuggling. They checked every inch of the donkey every time and never found a hint of evidence. On the man's deathbed the chief of police came and asked if he would finally admit to what it was he was smuggling. "Yes," he said. "Donkeys." The truth of what I need is always that close, and yet I'm always looking deeply past it, elsewhere.

I get dressed and take my heart to Club Español, where I meet Flo. I take unbridled pleasure in watching flaxen-haired Flo rack up the men to dance with her. Amid the tribal rites of connection this Thanksgiving Day, I completely forget my sorrow.

I have five days between the Saturday that I vacate the loft and the day I can move into my new place, so I've decided to take a trip to the famous Iguazú Falls up north in Misione Province, which juts into Brazil like a thumb poke. My fan-flapping Porteño friends all think I'm crazy to go in the heat of the summer, but I don't mind the long bus ride and I don't find the climate unbearable. I'm at ease in the Hawaii-like tropical wet heat. The bus, which is air-conditioned, is more comfortable than coach on any major airline. I've splurged for an executive "cama-suite" ($115 round-trip), which includes a seat that extends almost all the way back. The food is forgettable, but the hours fly by as I sleep or read. Tragically, I leave my Spanish notebook on the bus, three months of Tuesdays and Thursdays with Mariel, and my handwritten record of all my favorite sayings, verb conjugations, and *lunfardo*. I recall how Mariel felt like she lost a friend when she lost her books in a flood, and that's how I feel. It's irreplaceable.

Fifteen hours later, I arrive at Puerto Iguazú, and by this afternoon I'm on a paved trail to Iguazú's waterfalls, alone and having reconciled that that notebook is just another loss that will make me stronger. A comet—a blur of yellow and orange—flies across blue sky over the jungle canopy. But then I catch a glimpse of its beak. That's no comet, it's a *tucán grande*. I look around for someone to share in my excitement at seeing a toucan, but all I see is a cold-blooded black iguana that's crawling away from me as fast as it can.

The *tucán*'s colors and the jungle remind me of Tibetan sand paintings, lovely works of art that monks laboriously create then, in the sweep of a hand or breath, destroy as a lesson in impermanence. In the end, everything has to be let go, even vocabulary words, even cherished notions. *Even my breath*, I think, as I indulge my solitary moment to do some deep inhaling and exhaling. The noise I make catches the attention of a coati, who then carries on looking for insects.

At the end of the trail, I meet up with Iguazú's crush of tourists. I power past their airborne digital cameras to the spectacle of water falling from on high in great abundance. Thick white ribbons of falls crash down from a broad table of the Río Iguazú. I can see ten falls from where I stand, some of them blending into each other. Iguazú, from the indigenous Guarani words for "big water," consists of 275 falls in all, dispersed along nearly two miles of the Iguazú River. Well-marked trails thread through the thick jungle growth to various viewing areas. The falls drop from as high as 270 feet, though most originate from around the 210-foot mark. They are surpassed in height only by South Africa's Victoria Falls, which drop from more than 350 feet (and are more than a mile wide). They are higher than Niagara Falls (a mere drop in the bucket at 167 feet high), which I saw once thirty-three years ago. Argentines love that their falls are higher, and it delights them to no end when I say that I think theirs are more beautiful.

To hike to some of the falls, or *saltos*—Salto San Martín, Salto Mbigua, Salto Bernabé Mendez, Salto Bossetti, and Salto Dos Hermanas—I walk both the Inferior and Superior circuits. I start with the latter, wondering what Spanish conquistador Alvar Nuñez Cabeza de Vaca, the first European to spot the rushing water, must have thought when he arrived here in 1541.

The power and sound of the water crashing down all around make people positively giddy. The Parque Nacional Iguazú attracts thousands of tourists from all over the world, as does the Parque Nacional do Iguaçu on the Brazilian side.

Down at the Inferior (not a judgment, just a coordinate) circuit, the vistas are even more inspiring, if you prefer looking up at falls as I do. As soon as I reach the top I'm struck by another Dan memory: us in Yosemite on our yearly May visit to watch the falls gush over granite like giant fire hoses from Heaven as winter releases its icy grip in the Sierra Nevada. We often went in autumn, too, when the water ran thin and Dan would stand under Nevada Falls, risking rocks falling on his head. He would be in ecstasy here at Iguazú.

There is a free boat ride across the calm part of Río Iguazú to jungle-covered Isla San Martín. As I jump into the little motorized launch, I think of crossing the River Styx. I try to explain this to the two boatmen (grim reapers?), who laugh at me and ask me where I'm from.

"*Aquí*," I tease.

They laugh even harder.

"I'll swim back," I tell them when they drop me on the island's beach. I go for a dip in the warm water. I miss the cold San Francisco Bay that I swim in year-round at home, even in the winter, if only briefly, when the water temperature goes below 50 degrees.

I attempt to swim back across the "Styx," but get whistled at—not for being a bathing beauty, but for breaking a park rule. Okay, back inside the shallow baby water behind the rope I go. I'm tempted to risk another whistle and swim toward the falls—hell, Dan would—but it's late in the day so I decide to stay put. I'm tired, too, so the big kahunas—the falls at Garganta de Diablo, Devil's Throat—will have to wait until tomorrow.

I have found a dorm-style bed at the local youth hostel for thirty-three pesos (eleven bucks, breakfast included) a night. The common area is big and airy. I feel at home among the clutches of young people. They flop on old but comfy furniture reading, plotting shoestring budget itineraries, and listening to loud rock or Latin music. Watching them pound away at the keyboards on a bank of computers, sending emails around the world, I recall my European backpacking days when the only possible communication with home was paper mail delivery at an American Express. And even today, despite the fears and loneliness that arise, it is that state of being incommunicado, a state of moving meditation, that I treasure deeply.

The next morning, I hop the Green Train of the Jungle to shuttle to the Devil's Throat. Even the approach across the river is stunning. *This has got to be one of the most beautiful spots on earth*, I think, as I look across the river at Brazil. I've been told you have a broader vista of the falls from Brazil, but I didn't want to pay $100, a reciprocal fee for U.S. citizens to cross the border. But the view from here is amazing enough, and I vow that I'll return for that side in my future travels.

Devil's Throat crashes over a U-shaped indent in a cliff. It's quite magnificent architecture for a falls. The mist rebounds as high as five hundred feet. You can get so close—safely behind a rail—that you can drink the spray. Many of us tourists stand quietly watching the swallowlike silhouettes fly into the spray for sips, before the power of the big rushing water—or perhaps the negative ions—pushes them away. There are the requisite neon rainbows, pieces of them everywhere. I can almost hang from one that frames a few cumulus clouds in blue sky.

Iguazu boasts 430 bird species and many electric-colored butterflies (not to mention dun-colored mosquitoes). At trail's end, a metallic purple and orange one lets me touch it. For some five minutes it flutters in place as I gently run my index finger over its stained-glass wing, humming to it as if it were a messenger from nature to me. "I'm just a little caterpillar still," I tell it, "but someday I'll spread my wings again." I feel something primitive rise up in me as the urge to capture something beautiful washes over me, and I'm elated when it flies off before I lose control and snatch it up.

From the open-air train on the way back, some of us spot a strapping beast clumsily falling out of the jungle growth and into a stream of water. An Argentine passenger says it's a *carpincho,* a river pig, whose brushed-suede hide is sold all over Argentina. I'm entertained by all these comical-looking jungle critters. The graceless *carpincho,* the cartoonish toucan, and then, later that day, not far from the park entrance, I watch a pack of monkeys—capuchins—literally swinging from trees. They screech and laugh at the pod of tourists, and I can't help but wonder who's observing whom.

❧

I sleep most of the way back to Buenos Aires, except for two interruptions by the drug police, who pull us over twice. The police in Buenos Aires have the aura of school patrols, only more conspicuously armed. At the first check they walk the bus aisles with a ginger dog that they let me pet. He sniffs and sniffs and finds nothing incriminating or of interest. I can't help but recall Blanche's story about the donkey smuggling and wonder what might be hiding in plain sight.

The bus ride features a tasteless American movie with Spanish subtitles—about a woman who cuts off her husband's penis and he's trying to get it back (no doubt inspired by the real life Lorena Bobbitt's penis-ectomy). I raise my arms in disgust, looking for backup from the matronly woman in her sixties next to me. But she brushes off my protest and seems to say, "What's the problem? It's only a movie."

"But there are children on this bus," I motion wildly.

"So," she shrugs. I motion wildly again and she motions back. We're having an Italian moment, a body-language argument. We understand each other, but we are clearly not on the same page. "*Ah, managia-la!*" I brush the argument away in disgust with my favorite Italian cuss phrase, the equivalent of "damn it." There's something wrong with this picture—I'm the city slicker and she's a dowdy grandma from a province or suburb. But the attendant must agree with me and turns off the movie. I'm sure he's more concerned about my comfort than the content of the film, which is so bad it's not getting anyone's attention anyway.

As I return to my alpha state of rest, I think of one recent night when I had strolled to my Palermo park. I stumbled upon a completely different scene from my daytime visits. Apparently, that mile-long circular drive around the lake becomes a strip for transvestites and prostitutes to hawk their wares after a certain hour. They stand on calf-primping daggerlike spikes in full *scant* regalia, maybe twenty to fifty feet apart, as a parade of cars, at times bumper to bumper, drives by slowly. Many of the gawkers were not interested in buying, just looking or heckling occasionally. As if this scene were not eye-popping enough, there were many *normal* strollers like me out in the park, including young families with kids who were not paying a second's notice to the nearly naked ladies. I thought about the value of censoring certain things. Only in this country, I thought, could a dance with such primal content survive so long.

We approach the Retiro station in the early morning. I notice the adjacent *villa miseria*. The asphalt jungle, which I know to be a dangerous place, looks almost inviting. Its cracked abodes, laundry that hangs like Tibetan prayer flags, and trash alike are splendidly ablaze in the morning sun. I'm moving to a new place for the month of December and I feel richer than ever, not to mention spray-cleaned by the falls, and ready for something new.

Chapter 15

Life in the Pink Palace

Leave the past behind; leave the future behind; leave the present behind. Thou art then ready to go to the other shore.

—*"Cravings,"* The Dhammapada

My new but temporary home is called Casa de Deby. Located on Paraguay near Thames, in Palermo Soho, the inn is typical of long-term lodging here for tango-oriented tourists who want to stay in Buenos Aires at least a month in the care of a tango-savvy hotel-keeper. It's a three-bedroom apartment, two bedrooms of which are rentals and the other belongs to owner Deby Novitz. The inn, which Deby runs as a sort of bed-and-breakfast, is on the seventeenth floor of an elegant building with a twenty-four-hour porter. I'll be here through December, and then I'm off to yet another long-term rental in the Recoleta.

I'm home alone with Roxie, Deby's dog, the most mild-mannered pit bull I've ever met, gentle as the morning breezes that come off the Río de la Plata. I call her a big pussycat, though that's more than hyperbole since Roxie weighs as much as five house cats. She has the catlike habit of sticking out her long pick tongue and licking her paws clean, something she surely picked up from her two former feline housemates.

⋙⋘

I start calling Deb's place the Pink Palace about two days into my stay. The common area, a large shining dance floor, is uncluttered, with outer space–like pink walls speckled with tufts of cotton-candy white. It might have been the color of Deb's hair some years ago. Now she is a sassy blond, with a thick lock occasionally cascading over her right eye. Many mornings, I awaken to the sound of Carlos Di Sarli's "Bahía Blanca" as Deb and her coteacher, Fernando, give private lessons. Jane, a Taiwanese native from San Francisco, is their latest student. Tall, thin, and stately, she's a demure flight attendant for Northwest who comes to Buenos Aires frequently. I enjoy getting to know her.

I discreetly slip by them on my way to the terrace to have my coffee and *media lunas* with a view all the way to the Río de la Plata, a brown stripe on the horizon. Roxie sits beside me as if she owns the terrace. I admit to Deby that I was a pit-bull-o-phobe until I met Roxie. Deby is impatient with the undeserved reputation of the breed, which she believes is fostered by sensational journalism. Reporters glom onto the odd pit bull attack, when so many other breeds are potentially more dangerous. "It's all in the training," Deby says. "Roxie has never been hit." Interesting. I consider the fact that I, hit a lot during my upbringing, am more prone to violence than Roxie, who's blissfully unaware of her mandibular power.

Here on the seventeenth-floor terrace with Roxie I list the things that are gone from my life since leaving the loft: the unseen sax and flute players, the vocalist, the mysterious birdsong. In Casa de Deby, I hear the squeals of schoolchildren from the building across the street and the live folk guitar that blossoms nightly from the roof terrace of the hostel next door. Buenos Aires buzzes vertically and horizontally. It's another city up here—some of the rooftops, with their gaggle of antennae, wires, and junk, look like shantytowns.

Deby steps out to hang her laundry and tells me, "You might want to hang your fine lingerie here, too." I laugh and say, "It's all Gap—the dryer can't hurt it." She is a fashion plate. I could take a lesson or two from her, I'm sure. But I'm happy with my cheap costumes for now, and I'm not planning on submitting male eyes to my cotton skivvies anytime soon. The other Palace door is still locked tight—how fitting that I should be ensconced atop a seventeen-story tower.

One Saturday evening, I go with Deby to Talk-a-rama, a meeting of gringos and locals who help each other speak English or Castellano at a weekly social in Resto-Bar in the Puerto Madero barrio. I enjoy the chat and find that the riverfront walkway, with its neatly restored 1890s red-brick warehouses, is very inviting. Puerto Madero also has a slickness not present in other barrios in its high-rent offices and expensive restaurants, which makes it feel like Restored City Port, Anywhere.

However, it has signs of distinction, too. You can't miss seeing the Opera Bay when you're there, a building that looks like a bunch of giant overlapping seashells. It's modeled after the Sydney Opera House, but it's just a glitzy nightclub inside. Puerto Madero has redemptive value in having all its streets named for women who struggled for women's rights in Argentina. Its best-known bridge, Puente de la Mujer (Bridge of the Woman), is a neat pedestrian overpass designed by Spanish engineer Santiago Calatrava. Some of Argentina's best-known women, including Azucena Villa, founder of the Mothers of Plaza de Mayo, and Victoria Ocampo, whose memoirs I have been enjoying and whose life is worth at least as much notice as Evita's, have been honored with their own streets here.

Ocampo was the daughter of aristocracy and an outspoken proponent of women's right to vote. Victoria had five sisters (like me). She had big ambitions and was married briefly, leaving her husband after he secretly wrote to her parents that he'd get her pregnant and she'd forget about a career in acting. She loved France and spent a lot of time in Paris, where she met and fell in love at first sight with her husband's cousin, Julian. She writes provocatively of their torrid romance that lasted some thirteen years.

Although Eva Perón gets credit for finally procuring the vote for Argentine women in 1947, Ocampo did a lion's share of groundwork. She published her first essay at age thirty on the inequality among humankind in the Buenos Aires daily, *La Nación.* She was founder of *Sur,* a cultural journal that published the work of some of her greatest contemporaries, including Virginia Woolf, Julio Cortázar, André Gide, Thomas Mann, T. S. Eliot, André Malraux, Henry Miller, Octavio Paz, and Jorge Luis Borges. Writer José Ortega y Gasset called her the Mona Lisa of the Pampas.

Ocampo criticized the Perón government as undemocratic and, in 1953, the regime put her under house arrest for a month as a political prisoner with the charge of being an "oligarchic dissident." This would have been akin to Bill and Hillary Clinton having Gloria Steinem incarcerated for criticizing their welfare reform, but my Argentine friends, who are accustomed to such deep divisions, laugh at me when I get outraged about such things. The left is splintered irreparably, they tell me nonchalantly. Be that as it may, I tell my yogini friend, Carmen, that I'd love to see a work of art in which Victoria, the low-profile aristocrat, meets Evita, the rags-to-riches politico. Working-class Evita, who danced tango, would encourage Victoria to drop her highbrow view of the dance. Carmen shocks me when she answers, "It's been done—about twenty years ago." *Eva y Victoria,* she tells me, is a play by Monica Ottino that envisions how a meeting between the two women might have unfolded. Great minds!

It's good for me to be around people for a change. Deby's Porteño friend Marcelo, a schoolteacher, whose union is on strike for the day, stops by to chat fairly frequently. Michael, a congenial San Franciscan expat whom Deb calls "my gay husband," also pops in on a regular basis.

Not too far into my stay at Deby's, he becomes "our gay husband" when Deb and I share him on a stroll to Rosa's *parrilla* on Scalabrini Ortiz. It's so toasty that we decide to sit outside. Michael tells us about how he gave some money to a down and out young man he met at a gay hangout in Buenos Aires. He takes a long time to tell the story and when he is done he asks, "What do you think? Was the guy on the up-and-up? Or was I used?"

Distracted during his lengthy story, I'm momentarily bewildered by this anticlimactic punch line. But I have this startling moment of clarity as I suddenly recall a story Jack Kornfield, founder of Spirit Rock meditation center in Fairfax, California, planted in my head years ago. He told the story of a famous Argentine golfer who was coming out of an exclusive golf club. A woman begged him for money to help with her child who was dying and needed medical attention she could not afford. Please, she cried, my child is dying. The golfer's aides begged him to ignore her—she was an imposter, they said. But the golfer handed her $1,000. A few days later the aides indeed found proof positive that the woman had no child and was an imposter. They couldn't wait to tell him the news.

"You mean there is no dying child?" The golfer said.

The aides shook their heads. "No."

"Oh," groaned the golfer, "thank God."

Deb and Michael are silent—either awed or embarrassed for me. But then I see a connection register on Michael's face and I know I am looking at the magnanimous and compassionate spirit of the golfer. There is not a shade of the two officious aides. I feel good to have given him this belief in his own goodness, if not assurance that his young man was on the up-and-up.

We walk home slowly in the thick heat of the night, stopping to gaze inside Palermo's many boutiques. Furniture, clothing, jewelry, the soaring interiors of bistros and bars, it is all objets d'art in hipster Palermo Soho. Cowhide rugs, punky and classic jeans (from Ay Not Dead, Maria Cher, Rapsodia), tweedy plaids, Juana De Arco's textile scraps turned into one-of-a-kind garments, small designers like Lupe's denim jumpers, marine jerseys, canvas ballet slippers, Mishka's pumps, flats, and candy-apple sandals. Deby chose her neighborhood well. When she compliments my glad-rag outfits, I feel I've put something together right.

She herself is a paragon of successful makeovers for women hitting fifty. In 2004, she sold her three-thousand-square-foot home in Oakland, California, and moved to Buenos Aires after her eighteenth trip here. Many of her friends already thought she lived here and occasionally visited the States. On her blog, www.lavidacondeby.com, she describes the transition thus: "I went from being a high-powered computer geek to a tango dancing bed-and-breakfast owner and English teacher."

She suffered a fractured hip in a car accident several months ago and had to stop all activity while she was on the mend. It was a big setback for her dancing, her relationship with local teacher Robert Dentone, and her teaching, but her strong physical state and tough-mindedness pulled her through.

I call her the concierge to the city. She likes to tell her guests where to go—from where to get a decent facelift or tummy tuck to where to dance tango to where to eat good *parrilla*. While tourists flock to Comme Il Faut for tango shoes, she tells her guests about the many other places that charge less and are just as good or better but don't have a French name with such panache. A local daily, *El Clarin,* ran a one-page story on Deby before I met her, and among the many emails she received were four marriage proposals. She prides herself on knowing and dancing with only the crème de la crème (unlike me, who runs through the ranks high and low). At the *milonga* Lo de Celia, she introduces me to eighty-five-year-old Pocho, who adds me to his small handful of dancers. He saves me for the waltzes, the allegro ones, and then spins me in so many dizzying *giros* that I feel the centrifugal force create a vacuum all around us. He boasts how he never took a class, that he learned in the dance halls back when men and women were *damas y caballeros.*

Deby introduces me to Javier and Miriam, who hire English tutors whom they then send out to their clients. They sign me on to start teaching private classes. I run through a few students before I settle on just two—Vicky and Diego, a couple of young computer wizards. They're cool, unmarried (soon to be pregnant), and living with his mom and aunt in a small apartment in the city. They have a Siamese cat named Homer (after *The Simpsons* character). Diego has shoulder-length hair and likes T-shirts with sayings like DON'T BOTHER ME OR I'LL UPPERCASE YOU. They know I dance tango, so one day they present me with a gift, a book called *Che Boludo!* (Hey Asshole!), a lexicon with the *lunfardo* that originated in the tango milieu, as well as Italian hand signs that have infiltrated the Argentine culture. After that gift, I have no worries about showing up at Vicky and Diego's as the teacher who will teach them proper English, even if she is all dolled up for the *milonga*—which is where I head when I leave their home.

If *milongas* are countries, my journal begins to read like a tour brochure, my itinerary marked by men's names. In one week, I cover twelve "countries": La Glorieta, La Nacional, El Beso, Maipu 444, Los Consagrados, La Ideal, Hotel Dandi, Gricel, Español, La Viruta, Salon Canning, La Milonguita. Each *milonga* is followed by the first names of men I danced with, with pithy annotations (choppy style; strong breath; moves like a cloud; hated when he turned my head for me; *divino)*. I'm diligent about keeping track of these details in my journal when I return home, oftentimes early in the morning.

Another sardonic list I keep in the pages of my journal reads Dave, Dan, Alberto, Juan Carlos. I labeled it "would have been" then changed it smugly to "wood bin."

I'm in bed reading a few pages of Chilean author Isabel Allende's *Eva Luna* in the original Spanish. The protagonist, Eva Luna, is a twelve-year-old orphan who's been sent to work cleaning a rich woman's home. In a fit of pent-up anger, she pulls the hair of her surly *patróna* (boss lady) and is forced to live in the streets. It gives me pause to find my very act of frustration mirrored in literature. I have felt such a volatile cocktail of guilt, hurt, anger, and self-recrimination that it's oddly comforting to find it seemingly exalted by high literary form. Rather than feel justified for what we've both done, I focus more on what hurt I have in common with that parentless street urchin.

I lay the book and my journal on my night table and go to sleep, thinking of Dan. I wish I'd been more spontaneously generous with him, like the Argentine golfer who was only concerned that there not be suffering and not that people might be cheating him.

In these manifold *milongas* to which I travel, I meet an old friend who gives me a clue to a shortcut out of this vicious cycle. His name is Eduardo, another *tanguero* from back home. I know his solid carapace well from weekly *milongas* there. He has a tight, intimate *milonguero* style, but with many possibilities for *nuevo* moves that he is fond of trying on his partners—me included. He also dances salsa and Latin. He was born in Panama but grew up, like me, in the "Balkanized" east—Brooklyn's Bedford-Stuyvesant 'hood in his case. Having transcended my own family's low aspirations for females, I felt a bond in our parallel struggles to rise to the top and to follow our passions. From his modest roots, he's become a much-decorated engineer. He sells real estate now. He sticks out like a ruby among rhinestones at *milongas* where the dominant culture is white. He is often in such demand that he has to leave the room to get a break from all the women who want to be *cabeceo*'d by this dark, sensual dancer.

He emails to invite me to meet up at La Nacional, the *milonga* that always feels like a scene out of a David Lynch or Fellini flick. A very handsome man who looks a lot like Tony Curtis, except missing most of his left leg, is here this evening. He dances on metal crutches (no prosthesis) with a beautiful, shapely blond whom I study for signs of manhood (since the last gorgeous blond I saw here was Raquel, the transsexual). As I'm leaving, the man, who has striking hazel eyes, says, "I want to look as happy as you do when I dance." It turns out that he's Puerto Rican but lives in Atlanta, Georgia.

"Well, let's dance next time," I say. And we do, a week later, at Niño Bien. I put my hands on his upper arms and he leads with his chest, pointing with his heart where he wants me to go, as he balances with his hands on the crutches. It's quite a challenge and attempting it I have a greater appreciation for the blond who followed him very well.

Before we head out to our next *milonga* a few days later, I take Eduardo to my favorite Porteña *parrilla*, Cervantes. The swift-moving waiters in white shirts and black vests know me, the rare foreigner. They nod to my regular table. The chatter is strictly *español*—the waiters don't speak any English. The *bife chorizo* or *lomo* is succulent, the Malbec cheap—and some of Mendoza's finest. The food is so copious, the waiters will stop you from ordering too much. They expect you to share entrées—no charge for the extra plates.

I've supped on the fork-tender *peceta* (beef stew with potatoes), juicy pork chops, *tortilla española* (potato frittata), fried calamari, and the Cervantes salad—a rainbow conglomerate of veggies and protein. My bill is never more than ten bucks, wine and tip included.

As Eduardo and I sit eating under the glare of naked lights, between walls of faded green, I get to talking about Dan and how I wish to be free of my hatred toward Eveyln. When I tell him that I still love Dan very much, he says, "Send it out."

That should not sound so novel, but it does. So right there in Cervantes, with Eduardo's support, I send it out, giving it a little nudge over the equator. It doesn't matter whether Dan feels it or not. The fact is that I suddenly feel some upwelling of the lost bliss—a little flutter, the "wings" of hope that Emily Dickinson wrote of, perhaps. It lasts a few seconds. Then passes. Maybe it's the Malbec.

Eduardo recommends I read *The Power of Now,* by Eckhart Tolle. I tell him I'm not interested, thinking it is a businessperson's "how to be rich, spiritual, and happy" book.

"That's fine," Eduardo says, "there's nothing in it you don't already know."

"Well," I retract, swayed by his soft-pedaling, "if I can find a Spanish translation, I'll read it—just to get the new vocabulary."

I find it, *El Poder del Ahora,* the next day in the stacks amid the Greek columns at Ateneo bookstore. Over the course of the rest of my weeks at Deby's, with Roxie by my side, I read the book slowly, absorbing the new vocabulary and the message. Eduardo was right—I know everything in it. Tolle cites the teachings of Buddha and Jesus frequently. But I need to hear it all again and in a different way. In sum: Only this present moment matters. Happiness is a blink away, available to one and all right now. Heaven is here and now, not some mythical hereafter. Jesus (despite the modern-day distortion of his message) and Buddha and other mystics all said so. Dwelling on and agonizing over the past is a trick the ego/mind plays to give itself validity. Yet, we all have a *cuerpo de dolor* (body of pain) due to a past hurt that we were not present for, thus it accumulates and self-perpetuates. Therefore, we need to sit with and resolve that pain. "Time" is our nemesis to spiritual bliss. The future never comes—it's ridiculous to worry about it. Tolle means the artifice of time that we've invented and with which we measure everything with the precision of atomic clocks.

I keep the much-dog-eared book around for a long while, flipping randomly to different passages. It becomes my bible. I recall the blissful feeling I experienced for five easy heartbeats when, sitting across from Eduardo at Cervantes, I'd sent out my message. It was as if I'd put down all my bones only to snap them back up again, just like a dog. Who would I be without them to gnaw on? Tolle notes over and over how the experience of bliss, of "God," cannot be described (though many try) because it is a place of no-mind, of subtraction of intellect, of ego, of conditioning. It's a death of all our artificial constructs of consciousness. Learn to die now, and when the body's time comes it'll be a piece of cake. It's the main reason I practice Zen, which cuts right to the fact of our impermanence. *Great is the matter of birth and death/Life is fleeting/ Gone, gone/Awake, awake/Each one/Don't waste this life* is my other morning chant along with the Leonard Cohen lyrics about a crack in everything.

"The way is without difficulty, strive hard," some Zen sage uttered more than a thousand years ago, summing up the paradox of life and death. Bliss should be as effortless as my tango dancing is. I believe this.

As automatic as breathing.

I think of how my father slowly died from congestive heart failure. My father, the single person most connected to my *cuerpo de dolor*. I wanted him to talk to me more about the experience of dying, but it was clear he didn't want to. And I didn't push back. A devout Catholic all his life (even in the way he sinned and then went to confession), he respected and supported my "reversion" to Zen Buddhism. He knew I spent a lot of time watching my breath. One day in the throes of his sickness, he said to me, "Mia," calling me by my nickname, "I try and try to breathe and I can't get my breath to come." It was endearing and jarring to have him express anxiety. My father, the invincible patriarch of our large family.

"Dad, don't try to breathe," I said, "Just let it come, your breath comes on its own, it's an involuntary action." I watched as he considered, settled into it, and visibly relaxed. Then I added, "If it doesn't come, well, then, you know it's time." He smiled. A year later, on his deathbed, as we recited together "Abou Ben Adhem," a poem he loved about a God-fearing Indian, he remembered this.

We sat him up one day on a sofa and he said, "It's still working . . . if I relax . . . I can breathe the way you taught me to . . . "

"Good, Dad, just keep relaxing," I told him. We both knew the batteries to his heart were on their last charge.

It's evening now. Twilight time. I move *El Poder del Ahora* onto my small bookshelf, next to all my other bibles du jour, signifying that I've absorbed its message for the time being. I strip down to the skin and put on my most minimalist dress. It's black, the color of funerals, of mourning, the color of most attire worn in tango. Yet, it's that dark backdrop that allows tango to embody the presence of all colors, a prism through which dancers constellate every hue and nuance of their inner beauty to add up to white. To date, a space I whimsically call *tangolandia,* whose coordinates are somewhere inside my mind and body at dance, is the only place wherein I can effortlessly let go of the artifice of time, of ego, of intellect, of hate. Where I can lose consciousness and yet be so extraordinarily aware.

Chapter 16

Turning Points

Don't just do something, sit there.

—*Zen saying*

It is Día de la Virgen, a Catholic feast day of the Blessed Virgin and an important national holiday in Argentina. The *subte* is not running yet. It's 8 AM and I'm forced to catch a taxi to Junin 339, where Templo Serena Alegría is located. There I will meet my meditation group and we'll head into the nearby country for a few days' retreat.

On Tuesday or Thursday evenings for the past couple of months I have been hanging my *rakusu* around my neck and heading to the Temple of Serene Happiness to sit *zazen*. The group, usually about a dozen strong, is headed by Monk Ricardo Dokyu Gabriel. He's forty-eight, has studied in Brazil and Japan, and is trained in oriental medicine, shiatsu, and acupuncture. He teaches Soto Zen, the kind I practiced in San Francisco, which is usually distinguished from Rinzai Zen by its affinity for gentle gradual awakening.

Serena Alegría is inside a medium-size apartment on the ninth floor in the Once, a barrio that's lively with the young blood of college students. As Ricardo leads us through a half hour of stretching exercises, I often admire the pink sky of sunset over the city outside his window. I recall the pink sky of sunrise I'd see while chanting in the Buddha Hall in San Francisco. I feel good connecting with another urban tribe—other than *milongueros*. I've missed my Zen refuge in San Francisco. It was my own personal version of the drunk tank—a place to go when I felt too intoxicated with self-made delusions. I am glad to have found Ricardo's group. My mind and body need the stillness to complement the motion of my tango practice.

When we're done stretching, we each grab a *zafu*. We line up facing the blank white wall. We sit silent, eyes open, gaze held down at 45 degrees.

The room's stillness belies what I take as an article of faith now: All our minds are filling that empty space in front of us with a nonstop reel of thoughts and images. A major com-motion picture.

I sit in half lotus with my butt at the very edge of the cushion. For a few minutes I keep my palms down on my knees, my arms and spine a tripod of balance. When I feel my spine is ready to hold me upright, I bring my hands together in the mudra—left hand resting in right palm, thumbs forming a gentle drawbridge. I hold the mudra softly to my pelvis, locus of the second chakra, seat of rebirth. This position is my *salida,* as in tango, my exit of one time for another. A signal to enter the dance of no time.

Whether positioning my butt at the edge of a cushion or my torso against another torso, I enter a similar psychic space. In both cases, my mind seeks to empty, to not think, as effortless as water seeking its level. In both cases, I let my breath find its rhythm. (Like I told my dying father, if it doesn't come on its own, well, that's all, folks.) More often than not, as soon as I'm still, I'm amazed to feel how hard my heart has been pounding. It steadies as I sit. In both tango and meditation, my brain waves slow to an alpha state, fourteen to seven cycles per second. I have a long ways to go before they reach the Delta state of enlightenment, four to one cycles per second.

This morning I am doing tango and meditation almost back to back with about five hours between the two. I was at La Ideal until 3 AM helping Ángel and other *amigas* polish off two bottles of champagne. I wore my ragged-hem, strapless white dress (purchased for $15 in the Amargo barrio) and scuffed gold cloth heels. It was so hot—hard to believe Christmas is less than two weeks away. Someone had snapped a photo of me and Ángel striking a classic tango pose, my leg wrapped around his. Normally I hate having my picture taken. I never like the way I look in photos. But this time, as I studied my face in the window frame of the digital camera, I saw something I had never seen in myself before: the essence of *samādhi*—Sanskrit for "oneness with all," the state we all aspire to. The photo was taken before I touched the champagne.

Now I struggle with the usual physiological effects of alcohol and lack of sleep. Just my luck to get a chatty *taxista*. He must've drunk two *café dobles muy fuertes*.

"Today is the Feast of the Virgin, Argentina's patron saint," he announces.

"Uh-huh," I say. "*Sí, sí.*" I'm well versed enough to know that December 8 is the Feast of the Immaculate Conception, one of six holy days of obligation. It celebrates Mary's having conceived without original sin. I like to call it the Immaculate Concept. It's been exactly one year since I ceased keeping my relationship with Dan immaculate.

"What's your country?" he asks.

"United States."

"What's your country's patron saint?"

"Patron saint? Oh no, we don't have one. We have separation of church and state."

"*Clarooo*," he says with that intonation that means, *Of course, stupid.* "So do we, *más o menos* [more or less], but you have to have a patron. Every country has one. Ours," he says proudly, "is the Blessed Virgin."

"No, I'm sorry, we have no saints to guide us," I conclude, my brain exhausted by this short exercise.

"You must."

I can see he's not going to give up. "El Diablo," I say, which ends the conversation.

I'm relieved when we reach my stop, Junin Street.

⁕

Nineteen of us greet each other with kisses on the cheek and mill around waiting for our van to shuttle us to Vicente Casares, the countryside southwest of Buenos Aires. I am the only non-Argentine in the group. In the van, I lean against the window and sleep off the champagne while they chat all the way there.

With this group, I will be sitting my first Rohatsu *sesshin* in Latin America. Rohatsu means "eighth day of the twelfth lunar month," thus Rohatsu *sesshins*, which may be happening all over the world at this time, take place in early December. It commemorates Buddha's enlightenment, when he realized the Middle Way—the elusive sweet spot between asceticism and overindulgence—and attained full liberation under the bodhi tree. *Sesshin* is Japanese for "mind training." I have participated in many Rohatsus in San Francisco. They generally last seven days and are pretty rigorous, considering you "do nothing, just sit there." You rise at 5 AM and sit many forty-minute periods of *zazen* throughout the day until 9:30 PM. All but necessary speech is avoided. You eat your meals from special *oryoki* bowls in the *zendo*, cross-legged on your cushion. If you like forms and rituals—bows, incense, candles, gongs, bells, and chanting—as I do, it's very beautiful. It's also exhausting. It's also cleansing.

I sat my first *sesshin* in 1991, right after I met Dan. We were just starting to get involved, and in my strange but typical way, I wanted to trump one difficulty—entering an intimate relationship—with another. I had run several full and half marathons and completed several Olympic-distance triathlons. I could move to beat the race against any and all anxiety, but being still, the no-race, turned out to be a far greater challenge than any 26.2 miles I'd ever run.

We arrive midmorning at the retreat center in Vicente Casares. There are eight women, and we move to find our dorm and plop our packs and sleeping bags down. I take a top bunk. I know I'll sleep like the dead no matter what condition the mattress is in.

There are many spirits in the place—none more bothersome than my own. It's an old Jesuit mission from the 1800s now owned by a Korean couple who rent the space out to various groups. They are Christian leaders, and their staged annual-report-style photos hang everywhere.

It's a very cheap retreat, and now, when I see the state of disrepair, I understand why. There is no hot water. But it's very warm—in the high 80s—and humid. Cold showers are welcome. Cobwebs and bugs inhabit corners and the rafters of the high ceilings. Walls are chipped, peeling, and stained. The stone hallway is uneven and warped from settling. Electrical fixtures look like fire hazards. Windows are cracked and one shatters upon the touch of someone's hand.

Still, by the second hour there, because of the surroundings and the good energy of my fellow Zennites, this dilapidated place out in the country, far from the big city, feels like paradise.

The grounds are sprawling, lush, overgrown, sweet-smelling meadows. There are horses, frisky dogs, a braying donkey, some tall evergreens, and many old deciduous trees. Old sheds and other outbuildings are spread around. During breaks, many of us sit under the shade of the trees or on the mission's stone steps and watch the birds flying and swooping from trees. One species in particular reminds me of the hawks in my dreams of Dan and me.

Christina, the *tenzo*, or cook, who speaks some English, tells me they are *chimangos*, related to falcons. They're beautiful, cream- and russet-colored, and four of them fly low and close, as if teasing us. On our second day, when a great blue heron flies overhead, even the other birds seem calmed, cowed, or awed.

Ricardo's Rohatsu will last only three days for the mere fact that most Argentines cannot afford the luxury of taking too much time off of work. Although we rise at 4:30 each morning, it is not nearly as rigorous as some of the Rohatsus I've done that attract up to one hundred participants, all of whom are given various jobs, such as cooking, serving, washing dishes, hitting gongs, lighting incense, and such. We are only nineteen, including Ricardo, who does everything from ringing all the bells to hitting the wooden mallets to giving the daily dharma talk. We eat our meals sitting in chairs at a long table—instead of in the *zendo*. We talk and laugh when not in the *zendo*. We eat the most luxurious desserts at teatime.

In addition to nearly a dozen seven-day Rohatsus, I've done many shorter *sesshins* over the years. Almost all of them follow the same template of mental progression (which mirror the five stages of dying as defined by the late Elisabeth Kübler-Ross):

- Denial—Whose idea was this? I do not belong here in this *zendo*. I do not have issues to work on or think about.
- Anger—I'm "trapped." I've been lured here against my will.
- Bargaining—Okay, I'll sit just one day, hour, minute, and I'm out of here. Okay?

- Depression—I realize the overriding fact that all in life is impermanent and how there is no difference in life on the cushion or off the cushion.
- Acceptance—I feel serene. I wish this *sesshin* would never end. My body has adjusted to the rhythms and feels pampered by the slightest gift, one half-dollar-size sugar cookie, at teatime. My small mind has settled down and Big Mind holds sway. I feel so connected to the people sitting around me, whose little tics annoyed the hell out of me the first day.

I have had only one sitting in which I never got out of the denial phase and actually left and went home on some trumped-up excuse. Mostly, I get through all stages with varying degrees of grace (or lack thereof).

These three days are some of the most difficult I have ever sat, and I am perpetually awaiting the bell that signals the end of a period. Deep into each period of sitting I'm keenly aware of my own venom. Venom is a snake's response to fear of a threat, real or imagined.

My paranoia runs wild and deep.

What my mind projects on the speckled, faded wall in front of me are scenes from a hypothetical "Day in Court," starring me, the perpetrator, and Evelyn, the victim. I won't admit to feeling remorse for what I've done. She interprets this as evidence that I intend to kill her. Hearing dates are set, jurors are chosen, character witnesses are called. Mine line up around the block. She has only three, two of whom are her daughters. She shows up with a surgical mask over her mouth.

Counsel: Did you or did you not on the twenty-third day of August, 2006, in San Francisco Aquatic Park, pull the hair of the victim?

Me: I pulled it. I pulled it good.

Judge: Just answer the question.

Me: Yes, your honor.

Counsel: Did you or did you not say you wished to kill the victim?

Me: Well, yes, no . . . I don't remember . . . If I said "kill" it was the texture and color of a feeling, not intent. Certainly . . .

Dan is called in as a witness. But he pleads the fifth, doesn't want to take sides. He risks jail time. Everything goes black here. I'm unable to stop the continuous loop of my mind.

Why am I forgoing three nights of tango dancing to feel so lousy? This thought gives rise to a second brand of venom, picking on Self, which gives rise to infinite brands of venom. Venom begets venom. I feel consumed by my hatred of Eveyln. Only the slimmest margin of my mind believes that sitting here in the dark mentally out of control is doing me any good. I'm at once very miserable and very reassured. I know this process well. This is how it works. This is why *many are called but few are chosen* to Zen meditation. Maybe it's a homeopathic remedy—fight suffering with suffering. I call it "guided depression" sometimes, this space where I'm free to indulge my own dark side without doing harm to myself or anyone else.

I stare at the wall and try to quiet my mind by focusing on the black spots some careless paint-wielding cleric left long ago for my therapeutic use. If there are any Jesuit souls here caught between worlds they're probably scared witless by my demons . . . *Black spots, black spots, black spots,* I power-meditate . . . At last Ricardo rings the bell. We can get up and move.

We turn around and sit facing into the room to chant the Heart Sutra, or Prajna Paramita. I feel tears well in my eyes. They are not tears of powerlessness, but of gratitude. My foreign tongue blends harmoniously with those of my fellow Argentines in this old Japanese idiom—*kan ji zai bo-satso gyo/jin han nya ha ra mi ta.*

We hum like bees. I can almost hear the same buzzing far, far away in my home "hive." Possibly at this exact moment, my Zen friends and teachers are wrapping their tongues, hearts, and minds around the same vocal sounds at another Rohatsu *sesshin.*

My home Zen Center is named Beginner's Mind Temple after a basic teaching of founder Suzuki Roshi, who asserts that in the mind of the expert there are very few possibilities, while in the mind of the beginner there are an infinite number. Thus, as we chant, I try to return to my beginner's mind, that place where bliss is possible from myriad directions. I have only to let go of being an expert at the reasons why I need to suffer. *Dharma gates are boundless,* Buddhists also chant, and I know there is an invisible gate nearby that I am free to step through.

For now that gate is the doorway to the dining room for communion with my fellow meditators. Sitting meditation wears me out and gives me a huge appetite. I am starved for every meal, all delicious vegetarian compositions with variations of pasta, rice, quinoa, sautéed fresh vegetables. *These people know how to live,* I think, *especially when it comes to teatime.*

At about 3 PM, we take tea indulgently out in the meadow. We arrange chairs in a circle under a tree around a table with pitchers of melon water, herbal infusions, and a huge platter of freshly baked brownies and apple–ricotta cheese pastry. There is enough for each of us to have three big portions of dessert. In my *zendo* in San Francisco we're given but one cookie with tea. In the past it's reminded me of the well-known Zen parable of the man who is being chased by a tiger. He runs for his life and comes to a cliff. He hangs there by the limb of a small tree. The tiger approaches. A field mouse begins to gnaw at the tree's branch. Alas, he sees a single strawberry hanging from another bush over the cliff edge. One solitary piece of fruit, all ripe and ready to be eaten, within his reach. Even before he snatches it, he knows it will be the best berry of his life. I've always cherished the idea of how he lives a full lifetime in a matter of minutes. Even though there's plenty of dessert here for me, I savor it all with the zest of that man who knows death is imminent. In the grand scheme, I've got but a little more time than he. Still, the point is to savor each fruit of life like it's your last. Therein lies Heaven.

Although some of the conversation among the Argentines eludes me, I laugh and chatter along with the group. My favorite part is when Monk Ricardo calls for our attention and reads from an official document. Apparently, Daniel, one of the men in our group, is a human rights worker and has petitioned the Argentine government to make the full moon in May (already International Full Moon day) an official Buddhist holiday. The legislation is already moving through the bicameral government, the Senate and Chamber of Deputies, and will be official in a month or less. I misunderstand and think that every full moon will be a holiday, which prompts laughs from the group and the assertion that I have the true Latina Americana *espíritu*.

There is more sitting in silence with more "loud" discomfort and rumblings arising from my aversions. I do finally make it to the acceptance phase by day three, though not without struggle. What I accept is that no one—not Dan, not Evelyn, not any of my past encounters—can make me suffer. Only I can. This does not automatically end my suffering. But it lifts a huge weight, having only one person to blame, and it invites a sense of power. I don't yet understand that power. But I know it has a lot to do with finding my way back to beginner's mind and dropping everything I think I know about my suffering.

I meditate on a quote from Jorge Luis Borges that I came across at an exhibit of his life in the Galería Pacífico: *"Cuando me siento desdichado, pienso en la muerte, es el consuelo que tengo, el saber que no voy a seguir siendo, el saber que voy a dejar de ser."* (When I feel unfortunate, I think about death, it's the consolation I have, the knowledge that I will not go on being, the knowledge that I'll cease to be.)

I wish we didn't have to leave this mission, a place where I've allowed myself to confront my demons head on. I could live out my days, however many or few, and die happy here. I admit that I might find it hard to enter that dark meditation room where I have to face my unadorned Self. But the rest of the place, even with the bat in the rafters at night, the mosquitoes, and the many leaf-cutter ants, feels like a pit stop on the way to Heaven this last day.

Our final teatime is as lighthearted and delicious as the first. We share what has to be the sweetest foodstuff in the world—jelly rolls filled with *dulce de leche*. This one that I'm eating now, just made in the mission kitchen, is exceptionally ambrosial and oozes russet-colored, thick, and custardy onto my fingers. After all the restraint we've been practicing, I let myself go for a second huge slice, licking and licking my paws clean like a cat.

As always when I finish a *sesshin*, I have this wonderful sense of having been cleansed, even if the feeling only lasts for a day or so. But that's okay. I have found a new safe haven for tune-ups back in Buenos Aires: Serena Alegría Temple, where I will sit and sit again and again among these people whose still presence offers unimaginable support to my doing so.

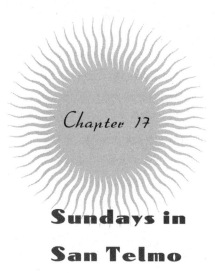

Chapter 17

Sundays in
San Telmo

Take care of things, and they will take care of you.

—*Suzuki Roshi*

Six of us have shown up this Sunday afternoon at Marcela's place in San Telmo, where weekly gatherings have become somewhat of a ritual of late. Her apartment on Chacabuco Street is a small but cozy temporary rental. By pure chance, no men have shown up this week, so we waste no time cutting loose from mixed-company protocol. In under a half hour I already know who can't go too long without sex or she becomes crazy; they know who (ahem) among us is abstaining for a year—maybe.

Marcela and her friend Sarah affirm how much Argentine men love to look, one of the harmless pastimes accepted, and often even embraced, by Argentine women. Elizabeth, a six-foot-tall beauty who reminds me of the lanky flappers of the Roaring Twenties, is visiting Marcela and her daughter, Carolina, whom she knows from New York. As we sit around drinking, eating, and talking, I'm reminded of the fun gab sessions we have when I get to hang out with my sisters—Terry, Grace, Lisa, Tina, and Donna—without our four brothers around.

Back in the apartment, we sprawl over couch and chairs as Marcela fills our glasses with Malbec. "¡A las mujeres!" the six of us toast.

"You look thinner than ever," Marcela says to me. "Have you lost weight?"

"No, I'm the same," I say. "Look who's talking, *flaquita,*" I hasten to add. Marcela is barely bigger than me.

I can see Marcela doesn't believe me. She disappears into her tiny kitchen and returns with platters heaped with fettuccine under a bolognese sauce made with tender Argentine *bolo lomo* and a savory rice-vegetable dish. The rap session is mostly in Castellano. Sometimes I am the translator between Polish-born Julia, who is one of Carolina's New York friends, and Marcela and Sarah, who speak very little English.

Sarah and Marcela, like so many Argentine women, endearingly inquire about how Julia and I have experienced the Argentine men. They want to know if there's been any maltreatment, anything that they might be able to clear up for us about the nature of the men here. We both assure them that we've encountered mainly respect.

Then I think of the young man who called me *"churro,"* a slang term for beautiful. I just smiled at him, envisioning the long, sweet donutlike dessert I've enjoyed mostly at football stadiums and baseball parks. Then there was a guy in Galería Pacífico. I felt the heat of a body an inch behind me. He breathed into my ear and muttered a string of obscene phrases—too fast to catch. The gallery was empty but for us. I turned, a bit intimidated, but curious, too. "What'd you say?" I really wanted to know. "You say that again, you, this time *despacio.*" He laughed and lurched forward to touch me. *"¡No me toques!"* I pulled away. *"¿Qué dijiste? Dime otra vez, más despacio."* I may as well have been talking to a dog the way I was handling the situation. Repeat! Do it again! Slower this time! He could've acted out his prurient interest with no one around, but my aggressive curiosity scared him off. "You don't need to know what I said," he laughed nervously, backing away under my overzealous stare. "Say it again." How's that for a creative way to get rid of unwanted attention?

Certainly, though, like most women, I've paid my dues with horrible, unwanted attention from men during travels. From butt grabbing and pinches in Italy to nerve-racking leering and touching in Spain to the masturbating driver in southern France. (This last one happened while hitchhiking with a friend. I was able to push her out the door, grab both our backpacks from his backseat, and roll out with her—Annie Oakley style—all in the quick seconds of coming to a halt at a stop sign.) I can't say I miss that kind of attention, which most often stems from a place of deep ignorance. And though now I can look on some of the more subtle calls and stares with more patience and understanding of cultural differences, the men who harass women have no idea what it feels like. Some of them might take a lesson from the elderly man who stopped to admire my yoga poses in the park a week ago. I thanked him for his compliments, and he moved on smilingly, respectful of my solitude.

⚜

Inevitably, the girls and I come to dishing the dirt about the *milongas*. We have our golden boys—Ángel, Osvaldo, Roberto—who can do no wrong. And then there are the bad boys, and those are the ones who get the lengthy reports. From the Buddhist view of "right speech," this is all babble, useless, idle, potentially harmful. But I issue myself a pardon. If girls just wanna have fun and the speech stays between four walls . . . never mind, I'll acknowledge it's wrong and just go to confession later. Just like in my good ol' Catholic schoolgirl days.

At the mention of the name Jaime, Marcela says, *"Le odio,"* which makes us laugh because it's so to the point, and because those four strong syllables, meaning "I hate him," are said in such a sweet voice. Dirt I would have never guessed true of him comes up, especially a few details about how he treated an ex-lover. It makes me uncomfortable to hear these things about a man I dance with. But if there is a time for everything, perhaps there's a time to not blindly accept all that's on the surface. Then Marcela proceeds to do a duck-walk imitation of how he dances. She captures his jarring lead spot-on. We're hysterical.

Even those we profess to love have some hidden flaws we handily expose. Marcela, Julia, and I all express our enjoyment of dancing with Octavio, a lawyer. Comparing notes, we learn that he feeds us all the same line when we ask where he learned to dance: "From the gods."

"No me diga," I say, "I believed him."

"He's so full of himself," says Marcela.

"Oh, *no me diga,*" I say again. I love this phrase, the equivalent of our "say it ain't so." "I've always thought so highly of him."

"Yes, *es buena persona,*" she agrees, "but he always waits for the last song in a *tanda* to invite me to dance."

"Me, too, come to think of it," I say. We all concur, and diagnose him: He's an agitated person, always jumping around, prowling the aisles, eyes out searching the crowd for someone better, running to the bathroom to change shirts (when one gets too sweaty). I learn Octavio is married and a *mujeriego* (womanizer), which disappoints me. But it pleases me that he's never come on to me, meaning he's only interested in my dancing—an integrity I'll settle for. Besides, skirt-chasing in the *milonga* is an accepted norm here. Julia says he has asked her out, but only after she made an overture, not knowing he was married.

"His car is dirty," says Marcela.

"No, it's clean," says Julia, "but he did wear the same shirt two days in a row."

"Maybe he didn't go home that night," I suggest. "Different *chisme,* please." I feel bored by the particulars, even though I wouldn't turn down getting the goods on some of the other men we dance with.

Marcela brings on the dessert—a huge, dense brownie cake and her infamous flan. It feels fitting to dish some sweets with the dirt. The conversation turns to Julia, who recently got in a fight with her boyfriend Hector.

"You made up yet?" Marcela asks.

"Tonight," she says, "we're gonna talk."

"*Es peligroso*" ("He's dangerous"), Marcela flatly says as she starts serving. Julia has only started seeing Hector a couple of weeks ago. He left the *milonga* on Thursday night in a fit of jealousy, which we all witnessed, because she kissed her dance teacher hello and not him.

"I'm setting a boundary," says Julia. "He can't come to *milongas* with me."

But Sarah and Marcela shake their heads. They have zero tolerance for his behavior and strongly advise she move on. They look to me for reinforcement. I say I agree, but that Julia's a big girl and has to make up her own mind. Clearly, Julia doesn't want to quit the guy yet. Also, and maybe this is obtuse, but I'm not reading danger in Hector's gestures, only hot blood and abandonment issues.

"Furthermore," says a defensive Julia, "I'm telling him he has to do something about that behavior—see a *psicóloga...*" We all turn to Sarah, the psychologist in the room. It's all quite funny, too, because Hector is a psychologist himself, and Julia's recommendation is that he see a female *psicóloga*.

I'm enraptured when Sarah and Marcela start talking psychoanalysis, proudly asserting that Argentina may be the world's most analyzed nation. Sarah says, "It's because we live in a society with so many rules and dogmas from the outside—religion, the military—we need something to guide us from within." It's an interesting connection in a country where religion and military have had enormous, sometimes detrimental, influence.

The Argentine model for analysis, Sarah says, comes from Europe, mainly France (Jacques Lacan, a neo-Freudian). She stops short of calling the therapy in the United States shallow, but says of our model, "They just want to fix a problem quickly."

Like cowboys with guns in their holsters, she says, which makes me laugh.

Even as a student of Zen, devoted to the experiential, I think there's room for both types of therapy. But I am attracted to the soul-searching societies, maybe because they spawn the best cafés and bookstores—centers for contemplating everything from *Is God dead?* to *Is tango dead?* And I gotta love a country where the most popular film director is Woody Allen, Mr. Psychoanalysis himself. He ranks higher up than Steven Spielberg here.

Marcela, who dove headfirst into married life at the tender age of sixteen, says eloquently, "We need analysis to address existential questions—what is the meaning of life, what do we want? We all have one burning question we want to answer. For me it's why do I end up feeling the same type of suffering with everyone."

Suffering is major currency for Zen Buddhism, so I see an opening, but I can't compose sentences fast enough. Coincidentally, Sarah is on to the onion analogy, a favorite of Zennites. "With psychoanalysis, you slowly peel away layer after layer, until you get to a nucleus." I adamantly want to differ—I would counter that there are evermore layers, and not even a nucleus. But my tongue and brain need more training to uncover the layers I'd love to be able to get into here, and so I stay quiet.

Besides, it's past dark and the most important subject of the night comes up. Dancing in the square, anyone? Yes, and with that we're up and on our way faster that you can say "*Vamos.*"

We are on our way to Plaza Dorrego. We stroll by the home of Mercedes, an architect who's just renovated her home and kept much of its 1880s Spanish colonial style intact. She's exposed the original wood beams and crumbling brick masonry but added ultramodern steel enforcements. The floors are stone or wood and the kitchen floor has Plexiglas panels through which you look down on a wine cellar. She has huge fireplaces. There is an inner courtyard, garden, and pool.

I notice a thick slab of rare *bife chorizo* that lingers on her indoor *asado* over cold gray ashes the way a stale croissant might in France, or a slice of cold pizza in Italy—waiting to be someone's snack later on.

Mercedes's home is big and sometimes *milongas* spontaneously happen here. But this evening we're there to pick up her and her friend, Liliana Belfiore ("the most famous dancer in Buenos Aires," says Marcela), to join us in our rendezvous to the plaza three blocks away. Liliana is a prima ballerina, formerly with the Teatro Colón, who now dances show tango and ballet. She is short and surprisingly thick around the middle for a dancer. She danced with the late Nureyev at Lincoln Center. Later that night she confides, "People tell me I look good, but I don't feel good inside." She has a beautiful face, but the excess weight holds some unhappiness, which I guess to be the stress and strain of an accomplished artist adjusting to middle age (she's fifty-six years old). But when I see her dance, especially the *chacarera,* so in tune with the music and her partner, the unhappiness I perceived earlier vanishes. She is radiant.

"Look, there's Osvaldo and Coca," someone says. They are our tango-dancing elders and are adored by everyone everywhere. Wiry Osvaldo, with his charming caved-in smile; Coca, who has the good-natured demeanor of an Italian grandmother. They must live in San Telmo, as I've seen them in the plaza a lot. Osvaldo always plants a passionate kiss on Coca's lips when they're done dancing, very much like my father loved to do to my mother in public.

The stars begin to come out. The CD player occasionally skips and the dancers shout, *"Mata el DJ!"* ("Kill the DJ!") About a hundred people dance or sit on the stone wall that borders the dance area along one side or at the outdoor tables that belong to the various restaurants that surround the plaza. I have my déjà vu experience that I've had repeatedly since my first day here. I've felt it time and again, whether it's because Buenos Aires is situated on the Atlantic Ocean like New Jersey and has tons of Italians, or because Marcela looks like one of my sisters. Maybe all it is is tango. Regardless, I feels as if I am one of the villagers and that I have been coming to this square for a hundred years.

Marcela, who lived in many places around the world when she was married, is telling me of the Australians who had the audacity to think Argentina was the end of the earth. For her, her barrio is the center of the world.

"For me, too, Marcela," I say. In my best-rehearsed Castellano accent, I tell her how grateful I am that she invites me to her home, to meet her friends, to hang out like this. She tells me it's not necessary to thank her, that it's a pleasure to have me. *"Adémas,"* she smiles, *"te quiero."*

"I love you, too," I reply with the ease and sincerity of speaking to one of my sisters. I feel such gratefulness for all of this before me. It has come to me free of effort, without any wild searching. It reinforces my Zen and tango precept to let go of looking and accept what's offered—in this case, a true-blue girlfriend, her professed love, a place to call home. With this thought my heart waltzes up through the starry night in time to the Biagi *vals* the DJ is playing, the one in which the violins, like my heartstrings, go higher and higher, getting happier and happier until they touch the sky and cascade back down to earth.

Chapter 18

Tango Rapture

"The stillness shall be the dancing and the darkness the light."
—*"East Coker," T. S. Eliot*

It's early in the evening of Nochebuena—Christmas Eve—and I'm walking the eerily empty streets of Buenos Aires. It's as if the city has downed tranquilizers en masse—it feels like Manhattan after a blizzard when no cars are out. Every self-respecting Argentine is at home with *la familia*. As I marvel at the quietude of the normally frenetic streets, I think how Christmastime has been a breeze to get through so far, a blessing after how hard Thanksgiving was.

I'm on my way to Carmen's apartment on Mancilla Street for a brief exchange of cheer. Carmen greets me at the door to her building, and we take the elevator to the eighth floor, where her small, uncluttered apartment is warmly lit.

My Carmencita has no contact with her *familia*. It's not a subject she likes to talk about, so I don't know the details. I've gathered that it's because they are rigid and Old World—and, in part, because they reject her chosen path as a healer and yoga instructor. I know all I need to know about Carmen, though, who is such a Good Samaritan, always helping others—she possibly even saved the life of a man going into cardiac arrest on a bus once with her knowledge of CPR. I love having someone who is so selfless in my life. I wonder how it's possible her family could not.

"This is awful. You must make peace with them—blood feuds are bad for your health," I tell her, speaking from pure Sicilian passion.

"I am at peace with them. If they want to reach me, they are free."

Her little place where she teaches people to release their pain is full of *buena onda* (good vibes), and I realize that this is true. She'd let them back in her life if they reached out to her.

She has Frank Sinatra playing softly in the background. She hands me my present, a ribboned scroll of paper, and before I even open it tears are streaming down my face. Frank sings "Try a Little Tenderness," a song on a set of tapes from the crooner's Capitol years, Dan's first Christmas gift to me long ago. I unfurl my gift to read "13 *lineas para vivir*" ("13 lines to live"), written by Colombian author Gabriel García Márquez. The first two:

Te quiero no por quien eres,
Sino por quien soy cuando estoy contigo

(I love you not for who you are
But for who I am when I am with you)

I'm most touched by these two lines in particular. It is one of
the most concrete pieces I've ever read by this writer of magical
realism. I paste it in my journal and will read it daily. Before sending
me off into the solitary night, Carmen gives me a bar of Argentina's
traditional holiday candy, Mantecol, a sweet similar to halvah, but
made from ground peanuts instead of sesame seeds. It will quickly
become my favorite local treat and energy food.

Back home at the Pink Palace I receive one other Christmas
present, a gift of initiation. Deby gives me a pair of pink panties. At
first I think it's because pink is her favorite color. But then I realize
that I've never seen a city so full of pastel pink underpants. They
decorate store windows more than the traditional red and green
during Yuletide. I learn it's a widespread ritual for women to give
each other pink *bombachas*. No one can tell me why this is so, but
it has a long history that apparently comes from Spain. So, perhaps
alongside thousands of women across the city, I wear *bombachas
rosas* proudly on Nochebuena.

The week after Christmas flies by, and although I've felt quite at
home in the Pink Palace, it's New Year's Day and time to move again.
This time I shed no tears. But poor Roxie may! She is so agitated to
see me packing up, she follows at my heels until Deby corrals her

and I close my bedroom door. I've never been this close to any dog, let alone a pit bull. I know we'll miss each other.

At 41 degrees centigrade (that's 105.8 Fahrenheit, folks), this feels like the hottest day of the year. As I pack my suitcases, I think how we dry-roasted last night in a blitzkrieg of fireworks that rang in the New Year with clouds of smoke over every corner of the city. I've never seen such unchecked launching of "artificial fire" in the States, though I was fortunate enough to have witnessed something similar last year in Prague, where I was visiting my brother Jim, who lives there. These two New Years' spectacles lead me to conclude that having survived dictators correlates with an urgent need for excessive pyrotechnic celebrations. As I watched the booming sparks spread out across the night skyline from Deby's balcony, I realized that I have never felt so relieved to have a year behind me.

Happy is what I feel as I cross town in a taxi with my five suitcases in tow. I love that it's summer in January here, and that I can expose a lot of skin and wear sandals and halter tops day and night—something that would lead to serious hypothermia during San Francisco's summer months. The heat wallops me as I step with my five bags from the air-conditioned taxi at 2599 French, an auspiciously named street in the Recoleta barrio. I take it as a nod to my lifetime as a Francophile. I am renting the eighth-floor apartment from Irina Larose, a tango dancer who lives in San Francisco. The apartment she owns is a sparsely furnished one-bedroom that has no air-conditioning and no TV, for which I'm relieved. It's about five hundred square feet, bright and airy. Its finest assets are a blond hardwood floor and two small balconies, one off the living/dining area, one off the bedroom. I keep their glass doors wide open day and night, and along with the two ceiling fans it creates that breezy living-in-the-outdoors feeling I covet. My surroundings are soothing: the sights and sounds of busy neighbors' lives in surrounding high-rises. I'm alone but not lonely.

⚜

I'm happy to be living alone again. I am happy even during the day. Even outside the circle of tango. Not just the skin-deep happy that I put on for social settings. It's the deep contentment I found as a quiet child who loved her own company. It's the "zone" or "flow" of the artist and creator. My "medicines" are working.

I mark the commencement of my own awareness of this sea change with that spontaneous photo of me with Ángel in tango repose, my white dress bleeding into his black suit like the yin-yang sign. I don't like photos of myself, but I've studied beyond the call of vanity this electronic image of me—the one I call "tango rapture."

Having *seen* in it my rapture for the first time, I was flooded with this thought: *If I can look that blissful, I can feel that blissful.* I've been set on this belief that only tango could allow me the experience of such bliss, but something has been moving and turning—perhaps since Thanksgiving, when my misery hit rock bottom and the choice was for me to stay there or climb up and out. Over the past month I've begun to realize that the golden center I find so easily in tango is available to me always.

Although I have been taught to sit meditation without a "gaining attitude," I know from years of study that, paradoxically, there is a goal to *zazen:* the ending of suffering. The way to end it is through removal of the major hindrances to joy: greed (or clinging, grasping), delusion (or lying, or denying), and the one I know all too well, hate (or aversion). It's this last one I can feel wearing down, reaching the end of its life span, and melting away to reveal what's always there, my rapture.

Not everyone subscribes to this subtractionist belief. Most of us go through life thinking we need to *add*, to *get* just one more thing, person, job, or whatever, and we'll be content. But I believe that somewhere within me I already know all there is to know about my own complete happiness and how to end my suffering. And it's right where I stand or sit; I needn't go off to faraway places. This lifelong process of removing the obstructions is what it's all about for me.

When I began to study tango, unconsciously perhaps, arrogantly maybe, I brought this concept with me: *I already know all there is to know about tango.* Tango, like bliss, was in my body. Every *body* has got tango. I understood that all I had to do was stay out of my own way. In other words, I had to *unlearn* things—like anticipation, thinking, desiring, judging, comparing—and just be present in my body.

After I had the basic steps of tango in my muscle memory (let's call this "knowledge"), I understood that what I needed most was to let the dance happen (let's call this "wisdom"), not try to make it happen. I have danced most of my life, and I have never met a dance like tango, a dance that has more to do with mind than body and yet which so unifies both mind and body wisdom—something that's so split in our culture.

Everybody's got tango—as well as bliss—in her or his body. I have seen a lot of anxiety among tango dancers for whom tango feels like religion—but one of those major world religions that allege we humans are wretched and deficient. Thus they constantly feel there is something they must *get* to really have the dance. I watch them learn steps and technique, acquire knowledge, and continue to suffer. They are hard on themselves, critical, self-negating. (This occasionally leads to sparks between dancers at times when one or the other projects their deficient feeling on their partners—just like in real life.) But tango, like Zen, is experiential, and I can't tell anyone to see it my way.

Hugo, one of my favorite dance partners, notices how much I laugh while I'm dancing. "You're laughing again, why are you always laughing?" *I'm the laughing Buddha,* I've thought. *Or the goddess of this galaxy.* But I don't tell him this. I couldn't begin to explain my rapture, that it's about feeling that *I* am gone and just tango and bliss remain before him. For simplicity's sake, I tell Hugo that dancing tango with him makes me happy—and this in turn makes him happy.

I have no sense of failure connected to tango, nor do I have a sense of accomplishment. In this way, it's as near a divine experience as I'll ever know. When people compliment my dancing, my first thought, always, is to say, "But *you got tango*, too!"

And so this reclaimed state of happiness I feel at the start of this new year in my new home seems connected to this expansion (or removal) of Self in tango. It gives me a new margin of headspace—which I need in order to work toward the forgiveness I want with regard to myself and Dan and Evelyn—in that order.

❧

In mid-December, a seemingly small incident had reinforced my ability to move toward the end I'm only now coming to fully grasp. When I left the States for Buenos Aires, I had agreed to check in with Dan periodically to let him know I was okay. But, since I stopped contacting him, or anyone he knew, after Evelyn's October email, he apparently had begun to worry about me, so much so that he called my sister Terry. When she wrote to tell me this, I decided it was time to write and explain my concern over Evelyn's email, which he told me he hadn't known about. He professed his love for me despite all, and I professed mine. I had no illusion that this meant we were getting back together, but it was an important reconciliation, one that allowed me this consolation: No matter what I have lost, something bigger and better has been gained.

I've been continuing to follow Pema Chödrön's advice of sitting down face to face with my aversion since that conversation with Dan. From what Pema says and from all the reading I've been doing, I've begun to understand that if love expands, hatred has no option but to leave the room, like the physics of hot and cold. Thus, instead of trying to quell my feelings of hate, I focus on that which was abiding and indestructible in mine and Dan's love. I've been able to think of all the good stuff that Dan and I had shared, things that will never go away. We had years of being there for each other in sickness, health, job stress, family crises, loss of loved ones, good times and bad. *That* love transcended the romantic love that had brought us together and was much deeper. And it was clear neither of us wanted to lose it. The essence of it, I realized, was like the dharma—pure and untrammeled. A few lines in particular of the *Metta Sutta* have helped me turn up the heat and expand the love not just to Dan, but out to others:

May all beings be at ease.
Whatever living beings there may be;
Whether they are weak or strong, omitting none,
The great or the mighty, medium, short or small,
The seen and the unseen,
Those living near and far away,
Those born and to-be-born,
May all beings be at ease!

And even in my most stubborn, self-clinging distaste for Dan's new girlfriend, somewhere deep down I knew she was a being deserving of that ease, too. But now it's already a few weeks into January, and as I stand on one of my little terraces in my new apartment and take a deep breath of the city whose name means Good Airs, I consider where I'm living. At $500 a month, I'm in the high-rent district. I'm tempted to call it "the poor woman's Paris," but that ignores the fact that I'd rather be in Buenos Aires than in the City of Light. And Paris can't hold a candle to the tango here. Paris was the crucible where tango was transformed by the young avant-garde into a highbrow craze. And it was the Parisian couturiers of that era, 1913–1914, who developed the dress with the slit up the side for freedom of movement, advancing it from Andalusian attire to art deco in a style that is reminiscent of the famous Erté. And so I give Paris its proper credit, but when it comes to where to dance in the here and now, Buenos Aires is it—hands down.

Like a true Argentine, I quickly become attached to my barrio, its quirks and its purveyors. There's my skeleton-key maker. He leans out a street-level window of a room with an old linoleum floor. There's Cambalache, who fashions my lumpy hand-rolled empanadas, and Nonna, from whom I get my cookie-cutter ones. Adriano, the cobbler, fixes my shoes and handbags and would love to cobble me a pair of tango shoes. When I pass by he never fails to step out to kiss me on each cheek and shoot the breeze. He reminds me of some South Philly guys I've known, and I'm dying to do my best Rocky Balboa—"Yo, Adriano!"—but it simply wouldn't translate and so I can only amuse myself with my impulse.

There's Dany, my pasta maker. "Dany," I tell him, "your pesto sauce is so flavorful, you must be Genovese, am I right?"

"No way, I'm Spanish all the way," he says proudly. "In Argentina, 80 percent of the pizzerias, pasta shops, bakeries, hotels, and garages are owned by Spanish. The Italians do the construction and metallurgy."

Hmmm. I've got to wrest back some of that claim for my heritage. "Well," I say, "but the bakeries don't have cannoli and tiramisu."

This gets Dany where he lives. "Yes," he hangs his head, "you need mascarpone and our bakers cannot afford it, it's too expensive." I feel like I've kicked a man when he's down. Because of the 2001 financial crisis, many people can't afford simple designer cheeses or gourmet foods that we North Americans take for granted, so they're in short supply. I buy a whole kilogram of his red pepper linguine.

But Recoleta residents can afford *paseadores* to walk their dogs, so my barrio is full of mini cattle drives, as I come to call them. The *paseadores* ride herd on as many as twenty-five well-behaved canines on leashes, a comical sight to see as the well-groomed charges strut the busy streets. The plazas and parks along Libertador are filled with every race of dog—either running free or tied to posts. Within my first few weeks in Recoleta, I'll see more unchecked doggy sex than I have in my life—which may be why Buenos Aires dogs are the happiest in the world.

I have a set route several mornings a week to my swimming pool at American Sport gym on Charcas. I always take Laprida so I can pass the *bomberos*, firemen, who are way more sexy in their black lace-up boots, formfitting attire, and oh, those velvet French tams, than their North American counterparts. Invariably, I share sidewise glances with two or three of them as they stand guard at their red fire engines.

I buy *El Clarin* every Saturday from the same kiosk, because that's the day it has the Spanish *New York Times* insert. I slow my steps every morning as I pass by the sidewalk flower stalls that also sell incense, one in particular that leaves an aftermath of rain showers. The booths are gardens laden with bouquets. For a buck fifty, I sweeten my home with jasmine, freesia, or daffodils.

I frequent the small produce purveyors and the mom-and-pop supermarkets run by Asians; Chinese women who speak less Castellano than I do run the beauty salon–cum–massage parlor on French.

Living in my new barrio, I realize my eyes are fresh again. I notice the rapture of others. The woman who irons clothes in the Laundromat, the man who sells loose herbs and spices, and the flower vendors. What they all have in common is a gourd of maté in their palms and a thermos of hot water nearby. Through the gold and silver *bombilla* they sip their elixir with a contemplative look and air of mystery befitting Sherlock Holmes and his pipe. Argentines talk of their maté as if it were a companion.

I drew back the first time I sipped it, but I'm a different person now. Amalia, one of my new Castellano professors (I've added two to complement Mariel), initiates me. She grabs a fistful of leaves and shows me the little *palos* (stem sticks) that add a dimension of flavor. "It's a question of personal taste whether you prefer maté with or without *palos*," she says.

Amalia loads the *calabaza* gourd with the leaves three-quarters full, covers the gourd mouth with one hand, inverts, shakes, and strikes it once with her other hand. She discards the fine powder that rests in her hand. She shows me how to slope the leaves in the gourd so as to not wet them all each time we add fresh water. We heat, but do not boil, the water. I love the blossoming aroma as we moisten the leaves. I sip through the *bombilla*. Then Amalia adds hot water and it's her turn. I love that that she does not wipe off the *bombilla*. This time it tastes nothing like turpentine. I taste naturally sweet things like artichokes and asparagus and a robustness of baked potatoes. I get a whiff of mountain misery or witch hazel, an aromatic plant that grows in the high Sierra. What I really taste now that I know them is the pampas that stretch for an eternity from Buenos Aires. I am becoming Argentine, and I am opening up to new ways of tasting rapture.

Chapter 19

Church of Tango

Volví por caminos viejos,
Volví sin poder llegar.
Grité con tu nombre muerto.
Recé sin saber rezar.

I returned to old roads,
I returned unable to arrive.
I shouted your dead name.
I prayed without knowing how to pray.

—"Milonga Triste" (1936)

Argentina is one of two nations (along with Uruguay) whose flag has a line-drawn face on it. On Argentina's flag, the yellow-gold sun emanates thirty-two rays and is centered along a stripe of cloud white that's sandwiched between two stripes of sky blue. The sun-face is pensive, its brow wrinkled, evocative of an Argentine wondering when the next crisis will hit. The Argentines are famously *quejosos*, complaining types, but who wouldn't be after all the trials their country has gone through—including the 2001 financial crisis that hit sometime after they finally got their democracy up and running.

But they're simultaneously optimistic, able to see the blue horizon no matter how dire the circumstances seem. They joke and rib each other, and make song, dance, and art. The subway entertainers always get a heartfelt hand, if not a handout, from passengers. Along Libertador Avenue, a multiple-lane artery running north to south along the city's east side, a young man on stilts amuses the drivers and himself at the red lights. At another corner, a boy and girl in striped stockings entertain the stopped traffic with their acrobats. Another day, a guy juggles a crystal ball. A vendor with a Marcel Marceau face holds up his whirligigs—some look like the sun-face—to catch the breeze and spin.

Vincent Lopez is a street that runs along the fortified brick wall of the Recoleta cemetery. The area is packed with revelers at touristy haunts—bars, nightclubs, cafés, restaurants, a cinema complex, and McDonald's ubiquitous McCafe. I'm stopped by a puppeteer's agile hands breathing life into his characters as he strings them along in a five-minute girl-meets-boy sitcom matched to a music soundtrack. How many hours did it take him to assemble these lifelike characters in their Spanish colonial garb? He conveys pathos and humor so effectively down those strings into cloth, wire, and papier-mâché that he disappears even though he is in full view.

The Recoleta cemetery opened for business in 1822, eighteen years after its Parisian counterpart, Père-Lachaise. Evita's art deco crypt is the necropolis's big draw for tourists. But a map at the entrance shows the final resting places of many other illustrious statesmen, explorers, writers, poets, military personnel, and clergy. There are 4,800 ornate vaults, some the size of a little cottage. A few blocks from my home, the urban graveyard is beautifully situated, with a sweet little church, green plaza, and the bustling terrace of Café la Biela nearby.

I find the less-visited and less-prestigious Chacarita cemetery across town more attractive with its broader tree-lined avenues. Juan Perón was buried there until his body was exhumed in late 2006 and reinterred in a mausoleum outside of Buenos Aires. Tango crooner Carlos Gardel, whose vault has a festive feel and is plastered with about a hundred engraved messages from his bereaved and posthumous admirers, is still there.

Recoleta's stone mausoleums cover what was once an orchard tended by Jesuit monks who built the sparkling white church next door, Iglesia de Nuestra Señora de Pilar, in 1732. When there aren't too many tourists, I come and sit here to meditate, as my Zen temple has limited hours.

The little baroque church's nave is bright and attractive with Moorish-tiled wainscoting. The side altars gleam with gold leaf and pretty statues. Six Corinthian columns of alabaster press into the wall behind the main altar, which is covered in an apron of silver with elaborate embossing. I have come to sit, relax, and empty my mind. Roger, a man whom I met only twice in San Francisco, is coming all the way to Buenos Aires for our third date. It's true: Our first date was dinner in a restaurant; our second was cycling in the Marin

Headlands. He loves biking above all, but he dances swing and is eager to learn tango, too, just because I do it. He is handsome, blond and blue-eyed, and athletically built. He'll arrive in a few days. I'm honored he'd travel so far to see me again. After searching around for a hotel for him and coming up dissatisfied with my choices, I have decided to open my home to him for a week; as for my heart, that remains to be seen.

I find this little church very welcoming, and I'm glad to have come full circle and be able sit here comfortably and not feel like a recovering Catholic, but a recovered one. No hard feelings. We both did our best all those years ago.

Gregorian chant from little camouflaged speakers in the corners fills the church. The choir's tenor voices spark a sudden visceral change in my whole being, the way only music can. The chanting reminds me of the priest's singing of the Kyrie Eleison during the high masses. Those seven syllables (kee-ree-aye-ee-lay-ee-son) were kneaded out to at least fifty as the priest's voice blossomed and billowed up concentrically over the faithful, filling the nave with reverberating sonar halos. The words mean "Lord have mercy" and I never knew it back then, but they are a Latin transliteration of Greek.

I still love their sound today.

The Zen Buddhists have a sort of high mass every month for the full moon, called a Bodhisattva ceremony. (Bodhisattvas are beings, saints of sorts, who forgo full Buddhahood and stay behind to wait for everyone else to be ready.) During the service, a cantor—called a *kokio*—chants a cappella in a soul-wrenching voice that makes my skin rise up and dance the *habanera*. The rhythm is like a dirge crossed with jazz riffs. Thankfully, the somber ceremony involves numerous prostrations on tatami mats, which keeps in check my urge to sway. The bows also let me wipe my tears.

When my friend Linda Fox tells me how she structures her day around tango "morning music" and "evening music" as if it were sacred—like Indian ragas—I feel validated in my own physical reaction to tango music, which I divide into marches, anthems, and hymns. The music often makes my mouth flood with saliva. My spirit coming, if I may indulge a double entendre.

I was not surprised to learn that there is such a thing as a tango mass. Luis Enríquez Bacalov, an Argentine composer, wrote "Misa Tango," a Spanish adaptation of the liturgy set to tango music. I love that Bacalov edited the mass so that it would appeal to Christians, Muslims, and Jews.

I have always felt so moved by music, as if it's the very voice of God whose universal call will unite us and save us all from self-destructing. Once, high up in the Marin Headlands, I came upon this feeling in the form of a woman, Lee Ellen Shoemaker. Calling herself the tunnel singer, she accompanies her singing with the Tibetan chiming bowl, playing it the way you play a glass of water with your finger. She lured me into the concrete manmade tunnel, near the national park's World War II bunkers. Her dark silhouette (the Pied Piper calling forth the peace in all of us) processed slowly back and forth in the penumbra of the hollow. I dropped my bike and sat in the duff of the nearby eucalyptus grove. At the sound of her music, my mouth and eyes began to water.

Holy art thou, music.

My parents, avid church attendees, disliked the folk music mass that came into vogue (after I stopped attending). So they sought out old-fashioned churches that clung to traditional hymns. I was in my midthirties when we were finally able to openly acknowledge that I had not attended mass in years. Still, I didn't mind attending, at their request, when I came home to visit.

As I sit in this house of God, I contemplate how tango is not a religion for me, nor is Zen, a nontheistic practice, meaning it neither admits nor denies the existence of a God. (You can be Christian, Muslim, Jew, or atheist, which is a form of religion, *and* Zen.)

I look upon this elaborate altar's Jesus, hanging from his pure gold cross, and feel, as always, a twinge of anxiety. Even though I've wandered far from the belief in Jesus as the literal son of God, I adore the Passion of Christ even today with the same schoolgirl trance. If it's *the greatest story ever told*, it's because it's a powerful myth for what we humans all go through in life, bearing our own crosses.

I can trace the anxiety I feel to the same overarching fact of death, or as we call it in Zen, impermanence. Time does run out. Things change—your parents die, your body ages, your lover leaves you.

But when I dance tango I am never anxious. I lose that sense of my mortal self. It is breathtaking to feel this month here, far from the place where I was born, in February the month of my birth: The dance is still as transcendent as ever for me. I give thanks to the God of this house for that.

Then my mind turns to the mythical story of Buddha touching his hand to the earth to bear witness before the demon Mara, who would dissuade him from his enlightened state. The earth shook in reply to that touch. I place my right palm, the very one that's met thousands of others' palms as we enter an unimaginable state of peace and joy, on the wooden bench. I shake and feel shivers in reply to the rightness of my being right where I am, right now.

Along Libertador, where I walked this morning, there is a bust of Mahatma Gandhi that I always pay homage to with a nod and bow of my head. When I passed it this morning, I wondered: *Do I dare equate my peaceful resistance in the* milonga *to violent leading, backbiting, and harmful speech with that giant's right actions?* I don't know, but I have thought about it often. *Beings are numberless, I vow to save them,* we chant in the Buddha Hall before lectures. If Mother Teresa were still alive and I tried to share in her work, she might say, had she seen Ángel and me dance, "You'll save more souls by dancing tango."

As I sit in my pew, stare at the virgin-white walls, and let go of all anxieties about Roger's visit, I have a small epiphany about what prayer really is: the ultimate photo op. You go blank as film paper and let the light—the Light, which might be nothing more nor less than your own unjaded Eye—burn an image on you. I have the impulse to call and tell my mother what I've figured out. She is the clearinghouse for the family's special intentions, always praying the rosary. I think what hard work that is for Mom, having to carry all our petitions in her body. Isn't it enough she carried us all in her womb? Prayer is, or should be—just like meditation and tango—the chance to drop all need, want, desire, hope, despair, petition, even intention. But I can also hear Mom's resigned sigh at the end of her prayers—*Your will, not mine*—my Mom, who put my father only slightly below God. *Although her way is not my way,* I think as I sit here and let the Light pour in, *I can see how I now carry Mom—and Dad.* A figurative lightbulb flashes and I see also how the dark space between them, where they didn't meet, didn't connect, but chafed, is mine too. What a photo op that is.

My mom doesn't see emptiness the way I do. Just as empty space in her home must be filled with gadgets and tchotchkes, empty space in her mind must be filled. She prays and talks to God a lot. I'm one of her enablers. I bought her a pair of rosaries from this very church during my 2005 visit.

But the essential art of Zen and of tango is nonthinking. The Fukan Zazengi, an ancient set of instructions for sitting *zazen,* describes how you do this. You take a giant step backward and give yourself some distance from the numbing rush of life's demands, and allow the light in. Prayer. Photo op. "The dharma appears of itself," says the Fukan Zazengi, which is actually about a thousand words of precise instructions on how and where to sit, as pertinent today as it was a couple of thousand years ago.

The way-seeking in Zen is like the way-seeking in tango in that the how-to is basic, streamlined. Following it takes no effort, just a lifetime of letting go—habits, ego, thought. Just sit there, don't do something.

Constantly seeking my way out of the dark cloud of confusion, I find happiness appears on its own time. Bliss radiates outward from my circle of dance and is enriching my life everywhere. The concierge in my building who sees me before and after I dance adores me and has taken to calling me *Camila el Sol*, Camille the Sun—and I love my new name. Even though I've followed my tango to some peccadilloes, it's a vehicle of grace for me. It's why I'm more centered, and why I committed to celibacy, not as a practice of denial or repressing libido, but as a rewarding way of refining my energy.

However, centeredness is a dynamic state. If I'm not vigilant, I will fall off axis, fretting. Worrying about Dan and Evelyn. As it is in tango, balance in life is a narrow place.

Last week I saw a cat die right in front of my eyes, then dreamed about him. I was walking down Junin, the street where my Zen temple is located. I had just sat a couple of hours of *zazen* with my Zen group. I was feeling soft and peeled of defenses. As the traffic roared by, I first heard the noise of the cat's body get hit. I turned to see him, a frisky little tabby, land on his feet and run to the curb. I ran to him thinking he was okay, but he stumbled to his side and cried out in pain before giving up his spirit. There was not a mark on his body. I'd never witnessed the actual passing of such a large sentient being. I sat there on the curb and let my tears come over me. I cried for the loss, for the pain, for the passing. When my father was drinking his worst, he would go into vivid emotional accounts of seeing men die before his eyes in the South Pacific, where he was stationed during World War II. All the booze in the world couldn't numb his misery. As I sat with the dead cat, I felt the critical mass of numbness that surrounded me—cars and buses speeding by, people going about their business, not even giving me a second look.

When the cat appeared in my dream that night, he was in a tropical place full of monkeys and bright blue and green birds. A peaceable kingdom. When I awoke and reflected on the radiant light in that sweet dream, I understood that I was grieving that cat as much as the death of part of me. The fact that he was alive again pointed to the rebirth that is ongoing for me. In tango, I'm often in a place that is as peaceful and playful as those monkeys. The light recalled the corona radiata, which surrounds the ovum, the unfertilized embryo. How fragile it all is.

My dreams are often filled with clear symbols and metaphors. Over the course of my time here I've dreamed about Dan and Evelyn often. Recently, I dreamed that they were not doing well. There was a lot of bright light. I have no reason to think they're not still together. In fact, given Dan's and my recent exchange, I have every reason to believe that they are still together. I'm sure they are moving ahead peaceably without me there. I am on the verge of being able to wish them well. But I'm not completely there yet. My commitment is to remain upright and way-seeking, in my *zazen* and my tango, both dances of improvisation, as well as in my life.

At one of the church's side altars, I step through what might have once been a secret door. It's a wormhole to another universe— what's called the Cloisters Museum. I hadn't noticed this little hidden door before today. And the spaciousness I find on the other side seems nearly impossible when you consider how large the church is from the outside. My parents would label this a miracle, similar to the time we were visiting Sicily and they had to go down on their knees to enter the musty grotto of Santa Rosalia and came out without a speck of dirt on their clothes. *The tunnel singer would love this place,* I think as I mount the uneven red-carpeted stairs. The ceiling is low and vaulted. The walls are lumpy, rutted brick. All is whitened with lime. The Gregorian chant is at a low simmer and though I know it to be recorded music, I almost expect to find the brothers on the museum's second or third floor.

Instead I find showcased an illuminated bible, many old handwritten church documents, pictorial history on the church's building, statues of dark-skinned Virgins, silver and gold liturgical instruments, and lavishly brocaded and embroidered priest vestments. There are more relics, too, including bone fragments from Saints Christina and Benedicta.

I keep following the music, all the way up to the third floor, but I never find its source—another miracle direct from heaven. My parents would call these invisible voices. I want to know what the friars are singing to me. Maybe they are chanting "Milonga Triste," a dirge: *Silencio del camposanto/Soledad de las estrellas* (Silence of the graveyard/Solitude of the stars).

I've spent two hours here and it's time to go home to have a bite to eat, shower, then dress for my other "church." The night is still hot and I'm off in a halter top and cotton skirt. I take the D Line three stops north on Sante Fe, and then walk ten blocks to Salon Canning.

A man died here some weeks ago. He stood up and keeled over stone cold dead of coronary thrombosis. He was sixty, overweight, a smoker. His name was Guillermo and he was known for wearing suspenders and no belt. He was not in the circle of dance when he fell. He had just finished dancing a lively *milonga,* and I've recently learned that he had appeared in *Evita* in a scene where he danced with Madonna, which turned all the other *milongueros* who auditioned at the casting green with envy.

When the floor catches my heel, I do a little stutter step. It's the very corner where Guillermo met his own fatal end, and it feels a bit wavy—his spirit grasping, caught between two worlds? I had been dancing somewhere else the night he died, but my friend, Turgut, who was present on the night of his death, has been upset ever since. *Impermanence: Can't live with it, can't live without it,* is what I think, glib as W. C. Fields taking up Zen.

Within minutes of entering the dance forum, I'm making the first *salida,* my exit from real time. I leave behind an average person who occasionally pulls ahead on the bell curve. In fact, I leave behind the bell curve altogether. The only curves are the three natural ones in my spine. I'm untouchable. Supreme. It's not breath-taking to feel this way. It's breath-giving. There is no competition, no comparative forms. No ego. Just a dance.

Sitting between *tandas,* I recall how a woman recently said to me at another *milonga,* "You did a *voleo*—don't do that!" I missed the memo that said no *voleos* in the *milonga.* But even if I hadn't, it's hard to allow for self-limiting rules when there is no Self to limit.

Tonight I make a point of dancing with new and old partners. I'm more patient than ever. I appreciate now how their beautiful minds work. They study the way women move to the rhythm of the music and then decide which woman they want to dance with to the beat of which favorite composers. I like to say they're making "algo-rhythm connections." Many men like my dancing to D'Arienzo and Troilo because I mark the "*compás*," or rhythmic beat, the way the Argentines do. Because it's in my blood as deeply as in theirs.

Oscar, a man now in my Top Three list of favorites, invites me to dance. He speaks English with a charming New York accent. Both of Italian extraction, we suddenly break into a heated debate—voices raised, arms flying, right on the dance floor—on how to cook the best marinara sauce.

When I regale him with a lavish compliment on his leading, he responds rather disarmingly, "Don't bullsheet me." So, for fun, I push the flirtation further: "Oscar, I want to show you a fruit tree. If you eat the fruit, you'll be like a God." And he replies in kind, "If Adam took one bite of the apple for Eve, I'll eat the whole fruit, tree and all, for you." I tell him that I'm referring to one of the four real kumquat trees in the beautiful Andalusian patio in my Palermo park. "Therefore, my *piropo* is more sincere than yours," I tease.

A few more *piropos*, a few more *tandas*. I'm easily satisfied this evening. As I head toward the exit down Salon Canning's long vestibule, a man I don't know and have never danced with catches up with me to praise my dancing. "You are excellent, elegant, beautiful. I've long watched you."

"*Qué amable, muchas gracias*" ("How kind, thank you very much"), I say, holding his hand and his eyes. A near identical thing occurred last night as I was leaving La Ideal—a man found me to lavish me with compliments. This time I know exactly what it is I must say. "Please find the men I danced with and tell them, too," I say to him. "*Sin ellos, soy nada.*" Without them, I'm nothing.

There is always a sunburst of kindness breaking through the cloud of meanness in the *milonga*.

Outside the midnight sky is lit up. I can almost see steam coming off the moon as I walk down Scalabrini Ortiz.

Young policemen stake out in the shadows of darkened stores. One of them steps forward and speaks to me.

"Señora, are you okay this evening?" It's not usual to be walking alone like this, on a dark street, so late. He still takes me by surprise and I'm touched by his concern. I can hardly find words.

"*¿Todo bien?*" he asks again.

"*Sí, señor, todo bien.*"

"*¿Segura?*"

"*Sí*, all is well. I'm sure." I point. "Look—the moon."

"*Sí, linda.*"

"*Muy linda.*"

There is a brief pregnant silence as I hesitate, wanting more connection. Because of the police abuses during the Dirty War, cops here are highly disdained and mistrusted. But this cop is a man who is so kind and beguiling, I can see us tangoing together. So, instead of an us/them stance I try to project *we*. He is saying something lighthearted that I don't understand. As I listen, I recall an unpleasant encounter with traffic police in the States last year when the cop was unnecessarily abusive. I'm back to *me and him*. I fall off my axis. But I hear some strains of music from a window or from a passing car, "Tango Mass" perhaps, and I recover quickly. I project *us* pressing our chests together, palm kissing palm, and the two of us dancing through the cloud into the blue, and behind us I envision legions of policemen dropping their weapons to better dance with their partners, all of us together rebirthing a whole nation, a whole me.

"*Gracias, adiós*," I say, and I turn to go home.

Tango Liaisons
and Lessons

Para mi el tango es un sentimiento, donde se fusionan el cuerpo y el espíritu del bailarin.

For me tango is a feeling, where the dancer's body and soul merge into one another.

—*Federico Paleo, professional tango dancer*

It's Friday, February 9, 2007, and hot as an August night in Sacramento. I'm in the middle of the first important ritual of my day, brewing my cup of joe. Slowly, I add the water, chanting my morning prayers. Maria Jose, my neighborhood shaman who helps me align my cycles with the moon, says I'm in my *hechicera*, or sorceress, phase as the moon wanes. This means I crave solitude more than usual. And my alchemical urge to transform substances, even just turn black grounds and hot water into a morning elixir, is extra strong.

Gotan Project's "Last Tango in Paris" pulses from my iPod in its speaker port. The music reminds me that I have a "tangover"—having danced nonstop *tandas* last night at Club Español until 11 PM, followed by three more hours over at Niño Bien.

My door buzzer rings and makes me jump as it always does. *What intruder treads there?* cackles my mind's crone, who is fast at work converting these black seeds into a drinkable potion. "*¡Hola!*" I shout into the lead-heavy black telephone that is my intercom.

"Fibertel," is all I can make out in the string of Spanish. That's enough.

"*Ah, ¡Sí! Momento, bajo.*" Coming down, I say. This is a *momento* biggo, indeed! The technicians are really here, as they said, to install my Internet service. I've been trying to get service since I arrived. I have to take the elevator down nine stories to let the installers in. No buildings here allow you to buzz visitors in without seeing them. It's an outcome of security problems due to a swell in the numbers of desperate and needy trying to break into homes where people might have had a little more, right after the 2001 financial crisis. Although that problem has abated quite a bit now, you still can only open a building's front door—from both inside and out—with a key. There are no fire escapes either. A U.S. fire marshal would have a seizure.

I sink my fat skeleton key into the lock and open the door for the two hard-hat guys in regulation gray jumpsuits. Yes, these are my boys: young, serious looking, and tech-savvy.

"We need to get on the roof," says the more serious of the two. They go about their business and I go back upstairs to my apartment to wait.

I'm back at my table drinking my coffee when I hear a knock. It's one of the techies. He stops just over the transom and looks around. I assume he's assessing where to put the cables, router, and modem, but it's quickly apparent that he's taking stock of all my tango accessories—my tango magazines and books, my "come-hither" spikes from Montevideo, my makeshift collage of tango dancers in various embraces.

"*¿Baila tango?*" he asks.

Do I dance tango? Does the pope say mass daily? "*Sí,*" I respond.

"*Yo también,*" he says, "*lo enseño.*"

What are the chances? A tango-teaching technician? Seconds later I am in close embrace with the dark stranger, dancing to Troilo's "Queja de Bandoneón," his selection from my iPod.

He smiles when we're done and switches immediately to familiar verb forms. "*Bailas bien.*"

"*Vos también,*" I say. "*¿Tenes una pareja?*"

As I could have suspected, he does have a practice partner. Probably many waiting in line. His name is Ramón. He's twenty-three and has been dancing for six years. *I'm old enough to be your mother, dude.* This is what goes through my mind as we dance around again in tight circles to Pugliese's "La Yumba." He's patient and knows how to milk the pause. On the last note he leads me playfully into a *sentada,* a jump into a sitting position on his knee. He keeps his hard hat on the whole time.

Ramón has a confident power lead. He is not tall, but that thigh that supports my *sentada* supplies a big, harmonious finish.

"*¿Dónde está tu amigo?*" I ask. But Ramón is unconcerned about his colleague walking in and finding us in *flagrante delicto*. There must be a ten-pound book on avoiding sexual harassment lawsuits in the United States. Rule Number 1,001: Never touch customers of opposite sex even if they touch you first. Rule Number 1,002: Never, ever dance close-embrace tango . . .

Ramón's partner, Hector, eventually shows and does the installation work while Ramón and I talk tango. Ramón tells me he lives in a barrio in Buenos Aires province, far outside the radius of regular *milongas*. I'm tempted to offer him lodging in my apartment so he can frequent the downtown *milongas* as I do. I want to support his tango practice. It's an impulse, one of so many I have here—to teach people how to recycle, how to let pedestrians have the right of way, how to protect consumers, how to make your government accountable—that is misplaced. I need to let him find his own tango.

And besides, I'm old enough to be his mother.

Hector doesn't seem to be bothered in the slightest that Ramón and I dance as he runs the cable from the roof around my doorway. When he's done they both sit at my iBook and check the connections. Next thing I know we're all watching tango videos on YouTube, including one of Gustavo and Jesica Hornos, an Argentine couple who teach in Sausalito, California.

"It's so easy to dance tango," Ramón is saying to Hector who doesn't dance.

"C'mon, Ramón, let's show him," I say and we dance a *milonga* to Ángel Villoldo's very upbeat "El Porteñito." We do another *sentada*. I give Hector my camera to snap a photo of us. I'm wearing a turquoise T-shirt, black running shorts, pink-, red-, and aqua-striped socks, and black shoes. I look like the Good Witch of the West. With Ramón in his white hard hat and gray jumpsuit, we make quite the hilarious-looking couple.

"How cool is this!" I write in an email to my family, in which I attach the photo. "Who among you has danced with a service guy who called at your home from some big corporate utility?"

My sister Grace writes back: "I'm a little confused. How many Buenos Aires repairmen does it take to install Internet? One to do the work and photography and one to keep you occupied so you don't realize how much time it takes?"

I sit at my wooden table and answer emails. It's great to finally be connected and not to have to go to the *locutorio*. In Buenos Aires, where everyone seems propelled to the smallest task with great purpose, I feel a sense of pride when I imagine my neighbors being able to see that I actually do work. I don't *only* dance tango, thank you very much. My neighbors, whose shouts frighten me out of my wits when their soccer team's winning or losing. My neighbors who probably thought, *¡Qué tipico!* when they saw me, an American living in Buenos Aires, dancing with a technician half my age.

I decide the room needs something, in anticipation of Roger's visit, and so I walk across the street to buy some naked ladies from the flower vendor. When I get back I put them in a tall clear vase in my bedroom, where I will let Roger sleep when he arrives the following day, while I sleep in the living/dining room on the futon.

After talking about this trip since September, Roger is finally here. He has chosen the week of Valentine's Day to visit, not knowing that my birthday falls just two days later. We waste no time getting him his first ever tango lesson. I start him with Oscar Casas, a tall elegant dancer I've watched and admired many times in different *milongas*.

"She is a precious stone, a piece of expensive crystal!" Oscar admonishes Roger in this first lesson. Roger is not manhandling me, but Oscar is using the metaphor that many teachers cite to help leaders forget themselves and focus on the follower as the all-important center of their universe.

Oscar is the son of dancers who organized popular *milongas* in the 1950s. "Feel the dance," emphasizes Oscar. He gestures toward his wife. "Dance with my beautiful wife," he orders. Marian, used to offering her assistance to novices, falls routinely into the follower's position with Roger. It's clear that her mind is still contemplating the task she was headed to, and when Oscar interrupts them to correct Roger, she picks up right where she was, continuing on her way like a spirit passing through. Their home is a huge century-old building with high brick walls covered in a gallery of Oscar's artwork. The corridor from the front door back to the living area seems to be half a mile long.

Marian is a blond delicate beauty whose equanimity is in stark contrast to Oscar's exuberance, which is evident in his many creative pursuits: acrylic, watercolor, and oil paintings overlain with his lyrics. He needs both words and images to express his *fuego*.

I think tenderly of what a fairytale romance they have—having met in the tango arena in Toronto, a place where Oscar was fortuitously waylaid on his way to Australia. He never got to Australia, but stayed in Canada and eventually married Marian. Once, after a trip they'd taken, when Oscar had returned to Buenos Aires before Marian, I asked him, "Are you glad to be home?"

"No, no, no," he hastened. "My home is wherever Mariana is."

I think about having a man say that about me, as I sit on the sidelines and watch Roger's long skinny feet. Upon arriving, Oscar took one look at Roger's street shoes and said, "Hold on just a minute." He disappeared and came back with a dusty old pair of sturdy maroon leather shoes with a basket-weave front. "Try these on, they belonged to my grandfather."

They must have been around since the 1930s. You could almost see and smell the old *milonguero* in them. They fit Roger's long narrow feet perfectly.

"A good sign," I told him. "If these don't make you dance, nothing will."

Oscar is teaching Roger a six-count *baldosa* (literally "tile") box, the foundational step of the *milonga* dance. I find Oscar's method to be simple and brilliant. He advertises something that no doubt makes other teachers blanche. He promises he'll have you up and dancing on the first night of your first lesson.

For the first half hour Oscar has Roger learn to lead in the six-count box. This starts with Roger stepping left on his left foot (the follower will mirror him on her right). Once Roger has this pattern in his muscle memory, Oscar teaches the ingenious part. He shows Roger how he can go from two to five, or five to three, or any such nonconsecutive steps in the box. It's a simple model, from which leaders can improvise their own patterns.

Roger, an engineer at Stanford Research Institute, silently takes it all in, digesting this out-of-sequencing approach. He tests the hypothesis (a mathematician doing his *algo-rhythms*) to find if there are any combos that can't be done. My brain's right lobe begins to hurt trying to follow his line of analytical thinking. He is a bit nervous, and so Oscar and I try to get him to forget the numbers and counting. But I can see that Roger is overwhelmed and wants to protect his right to keep on counting.

"This is how I learn," he says firmly. His lips mouth numbers as he steps, stops, steps, stops. One hour, a hundred pesos later, and too many numbers later, we are done. Whew.

For our first night together we have dinner at La Peña Colorado with my friends, Steve and Linda, from Santa Cruz. There is live music, a woman jazz singer from Peru.

The shared conviviality helps Roger and me ease comfortably into reacquaintance. We both sleep soundly and separately. I have given Roger my king-size bed, which is really two twins pushed together.

The next day, late morning, we arrive at Ángel's. The teacher starts in back leading Roger around his studio, saying his patented, "Feel me, feel me! I woman, you man." And "You, never first. Woman always first." I watch amused from the white couch.

Ángel is teaching Roger the eight-count *básico*. He shows Roger how to lead the woman to the all-important *cruzada*, a step where her left foot crosses over her right.

Ángel is very perceptive. "You've taken him to *another* teacher," he whispers to me accusingly. I plead no comment. Ángel tries to soften Roger's too-firm embrace as they dance together to Canaro's "Poema," a captivating song that always sounds like an opening or closing to some beautiful love story. As Ángel lays *ochos, cadencias,* and too many patterns on Roger, I sink into his cushy sofa, feeling weak-kneed. A wave of nausea overcomes me. I'm not one prone to illness, so I'm not sure what it is. But it passes.

As we leave Ángel's and head downtown to sightsee, I say, "Maybe I made a mistake in exposing you to two different teaching styles."

"I like both teachers," he says. "Both offer me something. I don't have a problem with it." I'm pleased with his openness to the travails of learning something new.

We stop by Victorio shoe store so Roger can buy his own dance shoes. It takes a very long hour, and I attribute my recurring nausea to a lifelong antishopping torpor. I've inherited it from my anti-consumer society grandma Catalano, an early paradigm for Reduce, Reuse, Recycle. But Roger ends up with a cool pair of dance shoes in that 1930s maroon with black patent leather.

We make our way to Café Tortoni on Avenida de Mayo, taking pictures of each other with the Obelisco in the background. I can't help but think of videos I've seen of the obelisk covered in a huge bubble-gum pink condom, an enshrinement in honor of Safe Sex Day a couple of years back. I would have *loved* to have been here for that.

At Tortoni, Roger gets the *bife lomo* and I get a turkey tart and salad. We order flutes of champagne and toast to our third date, which has been a sort of running joke between us.

"You haven't mentioned the naked ladies," I say, thinking this another opportunity to laugh.

"Oh yes, I meant to—very pretty."

"You seemed nervous at Ángel's," says Roger.

"Me? I thought you were."

"Hmm . . . no."

He excuses himself and disappears for a long while. Within an hour of his arrival he had informed me of his juvenile-onset diabetes, letting me know ahead of time that he'd have to vanish frequently to restrooms to inject insulin. He injects it at least four times a day, and the first time he did it in front of me I nearly passed out. He stocked up on candy—lots of Junior Mints. We'd have to eat frequently, he told me. No problem there.

While he's gone I reflect on how his condition limits him in no way I can see. He works long hours at a demanding job. Besides clocking a hundred aerobic miles of cycling a week, he sails his twenty-two-foot boat, *Solar Wind*, every weekend, often racing on San Francisco Bay. Two of his three sons (from a twenty-nine-year marriage) live with him, and he cooks dinner for them once a week. He's a poster boy for diabetics. His will to overcome limitation is attractive. A friend who introduced us matched us up well for our active lifestyles. He's sixty-one, an age group too prone to the pull of gravity.

It slowly dawns on me that what has been making me feel sick is that everything about Roger is so perfect. But I'm not ready for physical intimacy. He doesn't seem to mind the sleeping arrangements, but it's the third day of his visit and we haven't discussed any of this. Our touchstone of intimacy has been his blood sugar—and his tango lessons.

"So how long will you be here?" Roger asks when he returns. He knows almost nothing about my past—other than that I had a relationship come to an end.

"Let's get another round of bubbly," I say, thinking I'm not sure what the answer to his question is. I proceed to tell him the whole story about Dan, about Evelyn, and my violent episode. When I'm done I burst into tears. A cloudburst release of tension.

He hugs and comforts me, and the knot of nausea dissipates. He has had a postdivorce relationship he cherished end recently. It's becoming apparent that we are matched in our reserve about intimacy. He seems to be still recovering from his long marriage as well.

We pay our bill and stroll over to the pedestrian walkway, on Florida. It's crowded. Hawkers try to get the tourists to buy their *carpincho* leather. Roger stops at a dress shop and points at a red dress on the mannequin. "What do you think? You like it?"

"Yes, I do, it's nice. You have good taste." It's sleek, calf length, but with two discreet slits on either side. It ties around the neck and the neckline falls loosely into a V over cleavage if you have some. Silver-bead cables like chains run horizontally down both sides. It's formfitting with many tucks at seams that let the fabric lie flush against the body in flattering gathers.

"Let's get it," he says. Inside I try it on, but it's too big.

"Let's go," I say.

"Not so fast," he says. "They'll have other sizes." As it turns out they only have my size in black. I try it on and it fits like a glove.

"I like that color better," he says. Roger insists on paying the 100 pesos for it and we leave. I recall the not-so-distant past when I wouldn't accept a man's paying for things, hardly even a stick of gum, unless I saw some future for us. And while I don't feel that Roger and I will be like Oscar and Marian, I feel a kinship with him. Plus, he is entering into the dance of tango, which is a place of boundless generosity. I know I will return his gift in kind. I accept it with heartfelt gratitude.

And besides, it's Valentine's Day. I take the dress for a test drive at La Ideal that night. I love the way it looks and feels and that I get many compliments on it. I wear it two nights later on my fifty-sixth birthday, which we celebrate at the white-linen restaurant under Club Español. We're on a mission to keep Roger's blood sugar up and I'm more than willing to do my part. The following night we feast again at Divina Patagonia on lamb, deer loin, and beer-braised boar. It's all splendid. The last night we dine at my favorite place, Oviedo, starting with champagne and oysters. I order the suckling pig because Chinese New Year is just around the corner and it's the year of the pig.

The day Roger is leaving, we joke, but are half-serious, about what country our fourth date will be in. That night after he's gone, I find a large Junior Mint in my refrigerator and feel his absence. I sit on my futon and stare around my empty apartment. Every night for the week of his visit Roger had practiced tango, his lips moving as he counted, stepped, counted, stepped on my wooden floor. I feel more lonely than I anticipated now that he's gone. It was great having him as a roommate. I wonder momentarily if I should have pushed for a more romantic time. Then I recall the mantra I had with Dave before he and I practiced more than tango: *What's the hurry?* It was on my lips even as I fell from grace with him. I recall Flo's mom, who devoted her life to her children and found her true love at age sixty. It's all new for me to feel this slowed-down urge for intimacy, to not push for—or try to manufacture—the fairytale in my life.

And what a source of power. After all, on this night the moon is dark and I'm a *hechicera* in her transformative phase. The brief surge of loneliness subsides, and what finds me instead is the boundless spaciousness of mind-body I feel in my tango "hover zone," a place where I have now spent countless hours. It's the place from which I can move in an infinite number of directions. All I have to do is wait and be present for the invitation from the universe. It's an indescribable pleasure, but nothing less than Heaven here on earth. Now that's a potion I want to drink from over and over.

Chapter 21

Tango Without Borders

Far away in the heavenly abode of the great god Indra,
there is a wonderful net . . .

—*The Avatamsak Sutra*

March in the southern hemisphere is the equivalent of September up north. The kids go back to school and the scent of autumn is in the air. The energy of new beginnings abounds as I find myself regularly gravitating to a group of women I call Tango Divas. Carmen, who's been my close friend since the first weeks I arrived, is the only Porteña. There's Flo, my sunshine girlfriend from Los Angeles, and Rachel, a recent immigrant from London who bought and renovated a sturdy old apartment in the Montserrat barrio with access to her own private cupola. She spends her day orchestrating plumbers, painters, and other contractors in her burgeoning Spanish. Bobbie from Port Townsend, Washington, lived in Buenos Aires for a year with her husband, a *bandoneonista,* and their adolescent daughter, Madeleine, who went to grammar school in the Palermo. Now they visit a couple of times each year.

Having spent six months attending *milongas* mostly solo, it's a welcome change to go with a group of girlfriends. One night, we all head to the legendary Sunderland, a *milonga* in Villa Irquiza, an outlying barrio. Sunderland, far outside the downtown radius of dance halls, is in a quiet residential neighborhood where another famous *milonga,* Sin Rumbo, is also located. In the 1920s, at the city's hippodrome, an Argentine man gambled on a horse that was such a long shot its name was Sin Rumbo, meaning "without course." The horse won, and the man decided nothing was worthier of his money than a tango club. Sin Rumbo has been in the same spot for more than eighty years and one of its biggest claims to fame is that it's where actor Robert Duvall learned to dance.

Both Sunderland and Sin Rumbo are renowned for the Villa Urquiza style of tango, a smooth salon style wherein the partners take long strides and open up at times and do *sacadas, barridas,* and *voleos,* those punctuation marks in the otherwise straight catwalk. While Sin Rumbo is elegant with Andalusian features, such as black-and-white checkerboard floors, Sunderland is a hardcore sports club. There is not a shred of glamour in this barn of a school gym, with its sports equipment in place and garish lighting. But Porteños love the place and dress in their finest to scuff up their shoes on the hard gym floor. We arrive and take our seats at one of the long rectangular tables, reminiscent of the type you might see at a firehouse pancake breakfast. And we have a great time dancing until 4 AM.

A week later, we're all invited to a *milonga* in a clothing showroom for Tango Moda, located at the top of Palacio Barolo. Jorge Arias, an attractive man in his fifties and a regular denizen at *milongas,* sells his line of clothing and sporadically hosts *milongas* with food and wine in his classy showroom.

We make our way to the roof where many couples are sipping wine and enjoying the panoramic view of the cupolas of Buenos Aires. Over the course of the night, between dancing and drinking, we look at Jorge's line of clothing. What catches my eye is a sweater made of loosely woven beads, a cobweb of shiny points. It's stunning and reminds me of Indra's net. This ancient symbol illustrates the Buddhist concept of interdependency (like the "inter net"). Each of the net's single jewels embodies and reflects all the others. It makes me think of the way I share my accomplishments and compliments with my fellow dancers, sometimes silently, sometimes aloud. When my friends praise my *cabeceo*'s strength, I often say, "But it's yours, too." We reflect each other infinitely. It's rewarding to find myself opening more and more to the camaraderie that is possible around tango. I find this "tango without borders" to be yet another way to see Self and Other as one.

The unity I'm discovering is important, because we receive some really bad news—Club Español *milonga* will close in a few weeks. Actually, it's moving to another, less luxurious location due to a prohibitive rent increase, but that still spells death to an era—the era of Thursday nights at a venue reminiscent of a salon in Chateau Versailles. I'm not sure exactly how many years this *milonga* has been in operation, but it's long enough for everyone I know to have set foot in it many times to experience one of the liveliest, most flamboyant *milongas* in the city's recent history. While most *milongas* transpire under dimmed lighting, Espanol's took place under warm chandelier lights. Instead of tango black, many women were inspired to wear vibrant colors there. It was a good place for both foreigners and locals.

Despite this unfortunate turn of events, a few weeks later when the *milonga* opens at its new location in Club Galicia, the night proves auspicious for Diva Rachel. The first night at the *milonga's* new venue, on San Jose Street, Rachel meets Eduardo, a tall, dark Porteño who teaches tango. They fall madly in love, unbeknownst to the rest of us, right there in the circle of tango, and he moves into her place a week later.

When I see the look on Rachel's face I'm entranced by the gleam in her eye. We're in the doorway of the club competing for passing taxis. Rachel steps into the pouring rain with her umbrella, telling us that she'd prefer to walk—and splash—her way home. She glances back at us with eyes that sparkle like the jewels in Indra's net. She starts to sing in her Julie Andrews voice: "Raindrops on roses and whiskers on kittens/Bright copper kettles and warm woolen mittens . . . " I can't help but wonder how she could have fallen so fast and so hard, but I feel nothing but warm feelings. Whatever she has found reflects on me, too.

It's not too long after Club Español bites the dust that the Divas dissolve. Bobbie leaves town. Flo goes back to Los Angeles Carmen is busy spending time with Francis, a *tanguero* from Washington, who is her former beau, but ostensibly still her "soul mate." Rachel and Eduardo are inseparable, working with Tango TaxiDancers, living together and practicing for the tango world championships.

And so I'm back at the *milongas* alone. One night, I dance the last *tanda* with a foul-smelling man who happens to also be my best dancer of the night. Between songs, during the chat, I take a giant step back as he gallantly explains, "My style is different but I think you can do it well." My body language isn't lost on him, but he worries that I don't like his dancing. "No," I say, "*¡me encanta!*" I grab him in a premature embrace in an attempt to position my nose away over his shoulder again.

As I sit, the stench of an unwashed human will not leave my nose. I think suddenly of a man who kept poking my breastplate with his fingers as we chatted between songs and another whose lead was so full of dead space I wondered why he danced.

I realize that I'm having a spell. I still feel that the essence of tango is like grace and the dharma, pure and untrammeled. It's my body and mind that are prone to fatigue and negative feedback. Since coming here, I've pushed myself to not blame anyone for any unhappiness. But Mariel has given me this Spanish proverb: *Errar es humano, pero más lo es culpar de ello a otros.* (To err is human but to blame others is even more so.)

Instead of blaming the men, my mind drifts to Pema Chödrön, who writes in *Start Where You Are*, "There's a richness to all of the smelly stuff that we so dislike." She says that to awaken to our soft centers, we have to see the smelly stuff as our wealth, not as an obstacle.

I know she didn't have unclean dancers in mind, but still the learning applies to tonight quite literally and figuratively. For a long time I have held myself apart from those people who turn sour on *milongas*. Rather than acknowledge my own distaste has arisen, I've chosen to dig back in harder and more determined than ever to rise above the harmful speech, the pettiness, the triviality, the smelly stuff.

Where does a beginner's mind go? Back to sleep? There is a famous saying that's often taught to Zen students that goes like this: *Before they studied Zen, mountains were mountains and rivers were rivers; when they start to study Zen, mountains become something else, magical swirling cones or vortices, and rivers, too, become bodies and limbs of mystical energy; after they've studied Zen, mountains are once again mountains and rivers are just rivers.* What this little anecdote means is that once we start to study the dharma we want to shroud everything in an aura; we start to see only the aura and forget the mundane thing, the mountain or river, beneath it. As we come full circle back to a beginner's mind, we see the mundane thing and the aura, both as constructs of our mind.

I've been bending over backward—or twisting my body comical-ly—to avoid the smelly aspect of the *milonga* and clinging to its aura.

But the *milonga* is just another place where I run into my Self, which is a person losing her beginner's mind. Sometimes you have to let go of your mind. Sometimes the middle way is informed by the extremes. *If you meet the Buddha, kill the Buddha* is another famous proverb. It means if you come upon a big truth or amazing teacher, as I have in the shape of *milongas* of Buenos Aires—don't grasp and cling too hard, or sooner or later you'll fall off your axis, because truth is dynamic, ever-changing, so its opposite always occurs.

One night, Carmen's friend Francis, who is a bit of a monk-by-association (one of his brothers is a Zen master in Ojai, California, the other a former Jesuit priest), says to me, "You have to get away from the energy in *milongas* sometimes." Manjusri, the god of wisdom who cuts through the thick of delusion with his swift sword, couldn't have put it more succinctly.

So, affirmed in my own instincts, I take a whole week off—not from tango, but from the *milongas*. I allow myself to dawdle longer on those mornings when I go to my Palermo park, where I discover a talking stone bench. I sit under its trellis with its camouflaged motion sensors as a voice blossoms from two speakers telling a short story in Spanish.

Other mornings, I swim, spending more time at my pool developing a new twist on an ancient discipline—underwater yoga. At the pool's deep end I hang out in lotus. My lungs get more and more elastic and I'm able to stay down a long time, floating or sinking as I release air from my lungs. I place a floater between my ankles and do a forward stretch grasping my toes. Holding my breath adds another dimension of awareness—you can't mistake when to inhale and exhale in water. My joints rebound happier than on land. In the shallow end I do an elbow stand. Liquid weightlessness is my only prop—Iyengar yoga uses numerous props on land. At the pool wall, I do triangle pose. *Savasana,* or corpse pose, is a natural for the water—I have to be careful not to scare the lifeguard, though.

A couple of afternoons during my week off, I drop in on classes in women's and follower's technique. I have mixed feelings about them, because I prefer to hone my technique in situ. But Mimi Santapa comes highly recommended by everyone. In one of her classes, I notice a woman who cannot do the *cruzada,* the most basic step you learn on day one in the first hour of a lesson. It's not the holy grail, but it's key. Mimi doesn't make a big deal of it, but the woman sweats and seems overly nervous. She can't drop her fear, and I imagine that all our smiling, calm faces must appear like ghoulish grins. She suddenly walks to the outskirts of the studio, grabs her purse, and bolts without paying. The poor woman makes me think of how I could never have entered the meditation arena before I was ready to sit still and feel any anxiety as it arose. Nor could I have entered the tango circle before I was ready to see and feel, listen in a quietly intimate way.

On both Tuesday and Thursday nights, I walk over to Serena Alegría Temple on Junin Street. For years I've been meditating on Zen's ancient ox-herding pictures, and now I'm considering how they parallel my relationship to tango in terms of the stages one goes through in learning about Self—or about a dance. The pictures date back more than a thousand years to China and Japan. They are simple ink drawings of a child and ox, and each image is paired with a title: *Searching for the Ox; Seeing the Traces of the Ox; Seeing the Ox; Catching the Ox; Herding the Ox; The Ox Forgotten; The Ox and Child Both Gone* (I love this one—your eye is drawn to nothing but the white space of a full moon); *Returning to the Origin; Coming Home on the Ox's Back; Entering the Marketplace with Bliss-Bearing Hands.*

The ox represents the Self, or tango in my present state—something wild and mysterious that we try to harness and tame, perpetually. Considering my relationship to both Self and tango expands my awareness of the ways I tend to get overly identified with either—and dangerously cling to either. The ox-herding series can be symbolic of the relationship with anything that consumes you, defines you, takes you out of this world and then delivers you back, renewed, changed, different, whole, expanded.

You can master tango, but you cannot hold it still. You can know your Self, but if you hold it there, suffering comes. There is always a horizon. You are always walking the knife's edge with the likeliness of falling off to one side or the other. Being mindful of this is freeing. With bliss-bearing hands and feet, I'm ready to go back to the *milongas* having learned yet again that what is found was never lost in the first place. Beginner's mind is always available.

The air is as sweet smelling as it always was.

On Friday night, I meet Carmen at Maipu 444. Once again *soy la diosa de esta jodida galaxia*. The first man I dance with is Oscar. Now that I seek Oscar out, I recall how I assumed he was not interested in me. In true Zen fashion, he had only invited me when I gave up all hope. Not knowing his name, I called him the Eagle for his regal aquiline features. He stood out for his snowy waves of hair around a bald pate, his sensual walk, and the way he pointed and stepped on the balls of his feet, not to mention the way he filled his clothes. There is a tendency in *milongas* to begrudge the man or woman who won't dance with you. But in my spacious tango rapture, I never take lack of attention personally.

I always love watching the way Oscar studies the women and dances with the best. This evening at Maipu, he invites me to dance, not one but four *tandas*. Oscar's English is excellent, since he lived in the States for twelve years.

"You know I had waited for you for months," I decide to tell him during the first *charla*, unable to conceal my joy and feeling comfortable enough to share this.

"Well, you have to be still sometimes," Oscar says.

There must be an echo in this room, I think, stunned, as he adds, "You're always jumping up to dance with the first guy who asks."

"You're absolutely right," I say. "I don't like to say no to anyone because . . . " I trail off. The music has started and I cannot dance tango and talk. But also, I'm not sure I want to share with him that I have this Tango Precept Number Two: *to accept what is offered.*

It happens that Oscar and I are leaving the *milonga* together— Carmen has decided to stay longer and catch a few more *tandas*. He lives in the Belgrano barrio, which means he will take the same bus home as I. He invites me for coffee first. I chuckle, remembering that absurd *codigo* that he's really inviting me for sex. But Oscar and I have bonded over the knowledge of our Italian blood and our previous heated debates on food.

"I don't drink coffee at night, but I'll have a glass of wine," I say. I'm not in the least concerned about this white-haired, bespectacled man who, in his wool vest, looks more like a professor than a *milonguero*. And I must admit a part of me has been eager to chat with him outside the *milonga*. As we sit in the café, he tells me he's sixty-eight and has an eighteen-year-old son. He was never married to his son's mother. They are friends, but not romantically linked any longer. He's a Porteño, born in Villa Crespo barrio, the same one as the famous tango composer Osvaldo Pugliese, whose grandmother knew Oscar's grandmother. He becomes increasingly fascinating as I learn he just got his high school equivalent at age sixty-five and then went on for a college degree in philosophy, which he has not completed. He had left school at age fifteen to become a jeweler like his father, then in his midtwenties went to live in New York, where he learned the art of *la cire perdu*, or lost wax. He still makes jewelry models and trains apprentices in lost wax technique in his downtown workshop.

As he sips his espresso, he tells me one of the things he misses most about Manhattan is the Horn & Hardart automat. "I love their punkie pie," he says. Upon further inquiry, I understand he means pumpkin pie. He gains my trust, so I tell him a little about my coming to Argentina to get over my failed relationship and about my Zen practice. He listens with interest and takes it in. But then when I refer to him as a *milonguero*, he tells me he doesn't like to be called that—that here a *"milonguero"* refers to someone who doesn't have a life, who wastes away in *milongas*. Oh, but I tell him, where I come from the term conjures up a man who has tango so deeply in his body and soul, it's pure heaven to dance with him; he's like a god. "Someone like you, Oscar," I say.

Not for the first time, he replies, "Don' bullsheet me."

Which makes me laugh and give him a nickname, Oscar the Curmudgeon. But we cannot find a Spanish word for *curmudgeon*. The closest translation is *cascarrabias*, which really means grouch. So on this evening, Oscar becomes a *Sesame Street* character, Oscar the Grouch. We ride the 152 bus together, and I feel grateful to have a made a new friend, the first Porteño I've ventured to see outside the *milonga* since Juan Carlos, last November. I am learning the difference between healthy boundaries and unnecessary borders.

❧

A couple of weeks later, Carmen says we are invited to the home of Ana Maria and Hector, a married couple she recently introduced me to at Lo de Celia, a locals' *milonga*. They got a kick out of watching me never sit out a *tanda*. They have also invited Carmen's friend Francis, and Manuel, their friend, to the pizza party in their home in Caballito, a quiet working-class barrio.

"Don't tell me you're missing a night of dancing," teases Hector as he assembles the thick-crust pizza.

"Sad but true. I heard you wouldn't be there," I say.

Ana Maria hands me a glass of wine and says, "Here, *churro*." She's taken to using the old-fashioned slang that men flirting in the street use. All around their one-story home is Hector's artwork. Using wire and other basic materials, he's fashioned tango dancers. He captures curves of the way dancers really move, not as they might be taught in technique classes. You see the scoliosis, bellies that sag, curvature of spines, gripping embrace. I believe Hector has captured the tango rapture as I've never seen it.

After scarfing down about five pizza pies, we look at Hector's vinyl collection. He's got recordings five and six decades old of Pugliese, Canaro, Troilo, D'Agostino, and many more. The old photos and artwork on the album sleeves are fun to look at, too. And then we all dance—on a stone floor that was formerly a patio but now has a roof over it—until 3 AM.

"This is how *milongas* used to be—they just happened," says Carmen as I open the front door and step outside to think about this and the dance (and to get air because Ana Maria and Hector are chain-smokers). Of all the many dances I've done, only tango demands you show up fully. You cannot fake or fudge your part in the subtle and gross aspects of dialogue. As a follower, you may dance with your eyes closed, but you must have your mind and heart's eye open. It was easy to do things like open my heart when I arrived here with a sense of nothing left to lose. And now I do it because I find I have so much to gain.

Hector sees the door open. And I'm missing. He gets very upset. Carmen finds me and explains, "He was worried about you; you can't just open the door and step outside here—people can hurt you or try to break in." *Who? What people?* I've asked this question before, so I refrain. I don't doubt there is such crime. But why am I so lucky to not even come close to seeing it, to be enveloped only in the warmth, concern, and hospitality of people who get a kick out of me? I feel I am just starting to understand what there really is to lose—layers of Self I no longer need. And what there is to gain— friendship, love, sharing in the accomplishments of friends, and so much more. I am getting a taste of it as I ramp up for more tango with no borders—and I imagine I'll be insatiable.

Chapter 22

Breathing Lessons

If you're not living on the edge, you're taking up too much room.

—*Alison Wright, travel photographer/writer*

I'm being eaten by mosquitoes on the terrace of La Pharmacie, a restaurant in a former old drugstore on Charcas. But I wouldn't dream of wimping out and saying, "Let's go inside." My thick-skinned companions, photographer Alison Wright and writer Lynn Ferrin, live in San Francisco, where fog limits outdoor supping, and they want to eat al fresco. As uncomfortable as I feel, I realize I'd probably jump in the contaminated Río de la Plata if they asked me, so I sit tight.

Alison and I know each other peripherally, mainly through Lynn, who was my boss at *VIA* magazine until she retired in 1998. Alison's stock photos have illustrated some of my travel stories. They're hanging out with me before and after their cruise to Antarctica. Lynn had told Alison how I was down here practicing tango and Buddhism, so she sent me some emails asking what photo opportunities there might be along those lines. Since it's unlikely my monk friends would be seen dancing tango, Alison decides to follow me, perhaps the city's only dancing Buddhist, to my usual *milonga* haunts.

What an honor it will be to be shot by the same lens that captured the Dalai Lama, his head bowed, his hand gently around the rifle of a soldier who is smiling reverently back at His Holiness. This image of Alison's, for me, captures the way arms of peace will gently silence arms that lead to mass destruction.

Alison says she would not be alive today but for her ability to focus on her breath. In January 2000, she was in Laos on her way to a meditation retreat in India when her rickety old bus was hit by another bus and shorn in two. People died. She was sitting at the point of impact. Her back was broken, her spleen diced, her lungs punctured. Her left arm looked like it went through a paper shredder. She nearly bled to death. A British aid worker drove her over washboard roads seven hours to a makeshift hospital in Thailand.

She's convinced it was the "breathing lessons" at the core of Buddhist practice that helped her endure and survive the next three weeks of trauma and agony, including sutures with no anesthesia to her lacerated arm. Back home in San Francisco, it took many operations to remove glass and debris from her arm and lots of rehab to reassemble her. While still in physical therapy, Alison got a notion that she had to climb 19,340-foot Mount Kilimanjaro, which she did, defying all odds, just two years after the accident and a few weeks shy of her fortieth birthday.

This is what I'm thinking when I decide to let a few sharp-toothed mosquitoes gnaw on my legs all they want. It's so great to have Alison and Lynn here, just as my *milonga* world is starting to seem so small and insular. Their visit is a reminder of how big the planet really is.

Few onlookers could guess the number of vertical and horizontal miles my two companions have logged on this planet. Both Lynn and Alison have climbed to Everest Base Camp, about a thousand feet lower than Kilimanjaro. They've been to Tibet, Nepal, down the Amazon, into the heart of Africa, and all over Asia.

After we're done eating, Alison accompanies me to La Ideal, where I introduce her to Ángel. He invites us to sit at his "Ángel *y amigas*" table. She shoots plenty of photos of me and also furtively takes advantage of other ops—a pair of red sparkling shoes (Dorothy's ruby slippers on stilts), a creaky older couple stuck together with the glue of aged love and adoration. She calls me a "hottie" in my tango getup, but she's blond and so attractive that she has to keep fending off men who all seem to be under the impression that she can't wait to drop her equipment for them. "Sorry, I don't dance," she has to tell man after man after man.

The next evening I'm late in meeting Lynn at her hotel because the rainy season has kicked in—and that means occasional power outages. As I descended from the eighth floor the power went out. I made it safely out of my cage, but the other coffin-size lift held captive my neighbor, Laura. I called the concierge for help before

I left, but Laura later told me that she spent a good hour trapped between floors.

As Lynn and I feast on delicious *sorrentinos*, the Argentine version of ravioli with spicy sauce, and wine, I tell her how the elevator incident reminds me how blessed I am—finally. I'm leading the charmed life after a year from Hell, here in a perennially developing country where people constantly point their index finger to their eye and say *¡Ojo!*, meaning "watch for the dangers lurking everywhere!" Lynn shares with me how she loves Buenos Aires even as she recounts how she's been strapped with a few hundred counterfeit pesos. "I knew that change place was suspicious," she says, laughing it off, as she describes having to walk down a long, narrow dark hall to get there. But she was in a hurry to get smaller bills for the taxi driver who had no change for her bigger notes. It's refreshing to be in the company of a seasoned traveler who knows how to take these things in stride.

We talk about Dan a little, because Lynn has known him as long as I have. She thinks highly of him and believes that he and I belong together. With my newfound patience and equating the act of waiting as soul-building virtue, I tell her that may be so, but for now he's happy with Evelyn and I'm content here. Lynn says, "I can see that." Although she's with a group booked for a tango show, she'd as soon come watch me in the *milonga*. "You're the best act in town," she says.

What a good girlfriend she is!

Alison and Lynn leave for Antarctica, and while they're gone, I receive an email from Dan, telling me that his relationship with Evelyn has ended at her initiation. I read the email dozens of times, but it's simply informational, not invitational. I recall my dream about their having some trouble and wonder if I'm inheriting my mother's psychic abilities—her dreams have frequently been premonitions of birth and death. But I decide it's that Dan and I have a certain immeasurable connection that can't be so easily cut off.

Still, I'm surprised. I don't petition Dan for details, though. It's a bit of a conundrum: If he'd dropped her for me, wouldn't that feel great? But it's precisely because he is not frivolous, but loyal and constant, that I've felt devotion for him.

I call him one night and we talk for the first time in seven months. I offer comfort—and in doing so it feels as if the past year never happened. As I take his side I feel as if I'm arguing against a professional adversary. I tell him, "I can't believe she didn't know a good man when she had one." I can tell he's smarting by the turn of events and my words offer little consolation.

I recognize the five stages of *death of an affair*. I knew them well after Dave. DABDA is the handy acronym I came to know them by: *denial, anger, bargaining, depression, acceptance.* They don't come in any special order, and you cycle through them once, and again, back and forth, and sometimes all of them at once; time is not linear, nor is it cyclical, in dying; it's *webular.* I feel a little left out of his suffering, but I quickly recover and embrace my new position as his friend.

I think of the potential ammunition—*See, I told you so . . . serves you right . . . you got what you deserved*—none of which feels the least bit satisfying and all of which I let wash right over me. The profound thing about chanting the *Metta Sutta* and following all the other recipes for loving kindness is that they actually start to nourish you. I think of Alison's photo of the Dalai Lama's hand wrapped around the rifle's muzzle. It's not that my warrior is dead; she's just at ease, smiling reverently, dancing in close embrace with Her Holiness.

Dan's news has little effect on my dancing because it's always been the place where I don't even think, no less worry, about the past or future. This month, March, is when many tourists from North America and Europe begin to descend on the city for tango classes and events designed for foreigners. In a case of odd synchronicity, I run into two men I know from San Francisco. I run into Jorge and Tomás at different *milongas*, where both confide in me their female problems. Tomás's theory is that the problem stems from the fact that women want love first, then sex, and men pursue the reverse (reinforcement for my friend, John, from New Zealand). Carmen, a longtime student of astrology and numerology, says simply that Saturn is not in a good place for these men now. As for me, I take to the floors around town with Jorge, Tomás, and any other men who invite me, and soar above analysis and deconstruction. All those moves—*sacadas, voleos, volcadas, colgados, enganches*—that require warriorlike presence but no will, ripple through my body like breezes through a Tibetan prayer flag. I'm at peace, enough so to offer up a dance for Dan. And, *qué milagro*, one for Evelyn. I'm still as high as Mount Everest.

When Alison and Lynn return from Antarctica, I get together with Lynn again and tell her about Dan. She says when she gets back home she'll meet him for dinner. She asks if I want her to tell him anything. I ponder this for a minute or so. There's a tiny part of me that wants to make something happen, to leverage the situation to my *will*. But I feel my feet grounded on this Rioplatense soil, my lungs, heart, and blood oxygenated by its air, my tongue reshaped by its language. My right palm, from which sparks seem to fly when my female energy receives the male impetus, longs to touch the earth. I know the ground will shake with what I deem to be my only answer.

"That I love him . . . but he knows that." I tell her.

There's a little hole in my days after Alison and Lynn leave for good. I love my new friends down here, but there's nothing like an old girlfriend who knows all your history, good and bad, all your proud and embarrassing moments. I don't talk to anyone about all the shades of emotion running through me during these days following Dan's revelation.

One afternoon, I stand in front of my armoire's full-length mirror and recall the last time I sat in the little church next to the Recoleta cemetery. I had felt that forgiveness was possible because, in the end, I loved myself too much to carry the weight of hate and grudges. I'm grateful I felt it before I knew that Dan and Evelyn were a thing of the past. But still I need to ask myself, *Have you really put the bone down?* Or perhaps more aptly, thinking of Alison's photo, *Is your finger on the trigger or your hand on the muzzle?* It's dizzying to be suddenly without the primary reason I've been clinging to for being down here. It's disorienting, like when up and down are confused in a winter snowstorm whiteout. I come across a verse from an early Buddhist woman named Sangha that reassures me. In her poem, she writes of having given up her home, all that she loves, of packing up her desire, hate, ignorance, and even craving. "Now I am quenched and still," Sangha writes, describing perfectly the place I feel I have almost arrived at. It's frightening to think that were it not for Dan and Evelyn's affair I might not have left home. I might not have been *quenched and still.*

Do I feel like hopping on the next plane home to try to get back with Dan? Not even for a split second. It's not that I don't wonder what the future may hold for us as a couple. But what holds unswerving center is that sentiment of *What's the hurry?* It sways me like tango music and one of those moves that I want to milk for its beauty and goodness.

I study the row of well-worn tango spikes standing at ease on the top shelf of the armoire closet. *What would Lynn and Alison do in my shoes?* I ask myself. And then I look down at my hiking boots buried under a pile of street shoes and sandals and know exactly what they'd do. They'd run up a mountain.

So I book a week in the wilds near the stem-end of the earth, where Tierra del Fuego and Patagonia straddle Argentina and Chile. My sturdy feet and legs take me up the famous towers in Chile's Torres del Paine National Park. On the Argentina side, I come face to face with the icy spires and jags of Perito Moreno, a hulking Aqua Velva–blue glacier that rises massively some sixty meters (a twenty-story building) above the surface of Lago Argentino. In nearby El Calafate I hike around Laguna Nimez, where one hundred species of birds, mostly waterfowl—including a flock of Chilean flamingos, their vivid pink feathers dazzling against the sparkling blue waters—feed and breed on wetlands.

❧

I return to the big city refreshed and renewed as only time in wilderness can do. I'm quickly back up on my "stilts," telling my many Argentine dancing partners about their Patagonia land, which many of them cannot afford to visit.

I wonder often how Dan is progressing, but more important, I wonder how I'm doing deep down. It's nearing Semana Santa, Holy Week, and an opportunity arises for the stillness of meditation supported by the presence of others. Templo Serena Alegría will have a four-day *sesshin*, April 5 through 8, which is the day Buddha's birthday is celebrated. April 8 is also Easter Sunday.

A group of us, eight men and eleven women, arrive by van at Vicente Casares, an hour outside of Buenos Aires. It's great to be back in the country, training mind and heart. It's fall in the southern hemisphere, and the cottonwoods on the grounds of the former Jesuit mission are golden. At night, the full moon casts silver light that keeps the animals active. In a pink morning sky, the falcons cry out and circle close to us. The bat is still in residence in the rafters near the bathrooms. Leaf-cutter ants are marching in lines everywhere. With sharp head-shears the ants slice chunks of leaf about four to five times their body size. How funny when they fall over. They fall down a thousand times and get back up (like good Zen students).

The nineteen of us spread our *zafus* around the perimeter of the *zendo* and sit facing the wall hours after our arrival. I take my power spot with the same black splats on the wall. This time they recall a throw of the *I Ching*, that ancient Chinese system for giving order and meaning to what seems random and chaotic. I'm not sure yet what they're saying.

Thinking of Dan and me, I chant to myself, *Not knowing is nearest*, a Zen saying that helps one surrender to uncertainty's discomfort in a comfortable way. The longer I hold *not knowing*, the more freeing it is. I play with it: *Knot-knowing is knearest*. When I know my *knots* or *nots*, I should be prepared to learn what I need to know. *Stay close and do nothing, or you'll miss it*. Everything I need to know or see is right in front of me. All I need is vision as sharp as a leaf-cutter's head-shears.

Another line arises from the Jewel Mirror Samadhi, a sutra I've chanted hundreds of times: *When the wooden man begins to sing, the stone woman gets up to dance*. This phrase is open to endless interpretation. But for me it has always been a perfect haiku that describes a kind of eternal marriage, which someone in ninth-century China recognized. This couple finds each other. They know what they're made of. They both have hard parts. They work out a sort of vaudeville act together—*after* the children, after the divorce, after the affairs, after they've done the song-and-dance routine a zillion times and its pain turns to pleasure. The best part—they get married at the *end* of their lives, and live happily ever *forward*. I'm not saying I want us to get married. I'm thinking of the cracks and splits in Dan, me, and everyone, and how we all need to mend them, *tie the knot* (or *not*). The wooden man and stone woman have always felt like my own internal marriage.

Thinking of Dan's pain, I conclude that this is my second chance to embrace him fully, as I have so often wished I had done that January day when he was shattered over my affair. Which means to let go of everything, of every expectation, hope, craving, desire. Waiting was something that used to seem like punishment. But now, as an accomplished dancer, I know it to be a muscle, and through the grace of meditation and tango, I'm developing mine.

❧

Near dusk in the *zendo,* there is always a brief time when all the birds, horses, dogs, crickets, and other insects outside take an intermission and are still. My mind's thoughts, rising and falling, are the loudest sound. Then this chopping sound of metal scissors opening and closing—a bird—swoops by the window where I sit. *Cut it out! Cut it out! Cut it out!*

I have! I cut down and out much. I am more than halfway through my year here. My clothes are showing wear. I've retired yoga pants, my good-witch socks, underwear, and two bathing suits. Decay and half-life have stripped what my hands haven't—taking what's offered also means letting go of what goes. So little went into my suitcases. So much has come out—a thousand tangos, heartbeats, and breaths. All fit together like a Tibetan sand painting—a beautiful multicolored mandala, painstakingly assembled. Then gone in a flash. Impermanence has its upside. In museums I fatigue after an hour—all that "captured" art begins to weigh on me. Tangos and sand paintings, like breath, don't last long enough to oppress.

They last long enough to teach. Tango has taught me that humbleness is much richer, more spacious, more freeing, than conceit and pride. It has given me gratitude for the true depth and weight of time.

I think of an email that announced a tango seminar to teach "104,976 possible four-step figures" in tango. This astonishing numerical value belies one qualitative truth of all tango, meditation, and life—that with complete presence and mindfulness an infinite number of figures is possible (why stop counting at six figures?).

The Buddhists are fond of numerical values, too. There are 108 delusions, three treasures, four noble truths, an eightfold path, ten precepts, and a bunch of hindrances. But tango's points of entry, like the dharma gates, are boundless.

Just as the bell rings for dinner break, I feel another sense of gratitude arise—to Dan and Evelyn.

The *sesshin* food is simple and pure vegan again. What captures my imagination and senses is this small disk of saffron yellow *nabo*, or pickled turnip. They buy it in Buenos Aires's *barrio chino*, Chinatown. The flat little vegetable is meant to cleanse the empty plate, part of the *oryoki* eating ritual (in the States we use a *setsu*, a wooden stick with canvas at one end). The servers come around after we're done eating and slide a slice of *nabo* onto each plate along with a bit of boiling hot water. You pierce the *nabo* with your fork and polish your plate. Then you drink the water and eat the *nabo*. A wave of flavors ripples across the tongue. Fruit, smoke, hazelnut.

By the last day, my senses are so tuned up that the quarter-size disk explodes like a plate of black truffles soaked in a case of sake. I hold it in my mouth, suck it dry of flavor, then chew slowly like I would the Host. Oh, this must be what grace or redemption tastes like—very big. I dance and meditate, not just for serenity, but for this, to wake up to the infinitely rousing fullness of the moment, like this *nabo*'s spectrum of taste. Awareness is all-encompassing. *Moment* is a word that comes from the Latin *momentum*, for motion. Being present does not mean living in an artificial measure, a second or minute at a time. It means living in the whole moment*um* of life. I have called the entry to tango, the *salida*, an exit from real time. But I would like to revise that to an exit from artificial time.

Back in the *zendo*, I imagine a little gold disk to polish the soul. *Scrub, scrub*—I need to go deeper than last *sesshin*, when I got stuck with a hung jury in court. I focus my attention on three of the black spots. As always, distraction arises. My muscles feel angry or bored. I have no story to feed them. No day in court. We've settled. I know they are simply averse to stillness. I hold them, with my posture in an upright position. They scream at me. *Okay, okay,* I say. Without disturbing my neighbors a few feet away, I locate one muscle in the upper back, near the shoulder blade. There. I give it a good quiet isometric squeeze and direct the flow of breath. *Ahh,* I let go. Saliva floods my mouth. Something soft and ripe melts into my muscle. My *bodhicitta*, my soft, ripe vulnerable center, per Chödrön.

I know now that the paint splats are telling me there is still something deeper, some black marks on my soul I need to attend to. In order to have forgiveness you have to have sorrow. In order to have sorrow you must understand the Self—Buddhism teaches, *We study the Self to forget the Self.* This understanding has been long in the making, like a spring gushing to the surface: The rage unleashed toward Evelyn took up lodging in my body and mind long before she and I even met. I have traced it as far back as when I was four years old: *Standing in my front yard in Elizabeth, New Jersey, I am watching a little neighbor girl pull the hair of another little girl who pissed her off for some reason. I feel sorry for the little girl who runs home crying. But the overwhelming feeling is envy for the little girl*

who feels free to express ire without fear of severe corporal punishment,
with a belt or hand, as I would have suffered.

Even when I came of age and understood there are kind and
socially acceptable ways to express discontent, I went through much
of life envying that little girl, as I kept in check my many frustrations
and little angers, as if I might still get whipped for airing them.
Certainly I made progress toward unveiling my negative feelings,
but it was as if I were waiting for circumstances, such as those with
Evelyn, to provide me the opportunity to commit this one "crime of
passion" that I had long ago witnessed and admired.

The spots are saying that strong women who climb mountains
and have tough muscles must turn their strength inward. Just
because you can stop your life on a dime to leave hearth and home
doesn't mean you can't say *I'm sorry.*

I recall the tarot card from my second or third night here,
guiding me to give up "unforgiving hatred." I inhale deeply and
exhale fully. I stare at the stubborn spots. For a moment, I'm like
Lady MacBeth. I get out the *nabo* and scrub and breathe. It's on the
exhalation where I'm moved. It feels like the rock that rolls away so
that Christ could rise from the dead: "I'm sorry, Evelyn. And this
time I mean it." I almost want to run to a phone.

Monk Ricardo rings the bell and we chant the Heart Sutra in
Japanese, a song of compassion. And in this last hour of the *sesshin,*
the day Christ rose from the dead and the day Buddha was born
some two thousand, five hundred years ago, I say to myself, *C'mon,*
stone woman, get up and dance with that wooden man.

Chapter 23

Tango Grace

> *The important thing is not to think much, but to love much;*
> *and so, do that which best stirs you to love.*
>
> —*Saint Teresa of Avila*

It's May and the mercury is occasionally dipping into the thirties and forties. But, as the saying goes, it's always summer in the *milonga*, where the body heat is the same for all seasons. So I needn't alter my wardrobe too much.

There is a mysterious woman who frequents the *milongas* who has been in my peripheral vision almost since I've arrived in Buenos Aires. But I'm starting to pay her more mind. She doesn't dance. She's old. Maybe chronologically she's only in her late sixties, but she's very cronish. Her dress is dowdy and dated. Her taupe blond hair is rolled severely in the 1940s style à la Joan Crawford. The *milonga* hosts always seat her at the best tables. She drinks and eats daintily and watches. Dancers stop at her table to chat, but only briefly. Someone told me that she is important, that she is *la dueña* (owner) of tango. That sounded so impossible that I didn't want to have it explained further. ("A fact too good to check," one of my former bosses would say). Owning tango is like owning solar energy.

La dueña mostly watches through a calm poker face. There's something I like about her, I realize after all these months of not paying attention to her. I like when I feel her gaze on me as I dance by her table. I get the feeling I meet her approval, that she'd let me have an audience with her; but I keep my distance, not knowing what I'd say if we spoke. And I don't want to break this spell of her being the wise old crone right out of a fairytale.

The quality that *la dueña* most embodies for me is a big word—*sovereignty*—which I clearly remember learning at the freshly minted double-digit age of ten. I was watching a 1940s film version of the Celtic tale of the marriage of Sir Gawain on our black-and-white TV that seldom worked in those days. After slaying a white stag, King Arthur is accosted by a dark-hooded creature who says that unless the king can answer the question "What do all women most want?" he must die. In true courtly service, Sir Gawain sets to the task of finding the answer. He meets a loathsome, toothless old hag who says that she will give him the answer if he marries her. Gawain agrees and she tells him this: Women want *sovereignty*. My ten-year-old brain quickly intuited from that glorious final scene that this meant women want *their own way*. Gawain then breaks the spell on the hag by allowing her will to be done.

❧

It's a Thursday night and I'm sitting in Niño Bien alone between *tandas,* feeling my own wise crone energy. Most of the tourists have flown north with the snowbirds, but I am like *la dueña,* who sits across the salon from me tonight—a fixture, here for all seasons. I have decided to extend my stay through April 2008—another whole year. From a couple of phone conversations I've had with Dan, I understand that he's not interested in getting back together. He is interested in staying close friends, and I embrace this and extend an open an invitation for him to visit me here whenever, if ever, he likes.

I'm stretching that almighty peso in my choice to stay on, but I have faith that I can make it work. My savings have dwindled, and I'm only half-kidding when I say to friends who ask when I will return home, "When I can afford to live in the first world again." In my nine months here, I've spent less than what I would need to survive two months back in the States, but I have never felt richer in my life. I have not lived this much in the present since I was ten years old.

At Niño Bien, I am wearing some of my blue glitter, the sparkly makeup that Juan Carlos told me I should never wear so as to protect the men I dance with. I'm pretending to be *la dueña* and to *own* tango, though, and so tonight with my glitter I'm sending a message that the men who may be disingenuous with their wives had best not dance with me. I see dancing couples all around me, some sleepwalking, others awakening spiritually. I imagine myself going around the salon, a tango nun, telling them, "*Don't* leave too much room, the Holy Spirit likes to be cuddled." One of the blue sparkles I'm wearing flashes in my peripheral vision, and as I turn my head I see Alberto, my *príncipe azul,* who's bending to kiss my cheek hello with a flourish. I sense he'd kiss my ring if I asked—he, too, sees that I own tango now. Everything is copacetic between us—we exchange relaxed greetings. We've come a long way. Over the months, I've watched him fish—catch and release—many times. My distant smile conveys to him that I'd rather sit than dance with him.

He lingers with me for a bit before turning to fish elsewhere, and I recall with amusement how a month ago I was dancing at *milonga* Viejo Correo with Juan Carlos when Alberto stopped in with a woman. I'd never seen Alberto there before. As Juan Carlos and I danced, Alberto and the woman got up to dance, too. In the tight salon, they were inches away from us, nearly touching us. *In all of Argentina,* I thought, *I've known only two men in the Biblical sense. They don't know each other at all. What were the odds that the three of us would be circling together down the line of dance?*

Line of dance, wheel of fortune, street of dreams. This must be how you get to own tango—experiencing the *milonga* in all its sacred and profane incarnations. I've now seen it enervated and anemic, sometimes with bodies going through mechanical movements, and other times glorious and thriving as if from some divine provenance. It's no different from my experience in church or the *zendo* or anywhere. Owning tango really means owning yourself and all the perceptions you constellate.

I've watched the disenchanted dancers fall away, lose their faith. They call the *milonga* a scene or meat market or den of iniquity because they see themselves as separate (as I once did) from the smelly stuff, from the showing off, competition, and seduction. But tango is highly perishable, so they return to fish, to prowl. In the *zendo* we are admonished to sit with no gaining attitude. It's hard to convince people in the *milonga* that a nonjudgmental no-gaining attitude would bring rapture beyond their wildest dreams. But after all I've seen and experienced, I know this is so, down to the last marrow cell in my bones—as sure as I am sovereign of my own dance.

As I sit here admiring the flashy outfits, I recall another tale: Long, long ago, a woman—maybe *la dueña* of tango—lived in a seaside village and fished her whole life with a straight hook. People would pass by and laugh at her. "Why are you fishing with a straight hook, foolish girl?" But she just kept on fishing and fishing. For years she fished this way, and for years the world laughed. Eventually, she was quite old and white-haired, maybe even with a severe Joan Crawford hairdo. In a far away land, a prince—maybe a *príncipe azul*—heard of her, the foolish woman who had fished with a straight hook for years. He wanted to meet her. He was quite curious. He had his servants prepare for the long, arduous journey to find her in her humble village, maybe the Recoleta. On the morning of the day he arrived, the old woman was casting her straight hook into the Río de la Plata. The prince walked alone along the banks to find her and watch. "Excuse me, señora, can you tell me what it is you hope to catch with a straight hook?" The old woman turned to the prince, her face all sweet, all-knowing, and smiled, "You, my prince."

Tonight I am like *la dueña*, and both of us are here, fishing with our respective straight hooks. It would be easy to laugh at her, this woman who hangs out in a place of dance and doesn't dance. But I realize that if I dared tell my fellow dancers how I view tango as a spiritual practice, they might laugh at me, too. I'd let them, though, because my "prince" continues to show up when I least expect him, in the shape of breath-giving moments. I am a much happier—much better—person than I was when I arrived last August. I sit with this thought and watch the way the entire dance floor morphs before my eyes from a collection of separate couples into one unified organism of magnificent and harmonious motion.

The next morning I contemplate how I've changed over the last nine months. I walk to my Palermo park, inhaling the mild fall air through the tunnels of big jacaranda trees along Libertador Avenue. I walk briskly all the way until I'm at *la Pergola del Lago*. The long lakeside walkway is now covered in purple and red foliage of grapevines that wrap the supporting pillars and cling to the overhead trellis. This is where I've been doing my Stations of the Cross for some time now. Though instead of progressing through fourteen stained-glass windows as in church, I stop at each of the seventeen stone benches on the pergola. Lately, it occurs to me that I have been doing exactly the reverse of carrying a cross that gets heavier and brings scourging at the pillars, a crown of thorns, and much suffering. My cross has gotten lighter. The thorns are gone. No lashes or whipping from within or without. I am as light and carefree as that yellow-breasted kiskadee that watches me sit or stretch.

At each bench, I can mark a positive change—qualities like how I am calmer, slower, more patient, more open, more accepting, more present. When I recall how Miguel, the dancer I met months ago at

Salon Canning, tells me often, *"Linda alma, Camila,"* that I have a beautiful soul, I can't imagine he'd have said this last August.

I stop at one bench and sit in the dappled sun. I consider forgiveness and how it's come full circle. I've forgiven not only Dan and Evelyn, but also, importantly, myself. As I take in the beauty of this park, I feel the sheer joy of emptiness, not in our Western sense of impoverishment, but in the Buddhist sense of spaciousness—easy come, easy go. Thoughts and feelings are like waves lapping a shore. Last night, another man told me I was a *"junco."* A lily, daffodil, orchid, reed, bamboo? I guessed. No, no. Finally, using hand gestures, we got to a *rush* or a *bed of rushes* . . . lithe and lissome, he explained, which I took to be a remark on my suppleness. *Yes, inside and out,* I thought.

Several small rufous-crowned sparrows scatter from the next bench as I approach and sit. They remind me of the birds that sewed Cinderella's gown. This newfound sense of wholeness, the feeling of completion, doesn't mean that I've succeeded in getting rid of all anxiety. But it's a breeze to sit with it and see it through its shorter lifespan without any remarkable malfunction. I attribute this to my renewed experience of God-consciousness. (I never actually stopped believing in God, I simply expanded and refined the concept.) I know that time does run out, but there really is a place of no-time, a state of something eternal and immortal.

At the next bench, I think of how the exchange of male and female energies in tango is deceptively powerful and stirs every last *tanguero* I know. (Abandon all hope of ever being the same person, all ye who enter this dance.) I love to listen to newcomers to tango try to explain how alive and awake they feel, how their whole worldview is changing. They grope, as I have, for ways to explain this transformation. One handle, the most enlightened dancers share, is that the terms "leader" and "follower" are not quite accurate and don't describe what is ultimately accomplished in this dance. We cast about for terms—I suggest there is a starter step and then *lead* and *follow* disappear.

But I don't need to get stuck on semantics because the fact is that I'm pleased with how tango has taught me the bioenergetics of my hover zone, that waiting is active, uplifting, and enriching. I cycle through the benches until I reach the last one, my yoga power spot. Here I think about how tango is my transubstantiation. Just as the Latin words *hoc est* (this is) change plain flour and water into something divine, so my entering the dance circle with right mind, intention, and concentration changes me, the dancer in the plain brown wrapper, into something no less sacred than grace itself.

I'm getting ready for Salon Canning, where I'm meeting the dancer who's most captured my heart—like a tango soul mate. It's Oscar the Grouch. Like me, he's another dancer in a plain brown wrapper. He is now my favorite dance partner, and it seems the feeling is mutual.

Several days a week, Oscar sends me text messages telling where he'll be dancing that evening. We have now fallen into a steady rhythm of meeting up Monday nights at El Arranque, Wednesday nights at Salon Canning, Friday nights at Maipu 444, and Saturdays at Los Consagrados (which is the *milonga* held at Niño Bien). I love the creative spelling in his messages—*"mi, too"* or *"J'am late,"* he'll write. He gets his turn to chuckle at me when I write that he'll need a *paraguayo* (a Paraguayan), instead of a *paragua* (umbrella).

"You look beautiful," is his standard greeting. And when I arrive at Salon Canning, he doesn't disappoint. It's nice, this constant affirmation. We enter together and sit in our respective sections. We dance with others, but mostly with each other. Our energy is high and creative.

Oscar is about five feet, eleven inches, the perfect height for me. My head rests comfortably in the crook of his thick neck. His belt is in the right place, around his waist, not below a big belly. Watching the way his pants ripple as he dances, I am often moved. I think of the koan that asks whether the wind is moving the flag or the flag is moving the wind. Tango moves Oscar and Oscar moves tango. He rivals Ángel for torso-to-torso message delivery. Oscar is even more solid, with well-distributed weight. I love entering a *milonga* and scanning the men's section for the shine of his bald scalp and the blizzard of his thick long white hair all around the sides of his head and over his ears.

We have lively discussions between dances, and I like hearing his opinions, which are, like those of many Argentines, always strong, never lukewarm. He loves the composer Gobbi, even more than Pugliese. He tells me so many times, "I don't like Biagi"—the great pianist whom everybody else loves—that I finally tease him, saying, "Next time I'm mad at you, I'm going to call you a Son of a Biagi."

The following week, after dancing at Salon Canning again, we change our shoes and walk partway home together. I discover that while on the dance floor, he is sensual in an understated, irresistible way; off the dance floor he's got a clumsy, staggering walk. He keeps swaying into me. He holds my hand in a brotherly way, in one of his big fuzzy Shrek-like paws. This begins a new phase for us of walking around town, before, after, or instead of *milongas*. I call them "history walks" because Oscar has something to say about every street name or monument. He stops and sways like he's on a soapbox and gets lost in some history he's pouring forth as he recites various stories about Uriburu, the first president of Argentina, or Sarmiento, the education president, who wanted to put an end to the gaucho lifestyle, or Mitre, that right-winger who started the daily *La Nación*. At Plaza Evita, he says, "She wasn't beautiful, you know, like Madonna." Always Oscar ends with, *"Entendes?"* (You understand?) He means not only the content, but that his English is clear enough.

Along with the history walks, we inaugurate another ritual—Monday night dinners. I stop dancing at El Arranque on Mondays because my Zen group has started offering *zazen* at a new location in the Palermo. Oscar and I meet up at my apartment after he dances and I meditate to dine, as is the custom here, at about 10:30 PM. What with winter coming and the weather turning colder and damper as we move through June, my love of cooking kicks in. We eat and then talk. He's as cynical as the next Argentine about their government: "If Kafka were born in Argentina, no one would have heard of him, because his Kafkaesque nightmares would not hold enough surprise for readers here." But he's proud of one thing—that the country is now doing its own housecleaning of Dirty War killers, rigorously smoking out every last perpetrator and locking them up. I'm proud of Oscar for standing his ground on the necessity of this, unlike other Argentines who just want to close the book on that ugly chapter and won't even discuss it.

Over the next few Mondays, I warm and fill my home with aromas of my favorite winter fare—pasta with spicy red-pepper marinara or Dany's pesto sauce, whole wheat pizza with roasted peppers and basil, sausage with white beans and wine-braised cabbage. I roast the ubiquitous slabs of *calabaza* until brown and caramel sweet. And because *calabaza* is pumpkin, I concoct from sheer memory a rich punkie pie with a buttery whole grain. I give the entire thing to Oscar, who loves it, to take home. He calls me the next day to say it's gone—down his son's stomach.

We are seeing a lot of each other, but not every day, so Oscar doesn't know if I have a *novio* or not. One cold night at Maipu, which is currently our favorite *milonga*, Oscar asks, "Do you have someone to hug and keep you warm?"

"No, only my favorite *tangueros*," I answer.

"Oh, Camila, *qué lástima*," he says. He shakes his head and I can see that he feels truly sorry for me. I watch the way he sits back on his heels, his thick arms at his sides, and sways like a teenager. I explain that since my relationship ended, I haven't wanted a new one.

"How long it is?" he asks.

"A year in May."

"That's long enough to wait," he says.

"You're right," I say, "but I'm not looking."

I wonder briefly if he has himself in mind. I treasure our friendship and the ease of our meeting up to walk, eat, or converse. I don't want it to change. He often calls to tell me the news in the U.S.—some I could do without, like when there's a shooting spree by a sniper in Ohio. But he's entered the ranks of a very few people I'll let keep me on the phone just to shoot the breeze.

Our dancing continues to climb to new heights. It hits many high notes as the mercury continues to dip to record lows. It snows for the first time in some ninety years, on July 9, Argentina's Independence Day (achieved in 1806). Now I know why they blow all their fireworks on New Year's Eve. No one would come out to launch or see them in winter. The dailies run photo montages of the exquisite images of the one inch or so of wet snow on streets, trees, and cars, of the snowmen in plazas and parks.

It melts the very next day. And, as always, it's summer in the *milongas*. The following Wednesday at Salon Canning, Oscar and I dance a *milonga* to a Carlos Di Sarli song and it's so good the way we sway and do *quebradas* together. At the end of the dance Oscar bites my ear. This doesn't come as a surprise, and I like the way it sends shivers down one side.

"You little devil, Oscar," I say as he smiles like the cat that ate the mouse. It feels acceptable given our progressing closeness, hardly like an ever-creeping-closer game of seduction. We talk about the snow and the energy crisis, Argentina's fuel shortage that's all over the newspapers' front pages. We agree, there's plenty of body heat among us tango dancers. In the back of my mind somewhere, I am calculating how many months until the end of November, my year's celibacy mark. As if he's reading my mind, he says, "You know, Camila, good girls go to Heaven, bad girls go everywhere."

I smile and say nothing as I embrace him for the next dance.

The following Monday, he comes by to eat after dancing. I meet him at the building's front door with the big skeleton key, and we ride the elevator up facing each other in silence. His jowls and furrowed brow recede from view and I'm struck by how boyish he looks when he smiles impishly and his dimples get deeper. I brush my finger over one and ask what you call them in Spanish. *"Hoyuelos,"* he says. "My mother stuck her finger in my cheeks when I was still cooking."

"Oh, Oscar, *me encantan tus hoyuelos.*"

"Oh, Camila," he says, and we just giggle. We sit at my wooden table and talk about the coming election as we eat an omelet I've thrown together with leftover broccoli, cauliflower, cheese, tomatoes, basil, and a salad of arugula and red leaf dressed in lusty olive oil, lemon, and salt. When we're done eating, we move onto the more comfortable couch. We talk long about how Christina Kirschner will probably be the next president because she is a Perónist. We talk about the huge meteor that blazed across the sky when I was as a kid, the very month that Oscar moved to New York. It landed in the Bear Mountains. He says, *"Mí,* too, I saw this meteor." I know the way his deep-set blue eyes twinkle that he's playing. So together we create a fairytale of how we are *that* boy and *that* girl, the only two people to have seen its magnesium-blue flash. We've been looking for each other since. And we talk about our pasts. He's an only child and it sounds as if his parents did a number on him. His mother would point to other boys and say, "Why can't you be like them?"

"Wow," I say, thinking, *What mental cruelty.* "I only got hit."

"Yes, but you deserved it," he says so reflexively I can't help but laugh.

"Oh, Oscar, you clown!"

And with that he reaches over and gives me a bear hug that lasts a long minute, and then we kiss long and sweetly on the lips. We smile and then he leaves.

It's the new moon this evening, and very dark, when normally I sleep my best. But I'm wide awake after Oscar leaves. I sit up cross-legged and breathe. I think about Oscar and how much I care for him and feel in love, so unexpectedly. It's dizzying. My libido is rising like a tree's sap in spring. It's so splendid to be falling in love. That part of it is undeniably pure and untrammeled.

Then there's my monkey mind and its many voices: *He's too old; he walks with his right foot turned out. Ah, but he's smart, he likes artsy films. But he interrupts me a lot when I'm talking. Would he swim with me in the bay, or bicycle, or share any of my athletic interests? What about Dan—what if he comes back to me? I need to be able to travel. I need to get my finances settled before I jump into a relationship. What about that year of celibacy—three months to go. But he's so sweet, funny. He irons his own shirts. He dances divine.* Listening to my inner chatter, I conclude this is the closest I'll ever come to understanding how my parents had to listen to ten kids and synthesize their wants, needs, and desires into one harmonious family.

The following Friday Oscar and I meet up at Maipu, and, as I have been thinking all these things, and feeling the start of something, I ask, almost like a test, "Hey, Oscar, would you come swim in my pool tomorrow morning?"

"No, because you gonna hol' my head under the water, I know it," he says with that throaty New York Italian-immigrant intonation.

"Oscar, be serious."

"Okay, Camila," he says. "I be serious."

What I want to say simply is *I love you, Oscar.* Simple, straightforward, undemanding love is what I feel. And how grateful I am to be able to feel this love. But my writerly self takes over, waxing too poetic and abstract for him or anyone. What I say is something like how I feel like one of his lost-wax models for jewels, liquefied, remolded, reconstructed . . . he interrupts me, and I know from the look in his steel blue eyes exactly what's coming. "Don' bullsheet me."

I laugh nervously and remain silent as we finish the *tanda,* slightly annoyed by his predictable deflection. At the end of the night, I go home and email him an electronic image of the fuzzy green Oscar the Grouch in his trashcan. He phones me the next day to say he likes the image. "Yes, that's me, I live in a garbage can," says a man whose apartment is so tidy and spanking clean my compulsively neat mother would approve of it.

We have not defined what the kiss meant, or anything between us, but we continue with affectionate kisses, hugs, text messages. Our phone calls are always the same:

Me: I kiss you three times, once on your lips, one for each dimple.

Him: I kiss you four times.

Me: I kiss you five.

Him: I kiss you seven.

Me: You win.

I distill the little bit of anxiety I feel down to one overarching concern: Not to hurt Oscar in any way. For this reason, I won't say to him, *I love you, Oscar.* But I feel it deeply. And that is wonderful.

The next cold evening we're out dancing, we ride the bus home together. We sit next to each other, and I ask to run my fingers through his thick white hair. He says he's combed it the same way since he was a little boy when his mother would part it for him on the left side.

"What do you use to hold it down, gel?" I ask.

"I use *dulce de leche* or *mermelada* sometimes," he says.

"Oh, Oscar."

"Oh, Camila."

"Give me your comb," I say. He takes it out of his shirt pocket. I comb his satiny hair and he lets me, like a little kid.

The following Monday, it's still cold and we've had record rains that temporarily turn Buenos Aires streets into rivers. After a swim (in my pool, not the street) with some floating yoga, I sit to drink my coffee, read *Tricycle* magazine's Daily Dharma on my laptop, and open my other email. I spot one from Dan, which I eagerly open first. He writes that he'd like to come visit in November, if I'm still open to that. His niece Carol will come for the first week and then he'll stay so we can travel together, perhaps to Patagonia—taking that trip we would have done a year ago. I'm delighted. Dan and I have always traveled even better than we ever lived together. I'm excited about seeing them both and about showing him Patagonia. I'll get a freelance story out of it. They'll stay with me. I'll split the king bed back into two twin beds, and there's also the double futon. I can't say what my hopes are, but I feel very open to seeing what, who, how Dan and I are together after all that's happened.

Oscar comes by later as usual. We eat Swiss chard, Camembert, smoked ham, brown bread, and tomatoes dressed in olive oil, oregano, and salt. For dessert I whip up some *panqueques* (pancakes, a dessert here) of whole wheat–oat flour filled with walnuts, dark chocolate, *dulce de leche,* and raspberry preserves.

"I'm too full," he says, pushing away seconds. "You like an Italian grandma."

"Yes, that's me," I say, thinking of short fat Grandma Catalano who tried so hard to fatten me.

As we sit at the table, I tell Oscar that Dan and his niece are coming.

"But maybe you gonna go back with him," he says right away. "What if he wants to sleep with you?"

These are good, honest questions. "I love him like family, but I don't think he wants to get back or sleep with me. He's to me now like your son's mother is to you."

"If I would say *I love* my son's mother, I would be with her," he says.

I can see he's struggling with this. I say, "But you do love her; I mean you *show* love. Or you wouldn't continue to take care of her as you do." And then, because I know it won't sound corny to Oscar, I say, "Love is as love does." And hope that won't prompt a reply of, "Then, if you loved me . . . "

Even though I know there is love aplenty between us, the word has not yet crossed our lips, and his silence and look tell me he's not buying my view. I think about the way I feel—very turned on, *in love,* and yes, *in lust,* too—with Oscar. I *do* see him in my future, and I think how my love for Dan, and his for me, has not been very sexual for quite awhile. But there's no doubt in my mind I'd go running if Dan were in danger or needed me. With that thought, I suddenly recall the dream I had two nights before: In the dream, I'm watching Dan walking on a beach from afar when I see a huge tidal wave coming toward shore. My anxiety level rises and I prepare to dive into the wave and save him if I have to. There's not a second's hesitation, no doubt I'll do it. But then I see him safely on the shore, not swept away. When I awoke, I knew the dream was as much an affirmation of my newfound self-love as of the kind of love Dan and I mutually feel.

After a long silence, Oscar says to me, "Okay, I gonna ask him for your hand."

"Oh, Oscar," I say so endeared by how his mind works, since this pronouncement comes, no doubt, from me having professed the family bond I feel for Dan. "Maybe you should." I shrug my shoulders, as I recall how binary Argentine men can be. But Oscar's different—at least I hope so. We've talked about his renewing his visa and visiting me in the States next year. So in a mix of emotion spiced with his brand of humor, he goes off on a scenario, "So maybe I gonna come to San Francisco and we all live together. Doña Flor and her two husbands. You say 'Dan, oh you want apple pie? Okay,

I make you apple pie.' You say, 'Oscar, you want a punkie pie? Okay.' You make me punkie pie. Huh, right?"

"You're so funny, Oscar," I say because he is, even though I know his humor to be his armor.

"You know *Doña Flor and Her Two Husbands*?"

"Yes, I saw the film," I say. It's Brazilian and based on writer Jorge Amado's novel of a woman who adores her new husband but continues an affair with the ghost of her dead husband. Only a shaman can cure her. That would be my Oscar, zooming in on the precise reference.

I love him for these little traits and so want to tell him. I don't want him to worry. No matter what, I want to stay close friends. He's given me a huge gift—being able to feel love and in love again is way more valuable than being loved. I want him to come to the States, regardless. But I don't want to risk hearing him say, *Don' bullsheet me.*

At the end of the evening, he kisses me on the cheek and hugs me affectionately and leaves. I sit and feel my anxiety—shades of Dan and Dave again. *Wow, I'm too old for this,* I think. At age fifty-six, I no longer want to have to choose between two men. But when I sit still and upright in half lotus on my bed, the answer comes clearly that I'm golden. I have not made any false moves. And—what's the hurry?

Oscar and I continue to dance and see each other often, with only an occasional allusion to Dan's November visit. Everything seems copacetic.

Then, on August 8, three weeks away from my one-year anniversary date, I decide I will have a fiesta to celebrate. I start inviting all my friends. I try to reach Oscar to tell him, but he does not return my messages or emails, and he's not showing up at our *milongas*. When I finally reach him, he is distant and says he's busy with a student and will call back later. He eludes me for a whole week. *How could things change so quickly?* I wonder. Maybe he's just a *"milonguero"* after all, a fly-by-night, and not the good person I think I've known. The feeling of pending loss is big and distracting. It dominates all my meditations. But what to do? Call Dan and tell him not to come? No, I won't sell myself out. Oscar is not my keeper.

Oscar's complete boycott of me goes on, very painfully, for more than a week. I feel a loss. The old me would have moped around and made an inventory of *all I did wrong* to inflict this pain on me, but the new me knows I can't control everyone and everything, and that while pain is inevitable, suffering is always an option. So for this, at least, I feel grateful.

After ten days, I dig my heels in. I call Oscar and push him to tell me what's going on—in person. I deserve better treatment, I tell him. *Son of a Biagi!* You can't just vanish like this. "I miss you, Oscar!"

"Me too," he says quietly.

We meet at a nearby café. When he comes up the stairs from the subway, I squeeze him and kiss his dimples, I run my hand over his fuzzy Popeye-Shrek arms.

At the café, I notice how his tic, wagging his leg like a dog wagging its tail, is gone. He sits very still. I start right in. "Why are you ignoring me, Oscar? I don't like to be ignored. You have no idea what a button that is for someone who is fifth of ten kids."

"I sorry, Camila. I don't want to hurt you," he says. "My parents ignore me, too."

Seeing him so forlorn softens me, especially when he says, "I don't want to lose you." He explains how he doesn't want to be a placeholder and have me leave and go back to Dan's arms.

"We have to wait, Camila, to see what happens."

"I accept that," I tell him. I can't promise him anything yet, it's true. I need to not hurry. Apart from seeing Dan, I also need to go back to my country and see how it feels and settle loose ends. As for Dan, he and I need to see where we're at. We can't discuss or settle our relationship by phone or email. It may be just a friendship, but I need to leave my options open. Oscar and I have five months, but Dan and I have nearly sixteen years.

"I want you to come to my fiesta, Oscar, to celebrate my year anniversary here," I say.

"We see."

"I want to take you to the U.S. consulate to renew your visa for the States. I want you to visit me there next year."

"We see," he says again. And then that deadpan expression of his comes over his face and he says, "Maybe they not let me in if I say I know you."

"That's the Oscar I know and . . . like," I say. I reach across the table to rub his arm and want so much to squeeze him to me.

Oscar says he wants some time alone and I agree he should have that. We'll meet up the following Sunday at a new *milonga*, La Milonguita, in his barrio.

After he's gone I feel relief—he's still the same ol' Oscar—and sadness, like I'm losing contact with a really good friend. And a bit annoyed, too, as if there is an ultimatum: Be his lover or nothing.

In the coming week, I miss him and our conversations and easy time together immensely and can't wait to see him at La Milonguita. When I do, he's as happy as ever to see me. He greets me with the usual, "You look beautiful." Our palms meet, our torsos connect. And we disappear. There is no Oscar or Camille, only tango. We dance five great *tandas,* all wonderful, better than ever.

I'm ready to go home at about midnight, before him, so he takes me out front to wait for a taxi. As we stand in the dark listening to the music drifting from inside the salon, I say, "Oh, it's Fresedo, I love him, too bad we're missing him."

Oscar says, "I tell you something I don't tell many people. I used to have autographed photos of Fresedo, Di Sarli, Pugliese, all of them. My parents threw them out when I was living in the States."

He once told me he couldn't cry, but he looks like he could cry right now, and I can't help but wonder if his recalling this loss is connected to us. "Why did they do that?" I ask.

"Because they never respect me," he says.

"I respect you and I . . . hug you." I hug him instead of saying "love."

"Okay, okay," he says, as if to dampen my burst of affection lest he have to suffer its loss, too.

There's something different about his hair. "How come you look more handsome than usual tonight?" I ask.

"I stop parting my hair. I got rid of my mother, finally." I see it. He combs his hair, what hair he has around the sides, straight back.

"*Muy guapo,*" I say. And although I know he's done therapy for years, I can't help but feel that something in our budding friendship has sparked this long-overdue riddance.

"Oscar," I can't resist saying, "we'll always have Buenos Aires."

But he looks at me, uncomprehending.

"You know the line in *Casablanca?* We'll always have Paris."

"Remind me," he says.

"You know, with Bogie and Ingrid Bergman. They fall in love in Paris but—"

"Yes, yes," he interrupts. "I remember the movie but not the scene."

"It's during World War II, and then—"

"Yes, yes, she loves Bogie," he says.

"Yes . . . but her husband, whom she thought was dead, returns and so she says—"

"She *loves* Bogie? Right?" he interrupts again.

"Yes but . . . she had to go with her husband at the end—"

"But *she loves* Bogie, right?" He repeats in his richest *don' bullsheet me* voice. I understand now.

"Yes!" I cry out, *"She loves Bogie!"* I want to tell him that there are so many more types of love than what we're told, than what our parents, movies, and fairytales lead us to believe. But I don't, and we just exchange a knowing glance.

"I gonna call you next week to come with me to get the visa," he says.

"¡Genial! And my fiesta?"

"Okay, I gonna come, but don't make too much food."

"I'm sure I will," I say. I feel grateful as I realize he's not making me choose between him and Dan. I feel free and yet intimate with Oscar, my favorite tango dancer. It's a beautiful feeling, like the embrace of tango itself. It clears my misting eyes and I see a man ever more attractive, handsome, and younger.

"I like to go meditate with you sometime," he says. Although I know Oscar has a deep, pensive side to him, this takes me by surprise. I've talked of my Zen practice but never pushed it. It's almost too much for me—I'm not used to having this kind of influence over someone. I almost want to talk him out of it. What if he finds it too difficult and disappointing? Many are called, few are chosen. But I receive this request with grace and gratitude I cannot even express.

"You let me know when you're ready to be still," I say, as I think of his wagging leg.

"Here's your taxi, Doña Flor," he says with that edgy affection I love. I hug him and have time to kiss only one dimple. The right side, my favorite. I get in the taxi, he closes the door. I roll down the window and look at him and say, before the taxi rolls, "Oscar, *te quiero.*"

"*Mí,* too," he says.

As the taxi drives away, I wonder if there's another man in all of Argentina who would let me keep my sovereignty intact.

Line of dance, wheel of fortune, street of dreams. *Dazzling stuff,* I think, as the reflections and lights on Avenida Santa Fe flash by my eyes.

Epilogue

Three days short of my full year here in Buenos Aires, August 26, I held a wonderful fiesta in my small apartment that pulled together, among others, Oscar, of course, and my three best Argentine girlfriends, Carmen, Pato, and Marcela. Auspiciously, although I had invited twenty, there were only twelve of us total—seven women and five men, exactly the number and gender in my original tribe, my blood family, the one against whom all others are measured.

It fell toward the end of the long winter, and it was still chilly, damp, and rainy outside. My tiny place, though, was steaming with warmth. In the center of my wooden table, I put a bouquet of fresh daffodils, a pyramid of mandarins, and a buffet spread—crudités, sausage and beans, lemon-pepper chicken, brown rice, garlicky turnip and chard greens, pasta al pesto, cheeses and breads, fresh strawberries with crème anglaise, Brazilian chocolates, Spanish cookies, and plenty of Mendoza wine and champagne. Marcela, *por supuesto,* brought her empanadas, flan, and cream scones.

My friends came bearing gifts—extra-virgin olive oil from Mendoza, an azalea bush that bloomed for weeks, coconut cream bubble bath, and a book by Victoria Ocampo. But the best gift of all was the continuing friendships with these people whom I had known a short but intense time. Elena, a new friend from Austria, said, "You cook, you dance. Will you marry me?"

"Yes, Elena," I said, "I'll marry all of you! This is our wedding and we all have to dance." I put on the CD that Ángel gave me— Turkish tango waltzes that sound like wedding music from the Near East. I danced first with Oscar, who brought me two bottles of red wine whose label carries the same surname as his grandmother. Then everyone took turns in the ritual dancing on my small floor, where only one couple can comfortably fit at a time. We blessed that floor with our feet, making circles, figure eights, grapevines, and signs of the cross of the fertility dance.

We raised our glasses of champagne, and I tried to make a meaningful toast. But it was just like in my blood family and no one could be still long enough for me to get it all out. It was corny anyway. I wanted to tell them how I had come here with this frowning face—like the sun on Argentina's flag. But now, having burst through the layers of cloud, I'm more like the first crescent of the moon—a bright smile. Watch me wax and wane. The country and I both were broke when I arrived. All that the cracks in the sidewalks and streets required was exactly what the cracks in me required—a little bit of right Light, and a little bit of spinning in a dance that is still simple and mystical.

We ended the day in a *milonga* at the venerable Salon Canning.

※

Three days later on my actual anniversary, August 29, I had to ride the subway downtown to pick up my pay for my teaching gig. I saw that same little girl juggling in her clown suit, the one with the gorgeous thick black wavy hair. It was the first time I'd seen her in almost a year. This time I was seeing with new eyes, and I couldn't believe it was the same girl. She looked so healthy. She had a hint of steel blue in her black eyes. She made the balls fly like a pro and even looked a little bored with her routine. They hit the ceiling with the clack of the train. She juggled some more, this time turning in a circle. I knew she had horizons in front of her. People clapped before she was done. This time I saw no sadness in her. Her clown suit wasn't dirty. Her eyes were calm and centered. She didn't look forlorn. I didn't see her as a victim of her circumstances. I pulled out a ten-peso note, folded it, and pressed it into her hand, which I held for a couple of seconds so she would make eye contact with me. And she did. Our lips needed no prompting to move in perfect coordination together as we spoke to each other. I knew we were both going to say that one word that you never say to your tango partner in the *milonga* until the music has stopped and you're ready to sit down: *¡Gracias!*

Acknowledgments

There are so many people to thank for the many circumstances and supports, without which this book would not be in your hands, that I cannot possibly name them all. But let me start with my publisher, Seal Press, who has been recognizing great literature by women for more than thirty years. I'm enormously grateful that publisher Krista Lyons-Gould and senior editor Brooke Warner saw my story as bookworthy. Having Brooke, who has studied dance—flamenco—and lived in Spain, as my editor was a dream partnership for me. I needed her vision to keep me on course and track the important threads of my tango-Zen experience in a foreign culture. It was an added blessing to have as my copyeditor Marisa Solis, a diligent editor with whom I've had the pleasure of working before at Seal.

I could just thank all of Argentina for being there between Brazil, Chile, Paraguay, Bolivia, and Uruguay, and Buenos Aires for its comforting Italian culture—offering me the perfect refuge for the perfect storm in life. By name, let me thank my Argentine girlfriends—Patricia Jacovella, Carmen Iglesias, Marcela Caserio—who assisted me in so many ways to more quickly gain an understanding of and footing in their culture. I'm thankful to the Tango Divas—Carmen, Roberta Butler, Rachel Sloan, Flo Woodruff—for sharing of themselves as well as precious time in and out of the *milongas,* and our one accompanying Tango Divo, Francis Natali. Heartfelt thanks to Oscar Coda for finally inviting me to dance and for staying my friend—on and off the dance floor. Thanks to Ángel Cristaldo for his offering of some of the best (and underpriced) lessons on what the gold standard for the tango embrace should be.

Thanks to my Castellano teachers, Mariel Altobello, Demian Gawianski, and Amalia Fischbein, for their patience with my clumsy pronunciation of their tongue.

I'm grateful to my North American friends for their visits to the southern hemisphere and for stopping by to share the passion of tango with me: Lina Khatib, Jan Rowe, Arthur Fraser, Greg Frost, Eduardo Callender, Ed Waller, Roger Schmidt, Lynn Ferrin, and Alison Wright; and to Steve Pitzer and Linda Maxwell, part-time expats, for opening their home to everyone with delicious, nourishing feasts.

Deep bow to all of my Zen teachers and fellow *sangha* members at Beginner's Mind Temple (San Francisco Center)—Zenkei Blanche Hartman, Ryushin Paul Haller, Tenshin Reb Anderson, Dairyu Michael Wenger, Shosan Victoria Austin, and Lou Hartman—

without whom I would not have the enlightening dharma talks and Zen stories (some of which appear in these pages) that much inform my tango dancing. Deep bow to my Zen teacher in Buenos Aires, Ricardo Dokyu Gabriel of Templo Serena Alegría. Many thanks to Peter Esser for sharing his thought-provoking essay on Zen and tango; and to Kent Wade for attempting the impossible— to photograph my tango rapture.

Heartfelt appreciation to my wandering San Francisco–based writing group, the Itinerants (Bradley Charbonneau, Bill Fink, Connie Hale, Gayle Keck, Laurie King, Laura Read, Michael Shapiro), for kindly keeping me inspired, through our listserv.

Thanks to my mother, Carmela, for dancing with my father when I was still in utero; and to my multitude of siblings (Donna, Tina, Lisa, Tommy, Grace, Salvatore, Chuck, Terry, Jimmy), their spouses, partners, kids, and grandkids for keeping the home fires burning under the ravioli and the cannoli while I adventured, yet again. Extra thanks to Grace Becker for the $100 phone calls and to Terry Hennessy and Dan Gendel for shipping a three-month stash of Peet's French roast. Thanks to the Stephensons and Taaffes, my extended family out West, for moral support. Deep gratitude to Dan for everything, for more than I can ever repay.

Three people appear under pseudonyms in this book—Alberto (Chapter 4), Juan Carlos (Chapter 6), and Evelyn—and I wish to thank them.

© Marvin Parker

About the Author

Camille Cusumano, an editor at *VIA* magazine in San Francisco for seventeen years, has written for many publications, including *Islands, Country Living, Yoga Journal,* the *San Francisco Chronicle,* the *Los Angeles Times, Christian Science Monitor,* the *New York Times,* and the *Washington Post.* She is the author of one novel, *The Last Cannoli* (Legas) and several cookbooks, including *The New Foods* (Henry Holt), *America Loves Salads* (Literary Guild), *Tofu, Tempeh, and Other Soy Delights* (Rodale Press), and *Rodale's Basic Natural Foods Cookbook* (cowritten with Carol Munson). She edited the Seal Press anthologies *France, a Love Story; Italy, a Love Story; Mexico, a Love Story;* and *Greece, a Love Story,* and she has contributed to several other Seal anthologies. Her short story "Plot Theory," published in the 2006 summer issue of the *North American Review,* won third place in the Kurt Vonnegut fiction contest. When not on an adventure elsewhere in the world, she lives in San Francisco, where she practices tango and Zen.